SHORT COURSE SERIES

WORLD
TRADE
PRESS®

Professional Books for International Trade

THE SHORT COURSE IN INTERNATIONAL TRADE SERIES

*A Short Course in International Business Culture*

*A Short Course in International Business Ethics*

*A Short Course in International Business Plans*

*A Short Course in International Contracts*

*A Short Course in International Economics*

*A Short Course in International Intellectual Property Rights*

*A Short Course in International Joint Ventures*

*A Short Course in International Marketing*

*A Short Course in International Marketing Blunders*

*A Short Course in International Negotiating*

*A Short Course in International Payments*

*A Short Course in International Trade Documentation*

A SHORT COURSE IN

# *International Payments*

3rd Edition

How to use letters of credit, D/P and D/A terms, prepayment, credit and cyberpayments in international transactions

Edward G. Hinkelman

Published in arrangement with World Trade Press by

**ATLANTIC**

**PUBLISHERS & DISTRIBUTORS (P) LTD**

7/22, Ansari Road, Darya Ganj, New Delhi-110 002
Tel: 40775252, 23273880, 23275880, 23280451; Fax: +91-11-23285873
E-mail: orders@atlanticbooks.com; Web: www.atlanticbooks.com

**World Trade Press**
800 Lindberg Lane, Suite 190
Petaluma, California 94952 USA
Tel: +1 (707) 778-1124
Fax: +1 (707) 778-1329
USA Order Line: +1 (800) 833-8586
E-mail: sales@worldtradepress.com
www.WorldTradePress.com
www.WorldTradeREF.com (international trade and logistics)
www.BestCountryReports.com (business travel, communications and culture)
www.GiantMapArt.com (Giant maps for building lobbies, conference rooms and education)

**A Short Course in International Payments, 3rd Edition**
By: Edward G. Hinkelman
Series Concept: Edward G. Hinkelman
Cover Design: Ronald A. Blodgett
Text Design: Seventeenth Street Studios, Oakland, California, USA



ISBN 978-81-269-1253-7
**First Indian Reprint 2009**

This edition is for sale in Indian sub-continent only.



**Library of Congress Cataloging-in-Publication Data**
Hinkelman, Edward G., 1947–
A short course in international payments: how to use letters of credit,
D/P and D/A terms, prepayment, credit and cyberpayments in
international transactions / Edward G. Hinkelman.--3rd ed.
p. cm. --(The Short Course in International Trade Series)
1. Negotiable instruments. 2. Payment. 3. Documentary credit.
4. Foreign exchange. 5. Electronic funds transfers. 6. International trade.
7. Electronic commerce. 8. International business enterprises—-Finance.
I. Title: International payments. II. Title. III. Series.
HG3741.H56 2009
658.15'5--dc21

2009193354

Printed in India at Chaman Enterprises, 1603, Pataudi House,
Darya Ganj, New Delhi-110 002

# INTRODUCTION

The past 15 years have seen a dramatic fall in trade barriers, the globalization of markets, and a huge growth in international trade. Companies of all sizes are seeking to take advantage of the opportunities in this new world economy.

International transactions, however, add an additional layer of risk for buyers and sellers familiar only with doing business in their domestic markets. Currency regulations, foreign exchange risk, political, economic, or social upheaval in the buyer's or selier's country, questions of payment, and different business customs may all contribute to uncertainty. Ultimately, sellers want to get paid and buyers want to get what they pay for. Choosing the right payment method can be the key to a transaction's feasibility and profitability.

This book is designed to help both buyers and sellers learn about international payment options. The relative merits of the four most common types of payments are explained, and the two most common options—documentary collections and documentary letters of credit—are featured. This book also contains chapters on cyberpayments, Incoterms 2000, a comprehensive glossary, and a section devoted to documents used in international transactions.

To learn more about payment methods read one or more of the publications listed in the resources chapter and consult with the international trade finance department of your bank.

Edward G. Hinkelman
Petaluma, California

## ACKNOWLEDGMENTS

The author wishes to acknowledge the many bankers, freight forwarders, and international traders who gave their time to answer his incessant questions regarding the details of international payments and trade documentation. The book would have been impossible without their experience, expertise, and assistance.

Special thanks to the following:

Jeff Gordon and Britt-Marie Morris of Wells Fargo HSBC Trade Bank N.A. in San Francisco for answering questions and supplying a number of the forms used in this book.

Katrin Gretemer at SBC Warburg Dillon Read (Swiss Bank Corporation) in Zürich, Switzerland for permission to reprint a number of the forms used in this book.

Christoph von der Decken of Hapag Lloyd (America) Inc. in Piscataway, New Jersey and Susan Nalducci of Hapag-Lloyd (America), Inc. in Corte Madera, California for permission to reprint a number of the forms used in this book.

Karen Cross and Sandy Graszynski of Roanoke Brokerage Services, Inc. in Schaumburg, Illinois for permission to reprint a number of forms used in this book.

Vilva Kivijarvi at the Fritz Companies in San Francisco, California (now UPS Freight Services) for permission to reprint a number of the forms used in this book.

TABLE OF CONTENTS

CHAPTER 1

# Key Issues in International Payments

THERE ARE SEVERAL broad issues that affect what payment method will ultimately be used in an international transaction. Every participant in the transaction must consider these issues, though they will affect each differently and to a different degree.

Even after these broader issues are resolved, questions will continue to be raised throughout the transaction. Therefore, careful consideration of these issues can make a transaction go smoother, keep costs to a minimum, and ensure timely and efficient delivery and distribution of goods.

## Who Bears the Credit Risk?

In almost all business transactions the buyer would prefer to obtain easy, extended, and inexpensive (preferably free!) credit terms. Credit gives the commercial buyer the opportunity to resell the goods before having to pay for them. In many instances, the buyer will have a market for goods but not possess sufficient working capital to make an outright purchase and payment prior to their resale. Credit makes many such transactions possible.

At the same time, the seller has a different set of priorities. Having paid for product development, raw materials, component parts, labor, and overhead, the seller needs to get his investment back. The seller may not know the buyer or may not trust that the buyer is financially stable enough to make payment at a future date. International transactions are not as stable, secure, transparent, or reliable as domestic transactions and many things can happen between the time of the sale and the expected time of payment. For these and other reasons, the seller will always prefer to be paid immediately; either at delivery or even prior to delivery.

- BUYER/IMPORTER: Prefers that the seller bear the credit risk and wants to make certain that he receives the goods once he has paid
- SELLER/EXPORTER: Prefers that the buyer bear the credit risk and wants to make certain he receives payment for goods shipped

## Who Finances the Transaction?

In an international transaction it may take from several weeks to several months for merchandise to find its way from the warehouse of the seller to the warehouse of the buyer. Goods must be prepared for export, trucked or sent by rail to the port, export cleared, shipped to another port, possibly transshipped to the final port, warehoused awaiting customs clearance, inspected, customs cleared, sent overland to the final destination, and finally inventoried at the buyer's warehouse. The seller has already made a substantial investment in manufacturing the product and doesn't feel that he should bear the brunt of the costs of financing.

The buyer, on the other hand, knows that it may be one or two months before he even sees the goods in his warehouse, another one or more months before he sells the goods, and another one or several months before he gets paid from his customers. Why should he pay for goods or pay for the financing of goods he doesn't even have in his warehouse?

Although both buyer and seller would wish that the other party finance the transaction and pay for the costs of financing, the realities are that both buyer and seller typically need to compromise somewhat in order to make the transaction happen.

- BUYER/IMPORTER: Needs funds for payment and during the period before resale of goods, and prefers that the seller finance the transaction
- SELLER/EXPORTER: Needs funds for production and the period before payment is received, and prefers that the buyer finance the transaction

## In What Currency will Payment be Made?

The currency specified for payment in a contract can have a significant effect upon the ultimate profitability of the transaction for either the buyer or seller. If the value of the specified currency appreciates between the contract date and payment date, it is a hardship for the buyer. If it depreciates, it is a benefit to the buyer.

In most instances, the specified currency of the transaction will be a "hard currency," such as the US dollar (US$), the European euro (€), the Swiss franc (SwF) or the Japanese yen (¥).

In some instances, however, it will be impossible to conclude a transaction in anything other than a local, less stable currency. In these instances, it may be possible to "hedge" the foreign exchange risk. See "Hedging" in Chapter 4: Foreign Exchange Basics.

- BUYER/IMPORTER: Wants (typically) to make payment in own currency or in a currency that is expected to decrease in value between the date of the contract and date of the payment
- SELLER/EXPORTER: Wants (typically) to receive payment in own currency, a hard currency, or in a currency that is expected to increase in value between the date of the contract and date of the payment

## What are the Political and Legal Risks?

The political environment in both the country of export and the country of import can have disastrous effects on international business transactions. Political instability can lead to changes in trade policy, restrictions on foreign transfers, restrictions on the importation or exportation of certain goods, changes in monetary policy leading to devaluation of the local currency, and riots or civil unrest causing loss or damage to merchandise potentially not covered by insurance, among other problems. Although political risks are generally outside the direct control of either trader, they can sometimes be predicted in the short term and managed to a degree.

Legal risks can also affect an international transaction and can only be managed through extreme diligence. Lack of comprehensive knowledge of legal issues can precipitate problems unimaginable in the local marketplace. These include unknown procedural restrictions, import regulations, and more.

EXAMPLE: A contract signed in a foreign country was ruled invalid because the trader was improperly in the country on a tourist visa.

EXAMPLE: A shipment of encyclopedias published in the United States languished in customs in Calcutta because a map of India showed the "de facto" border with Pakistan, indicating Pakistan's gains from a long-simmering boarder war, rather than the government approved map that indicates all the territory as part of India.

- BUYER/IMPORTER: Considers political risk to be minimal in part because he lives with it every day and understands it
- SELLER/EXPORTER: May consider political and legal risks to be significant, especially if the country appears to be unstable by his own standards

## Who Will Bear Transportation Costs and Risks?

Who pays for transportation and who assumes the risk if goods are damaged or lost in shipment is also a major issue in international transactions. This is especially true in transactions involving high-value or perishable goods and unusual destinations. Both the cost and risk increase as goods are shipped to remote locations or transshipped or handled over and over again.

The seller probably feels that his quoted price is excellent and that it is the problem of the buyer to get the goods to the buyer's home country market.

The buyer, on the other hand, doesn't think in terms of the sale price in the country of origin, he thinks in terms of the landed cost in his own market. If the goods are heavy or bulky and are shipped from Chicago, in the United States, and are going to Uzbekistan, the transportation and insurance costs will be high.

Even if the buyer agrees to handle insurance coverage, the seller may have "insurable interest" in the goods, especially if they have not yet been paid for.

Timeliness may also be an issue of risk as some goods are time-sensitive.

EXAMPLE: Christmas merchandise needs to be on the shelves no later than early November. This generally means that it needs to be received by distributors and wholesalers by no later than mid-October. If the goods arrive on the dock in early December the selling season has been lost.

- BUYER/IMPORTER: Wants (typically) the seller to bear the transportation and insurance costs and to have the goods delivered to a local, home-country delivery point where ownership is assumed
- SELLER/EXPORTER: Wants (typically) the buyer to bear the transportation and insurance costs and to deliver the goods and transfer ownership at his own warehouse or at a local port

## What Are the Costs of Each Method of Financing and Payment?

Every moment the goods are not paid for costs the seller money in financing, while every moment the goods are not resold in the end market costs the buyer money in financing. Who assumes responsibility for the goods at what point in the transaction will affect the availability and terms of financing.

Each method of financing and transfer of payment has a greater or lesser risk for the buyer, the seller and the banks involved. Costs are directly related to the risks and someone has to pay. The following chapters introduce the buyer and the seller, and then detail the various methods of international payment.

## Special Cases

- Multinational affiliates shipping raw materials or merchandise to each other will normally do so on open-account terms, although they might be hesitant to accept these payment terms from any other international customer.
- High-value or perishable goods normally require special payment arrangements, such as advance payment or inspection after arrival of the merchandise and before payment is made.
- Transactions in a developing country, which can be difficult though profitable, often require cash or confirmed letter of credit terms. To consider any other method of payment would probably be a mistake.
- In new trading relationships it often makes sense to start on more conservative terms and, after experience and greater familiarity, proceed to deal on more liberal terms.

CHAPTER 2

# Introducing the Buyer and the Seller

AT THE HEART OF every business transaction is the buyer and the seller. Both parties have one thing in common: to profit from the transaction and to expose themselves to the least risk possible. All transactions, no matter how innocent, expose buyers and sellers to risk. In this chapter we will discuss the business concerns of the buyer and seller and how these concerns affect decisions relating to which payment method is used in an international transaction.

Fundamentally, the concerns of the buyer and the seller are the same in both domestic and international transactions: The buyer wishes to get the goods ordered and paid for, and the seller wishes to get paid for the goods shipped. International transactions, however, add a layer of uncertainty and risk for the buyer and seller that does not exist in purely domestic transactions. The buyer and seller are separated by long distances, differences in culture and business tradition, different government and economic systems, different currencies, and different banking and legal systems to name but a few.

In this chapter we will discuss issues and concerns from the perspective of both the buyer and the seller. If you are already a buyer or seller many will be familiar with some or all of them. You may also be introduced to new issues of concern to the other party. Understanding the needs of your counterpart will help you in structuring a transaction that works for all concerned.

If there are any conclusions to be drawn from this analysis of the buyer and seller, they are: (1) you should know as much as possible about all the parties to a transaction in which you have an interest, and (2) no matter what protections are in place, a degree of trust in the other party will be required.

## Introducing the Buyer

The buyer is in the business of purchasing or the brokering of raw materials; component parts; finished goods; or services for manufacturing, assembly, or resale to others. The realities of the buyer's financial situation, type of business, physical location, country of business operation, position in the chain of distribution, and type of goods purchased dictate the manner in which he or she is able to conduct business and make payment.

### ISSUES AND CONCERNS OF THE BUYER

- **ASSURANCE OF DELIVERY AND CORRECT COUNT** The most fundamental concern of the buyer is certainty of securing delivery of the goods purchased. What if the buyer orders and prepays for goods that never arrive? What if the buyer orders one hundred units and receives only eighty-eight units?
- **QUALITY OF GOODS** The buyer will always want to receive "quality" goods. What if the buyer orders one quality and receives a lesser quality? Who is the arbiter of what "quality" means when dealing with people from a different culture?
- **CONDITION OF GOODS** The buyer will always be concerned that the goods arrive in good (usable or salable) condition. What if the goods arrive damaged and in unsalable condition? What if the refrigeration unit ("reefer" container) malfunctions and perishable goods spoil en route?
- **TIMELINESS OF RECEIPT OF GOODS** The buyer wants to make certain that goods ordered are shipped and received in a timely fashion. What if Christmas merchandise scheduled for arrival in October is delayed and arrives at the port in mid-December, much too late to make it to the store shelves for the Christmas holiday selling season? What if component parts arrive late and a production line is held up?
- **LAG TIME** The buyer and the seller may be separated by many thousands of miles. What if it takes sixty days for the goods to arrive at the seller's warehouse? Is the buyer going to be required to pay prior to receipt of the shipment? Who will pay the financing costs while the goods are in transit?
- **FINANCING THE TRANSACTION** In almost all business transactions the buyer would prefer to obtain easy and free long-term credit. In many instances the buyer will not possess sufficient working capital to make an outright cash purchase of goods.

  What if the buyer's cycle of getting paid is extremely long and he needs time to make payment?

  What if the buyer has the ability to successfully market the goods as well as the willingness to make payment at a future date after resale of the merchandise but doesn't possess the capital to make immediate or prepayment for the goods?

---

EXAMPLE: In the book publishing business, it may take the wholesaler three to four months to collect on a shipment of books sold to a retail bookstore.

---

- **BUYER AS BROKER** The buyer may be acting as a broker and unable to make payment before getting paid himself. What if the buyer's buyer is unable to pay before the buyer must pay the seller?

  The buyer acting as a broker may also be working on a small margin. What if unexpected "incidental" costs eat up his entire margin of profit?

- **TRANSPORTATION COSTS AND RISK** The cost and particulars of transportation will be of great concern to the buyer, especially if great distances are involved and if the risk of loss is great. Who will bear the costs of transportation? Also, at what physical point will the buyer accept responsibility for transportation? From the factory door of the seller? From the port of export? From the port of import?

  In international transactions it may take as long as several months for merchandise to find its way from the warehouse of the seller to the warehouse of the buyer. The cost of this transportation may be high, especially with heavy, bulky, perishable, or high-risk goods requiring special handling. What if the cost of transportation is very high in proportion to the sale price of the goods themselves?

- **INSURANCE** The cost and particulars of insurance will be of concern to the buyer, especially when the terms of the contract specify that the buyer is responsible for insurance costs from the seller's door or from the port of embarkation of the seller's country.

  The cost of insurance for goods in transit may also be a concern for the buyer, especially with heavy, bulky, perishable, or high-risk goods requiring larger insurance premiums. What if the buyer finds the costs associated with insurance to be extremely high compared to the sale price of the merchandise?

- **DISTANCES** The buyer and the seller may be separated by huge distances requiring several modes of transport. This can both add to the cost and risks of transport as well as to the time it takes the buyer to receive the goods and begin the process of manufacture, assembly, or resale.

- **CURRENCY OF THE TRANSACTION** International contracts for the sale of goods or services need to specify in what currency the payment is to be made. If the specified currency *appreciates* between the contract date and payment date, it has the effect of increasing the cost of the goods or services purchased by the buyer.

---

EXAMPLE: Assume that a Korean company, conducting business primarily in Korea and in its national currency (the Korean won) agrees to purchase goods from a US seller with payment to be made in US dollars. If the Korean won depreciates 40 percent, (as it did in the fall of 1997) the Korean company will have to pay 66 percent more than it expected for the US dollars to make payment.

---

## Introducing the Seller

The seller is in the business of manufacturing, selling, or brokering raw materials, component parts, finished goods, or services to the buyer for eventual manufacture, assembly, or resale to others. The realities of the seller's financial situation, type of business, physical location, country of business operation, position in the chain of distribution, and type of goods purchased dictate the manner in which he or she is able to conduct business and secure payment.

### ISSUES AND CONCERNS OF THE SELLER

- **CERTAINTY OF PAYMENT** The most fundamental concern of the seller is certainty of getting paid for the goods sold. What if the seller ships goods and never gets paid?
- **ASSURANCE OF DELIVERY AND CORRECT COUNT** The seller wants to make certain that goods shipped equals goods received. What if the seller ships one hundred units and the buyer claims receipt of only eighty-eight units? Does the seller have to make up the difference?
- **CONDITION OF GOODS** The seller wants to make certain that the goods arrive in good (usable or salable) condition. If the goods arrive in an unusable condition it may affect the ability of the buyer to make payment. What if the goods arrive damaged and in unsalable condition? What if the refrigeration unit ("reefer" container) malfunctions and perishable goods spoil en route? What if the buyer claims that he is unable to make payment because he is unable to resell or use the goods shipped? Although the seller may think that this is not of concern if the goods are already paid for, unhealthy buyers will ultimately have an unhealthy effect on sellers.
- **TIMELINESS OF RECEIPT OF GOODS** The seller will want to make certain that goods shipped are received in a timely fashion. If the buyer's shipment is delayed it may affect his ability to pay the seller.
- **FINANCING THE TRANSACTION** If the seller is the manufacturer of the goods he or she has invested in product development, raw materials, component parts, labor, and overhead. As a result the seller is likely to prefer to be paid immediately; either at or even prior to delivery of the goods. But what if the buyer is simply unable to buy unless there are credit terms? What if the buyer has the contacts and business structure to sell the goods if only they are made available on credit terms? Also, what if the seller has a great product that is in demand but does not possess the financing to start manufacturing?
- **SELLER AS BROKER** The seller may be acting as a broker and be unable to ship the goods before making payment to his supplier, or the seller may be unable to make payment before getting paid himself.

  The selling broker may be working on a thin margin and unable to extend credit. The buyer acting as a broker may also be working on a small margin. What if unexpected "incidental" costs eat up the entire margin of profit for either?

- POLITICAL RISK The seller may be contemplating a sale to a buyer in a politically or economically unstable country. Political instability can lead to changes in trade policy, restrictions on foreign transfers, restrictions on the importation of certain goods, a change in monetary policy leading to devaluation of the local currency, or riots and civil unrest that can cause loss or damage to merchandise (potentially) not covered by insurance, among other problems. What if the sale is made, goods shipped and received in good order, and then a revolution occurs? Or civil unrest destroys the goods and therefore the buyer's ability to pay? Or a change in the country's political or economic policies makes it impossible for the buyer to pay? What if the country of importation suddenly imposes a political or economic policy that forbids the transfer of payments from the buyer's country to the seller's country?
- LEGAL RISK The seller faces legal risks unknown in most domestic deals. What if the transaction, normal and harmless by all accounts, is suddenly found to be against the law in the country of import, and the buyer is unable to make payment because the goods have been confiscated? What if the goods do not conform to an obscure legal requirement in the country of importation and cannot be sold?
- TRANSPORTATION The cost and particulars of transportation will be of concern to the seller, especially when the terms of the contract specify that the seller is responsible for transportation costs to the buyer's door or to the port of entry of the buyer's country. What if the goods are lost or damaged in transit? What if the goods are stolen by the ship's crew or pirates on the high seas? (It does happen!) What if the goods are perishable, and the seller is concerned that if he ships them without advance or guaranteed payment the buyer will "hold him hostage" demanding a lower price for the goods, knowing they will spoil on the docks?
- INSURANCE The cost of insurance for goods in transit is a concern for the seller, especially when the terms of the contract specify that the seller is responsible for their insurance up until they are received by the buyer or delivered to the port of destination.

  What if something happens to the goods in between the seller's insurance coverage and the buyer's insurance coverage? What if the buyer has neglected to secure proper insurance, the goods are damaged or lost in transit, and the buyer is unable to pay?
- DISTANCES What if the buyer and seller are separated by huge distances requiring several modes of transport? What if the lag time means an extra sixty days before payment can be made? Who will pay for the financing costs?
- CURRENCY RISK The currency specified for payment in a contract can have a significant effect upon the ultimate profitability for the seller. If the specified currency depreciates between the contract date and payment date it has the effect of decreasing the payment value of the goods or services sold.

CHAPTER 3

# Introducing Basic Terms of Payment

TO A LARGE EXTENT, payment methods in international trade are similar to those in domestic business. However, due to the added risks and complexities involved in crossboarder transactions, certain terms are more often seen in international trade. In international trade, the means of payment are frequently known as the "terms of payment." There are four commonly used terms of payment, each of which offers different levels of risk and stability for buyers and sellers.

## Key Factors in Determining the Payment Method

The terms of payment used in an international transaction will depend on the relationship between the seller and the buyer, the nature of the merchandise, industry norms, the distance between buyer and seller, the potential for currency fluctuation, and political and economic stability in either or both countries. All of these factors must be considered before deciding on a method of payment that is acceptable to both parties.

The single most important factor, however, is the nature and length of the business relationship between buyer and seller. Trust and confidence in the other party go a long way in both parties' willingness to accept payment terms bearing a higher degree of risk.

## Relative Security of Payment Terms

It is, of course, the desire of all parties for a transaction to have absolute security. The seller wants to make absolutely certain he gets paid, while the buyer wants to make absolutely certain he gets the merchandise as ordered. In fact, there can't be absolutes of certainty for both parties to a transaction. If one has absolute security (seller gets prepayment or the buyer gets the goods before making payment) the other party correspondingly loses a degree of security. Also, a buyer or seller who is insistent about having the transaction work only for themselves will find that they are losing a great deal of business. International transactions, therefore, often require a compromise on the part of the seller and the buyer that leads to relative security for both.

## Four Basic Terms of Payment

There are four basic terms of payment used in international trade. All have variations and permutations that are the subject of this book. These four are described briefly below, in greater detail in the pages that immediately follow, and exhaustively in the chapters of this book. Ranked in order from most beneficial to the seller to most beneficial to the buyer, they are

### CASH IN ADVANCE

- Provides greatest security for seller and greatest risk for buyer

The buyer simply prepays the seller prior to shipment of the goods. This term of payment requires that the buyer have a high level of confidence in the ability and willingness of the seller to deliver the goods as ordered.

### DOCUMENTARY (LETTER OF) CREDIT

- Security and almost equal risk for both buyer and seller
- Added costs (for the handling of the documentary credit) to buyer

A letter of credit is a bank's commitment to pay the seller a specified sum on behalf of the buyer under precisely defined conditions. The buyer specifies certain documents (including a title document) from the seller before the bank is to make payment, and the seller is assured that payment will be received after the goods are shipped so long as the specified documents are provided.

### DOCUMENTARY COLLECTIONS

- Security and almost equal risk for both buyer and seller.
- Less costly and easier to use than a documentary letter of credit.

A documentary collection is similar to an international cash on delivery (COD). The seller ships goods to the buyer but sends the documents, including the bill of lading (title document), through the banks with instructions to release them to the buyer only upon payment. When the buyer obtains the title documents, he has the right to take ownership of the shipment.

### OPEN ACCOUNT

- Provides the least risk for the buyer, and the greatest risk for the seller

The buyer agrees to pay for the goods within a designated time after the shipment, usually in 30, 60, or 90 days. The seller is thus totally reliant on the buyer's ability and willingness to pay for goods already shipped.

## Cash in Advance

Payment by cash in advance requires that the buyer pay the seller prior to shipment of the goods ordered. Cash in advance provides the seller with the most security but leaves the buyer at great risk that the seller will not comply with all the terms of the contract. The cash payment is received before, and independently of, shipment of the goods. If the goods are delayed or of inferior quality, the buyer's last resort is to take legal action on the basis of the sales contract, unless the seller makes a satisfactory adjustment. Due to the high degree of risk, the buyer should always consider whether any alternatives are available before agreeing to cash in advance terms.

Cash in advance payments are made either by bank draft or check or through a wire payment to the bank account specified by the seller/exporter. If receiving payment by check, the seller should verify that it has been cleared by the buyer's bank before proceeding with shipment.

Generally, only two categories of sellers can require cash in advance terms: those fortunate to have unique or high-demand products, and sellers receiving orders from unknown buyers in unstable countries.

Cash terms can sometimes be asked when shipping a small sample order to a buyer. Also, in some cases involving a large buyer, a small seller, and a large order, the buyer may be willing to make an advance payment to help the smaller company carry out the manufacturing process. In addition, in some situations, such as when the relationship is new, the transaction is small, and the buyer is unwilling to pay the costs of documentary payments, cash in advance terms may be called for.

Overall, cash in advance payment terms cannot be required from buyers and this type of payment constitutes a small proportion of payments made in international transactions.

### QUESTIONS FOR THE BUYER

- Are cash in advance terms the only option available?
- Will the seller comply with the terms and ship the goods as promised?
- What recourse is available if the goods are not shipped as ordered?
- Are there economic, political, or social instabilities in the seller's country that may increase the likelihood that the seller cannot ship as promised?

### QUESTIONS FOR THE SELLER

- Is the product unique enough or in high enough demand to "get away with" requiring cash in advance terms?
- Is the buyer willing to pay at least some proportion in advance?

## Documentary Letter of Credit

A documentary letter of credit is a bank's promise to pay a seller on behalf of the buyer so long as the seller complies with precisely defined terms and conditions specified in the credit. A documentary letter of credit provides almost equal security to both the buyer and the seller and is second only to cash in advance in terms of security to the seller.

When a letter of credit is issued by the buyer's bank, the bank assumes the payment responsibility for the buyer, thereby placing the credit standing of the bank between the seller and the buyer. With use of a letter of credit, buyer and seller do not communicate directly. The bank(s) act as intermediary(ies) between the two. The bank, however, deals only with the documents regarding the goods rather than the goods themselves. This latter point is critical and will be discussed later in detail.

Letters of credit are the most common form of international payment because they provide a high degree of protection for both the buyer and the seller. The buyer specifies the documentation required from the seller before the bank is to make payment, and the seller is given assurance that payment will be made after shipping the goods so long as the documentation is in order. The key document is the bill of lading or title document that authorizes its holder to take possession of the shipment. If the buyer and seller have a subsequent disagreement regarding the order, however, it is handled between them, independently of the banks or of payment.

Consistency and accuracy are paramount in preparing and submitting documents for payment under a letter of credit. The documents presented for payment by a seller must conform precisely with the wordings specified in the letter of credit or the bank will not make payment. Many documents presented under letters of credit carry some sort of error (small or large) that can delay or prevent fulfillment of the credit.

### QUESTIONS FOR THE BUYER

- Is my bank experienced in documentary credit transactions?
- Am I prepared to amend or renegotiate terms of the credit with the seller?
- Am I certain of all the documents required for customs clearance?

### QUESTIONS FOR THE SELLER

- Will I take care to confirm the good standing of the buyer and the buyer's bank?
- Will we carefully review the credit to make sure its conditions can be met?
- Am I committed to properly prepare documentation for the credit?
- Can we comply with every detail of the credit?
- Am I prepared to amend or renegotiate terms of the credit with the buyer?

## Documentary Collections

A documentary collection is an order by the seller to his bank to collect payment from the buyer in exchange for the transfer of documents that enable the holder to take possession of the goods.

Under a documentary collection, the seller ships goods to the buyer but forwards shipping documents (including title document) to the forwarding bank for transmission to the buyer's bank. The buyer's bank is instructed not to transfer the documents to the buyer until payment is made (documents against payment, D/P) or upon guarantee that payment will be made within a specified period of time (documents against acceptance, D/A). Once in possession of the documentation, the buyer may take possession of the shipment.

Like letters of credit, documentary collections focus on the transfer of title documents to goods rather than on immediate transfer of the goods themselves. However, unlike letters of credit, banks involved in the transaction do not guarantee payment but act only as collectors of payment.

Documentary collections are excellent for buyers who wish to purchase goods without risking prepayment and without having to go through the more cumbersome letter of credit procedures. Documentary collections are easier to use than letters of credit, and bank charges are usually lower.

Documentary collection procedures, however, entail some risk for both sellers and buyers. For sellers, risk is incurred because payment is not made until after the goods are shipped; also, the seller assumes risk while the goods are in transit or in storage until payment or acceptance takes place. Also, banks involved in the transaction do not guarantee payments. For buyers, risk is incurred when the goods shipped by the seller are not the quality or quantity ordered. Therefore, from the seller's standpoint, documentary collection falls somewhere in between a letter of credit and open account in its desirability. This term of payment is generally utilized when the buyer and seller have an established and ongoing business relationship, and when the transaction does not require the additional protection and expense of a documentary credit.

### QUESTIONS FOR THE BUYER

- Do I trust that the seller will ship the quality and quantities of goods as promised?

### QUESTIONS FOR THE SELLER

- Do I know the buyer well enough to trust that he/she will pay for the documents?
- If the buyer refuses to pay for the documents, are the goods we are shipping easily marketable to another client?
- Is our company committed to prepare documents correctly?

## Open Account

Purchase on open account means that the buyer agrees to pay for goods ordered within a designated time after their shipment. Common terms are 30, 60, or 90 days although longer terms of 180 days are not unheard of.

Open account provides the buyer with the greatest security and flexibility but leaves the seller at greatest risk that the buyer will not comply with the terms of the contract and pay as promised. If the buyer does not pay, the seller's last resort is to take legal action on the basis of the sales contract. Due to the high degree of risk, the seller should always consider whether any other alternatives are available before agreeing to open account terms.

Open account terms give the buyer time to receive the goods, market them in his domestic market, receive payment, and make payment to the seller without direct investment of his own funds. Open account payments are made either by bank draft or check or through a wire payment to the bank account specified by the seller/exporter.

Although open account terms are common in domestic trade, where the legal system provides ready recourse against defaulting buyers, these terms are much less common in international trade. Winning and collecting a judgment abroad is at least several times more difficult than the same procedure domestically.

Generally, open account terms are utilized only when goods are shipped to a foreign branch or subsidiary of a multinational company or when there is a high degree of trust between seller and buyer, and the seller has significant faith in the buyer's ability and willingness to pay. If the transaction is with an unknown buyer, the seller is advised to find a different payment method.

Overall, open account payment terms cannot be expected from sellers early in the relationship.

### QUESTIONS FOR THE BUYER

- Can I convince the seller of my ability and willingness to pay on open account terms?
- Is my marketing or distribution strength and reputation in my domestic market attractive enough to the seller to justify open account terms?

### QUESTIONS FOR THE SELLER

- Are open account terms the only option available?
- Does the buyer have the ability and willingness to make payment?
- Will economic, political, and social instability in the buyer's country hinder the buyer's ability to pay?

CHAPTER 4

# Foreign Exchange Basics

IN INTERNATIONAL COMMERCE, payment for goods and services usually involves the currencies of more than one country, and the problem of which currency to use can become a serious barrier to completing a deal. There would be no problem if the currency of a seller's country could always be bought and sold at a fixed and invariable price compared to the money of a buyer's country. However, in most cases, the relative value of currencies is constantly changing, and some are quite volatile.

If the value of a currency changes between the time a deal is made and the time payment is made it could have a serious impact on the profitability of a transaction. For example, if a trader has made a deal to be paid in a foreign currency and that currency devalues before payment is made, the trader will receive less value for the goods than originally anticipated. Of course it is also true that extra profits could be made if the foreign currency increases in value. In any event, this is a risk most traders would prefer to avoid.

There are many ways of dealing with foreign exchange risk and the simplest, if you are the seller, is insisting on payment in your own currency. This strategy lays the risk at the buyer's door, but it may not always be a viable option, and traders may have to accept payment in foreign currency in order to make a sale. If full agreement cannot be reached, it may be possible for both buyer and seller to share the risk by arranging for a portion of the payment to be made in one currency and the remainder in another.

If it is absolutely necessary to take on the foreign exchange risk, traders can protect themselves in a number of ways. One way is to build the estimated cost of a currency fluctuation into the deal to guard against potential losses. However, as this is simply an estimate it will rarely fully protect the trader.

## Using a Third Country Currency

While banks will undertake to assume the risk of currency fluctuations under foreign currency letters of credit, they do charge fees for this service (which can be hefty, especially if a company conducts many smaller foreign trade transactions). Since it is unlikely that either buyer or seller will agree to assume the risk of currency fluctuations, many international trade transactions are invoiced in a strong and stable currency—even if it is that of a third country. For this reason the US dollar (US$), the European euro (€) and the Japanese yen (¥) are all widely used in international payments. In fact, more than half of world trade is denominated in US dollars, although the Japanese yen is widely used for trade throughout the Pacific Rim. The euro is making inroads against both.

## Hedging

The management of currency in international transactions is often accomplished through hedging. A hedge is a contract that provides protection against the risk of loss from a change in foreign exchange rates. There are three common methods of hedging.

### 1. FORWARD MARKET HEDGE

A trader can lock in the rate at which he can buy or sell a foreign currency by buying, at the time the original sale of merchandise (or services) agreement is made, a forward contract to sell or buy that currency with delivery set at the anticipated payment or receipt date.

### 2. MONEY MARKET HEDGE

A trader can reverse a future foreign currency payment or receivable by borrowing domestic currency now, converting the currency into foreign currency at today's exchange rate, and investing the proceeds in foreign money market instruments. The proceeds of the money market instruments upon maturity can be used to meet the foreign currency needs payable at that date.

### 3. OPTIONS MARKET

There are two types of foreign currency options available to manage risk. A "put" option gives the buyer the right, but not the obligation, to sell a specified number of foreign currency units to the option seller at a fixed dollar price, up to the option's expiration date. A "call" option, on the other hand, is the right, but not the obligation, to buy the foreign currency at a specified dollar price, at any time up to the expiration date.

### RISKS OF HEDGING

While hedging can reduce a trader's exposure to foreign currency fluctuations, the costs of such instruments must be balanced against the risk of loss. Their usefulness is also limited by the fact that they are only available for major currencies and for certain maturities, which makes their use difficult for traders with substantial exposure in developing countries. However, since most trade is conducted in the major currencies for which options are available, and many international payment terms are consistent with the maturity terms of currency hedging instruments, they are usually a viable alternative.

### COSTS OF HEDGING

For a trader that has frequent exposure in many currencies, hedging every transaction is counterproductive, since the likely outcome of the gains and losses under an unhedged position will approach zero. Unless the exchange market is perceived to be grossly distorted due to undue government intervention or some other reason, a policy to hedge all exposures is likely to be as costly as the expected exchange rate changes. If hedging a large number of transactions will produce the same outcome as the unhedged position, then the overall gain from hedging operations is slightly negative because of the cost of arranging the protection.

## HEDGING RISKS FOR BUYERS

Since most traders prefer to avoid the risk of currency fluctuations, they usually shift the foreign exchange risk to commercial banks. If a buyer arranges to establish a letter of credit in the seller's country, the payment to such seller will be made in the seller's own currency by a designated overseas paying bank in the seller's country. Upon receiving the documents from the opening bank in the buyer's country, the buyer is required to supply domestic currency equal to the amount of foreign currency paid by the overseas bank.

If the conversion of currency occurs on the same day as payment is made, it is usually based on the exchange rates of the two currencies on that day. The buyer's bank just sells the foreign exchange to the buyer at that day's rate—called the spot rate—and credits the foreign exchange account of the overseas bank.

However, if the buyer wishes to eliminate any unfavorable exchange risk arising from currency fluctuations between the time the buyer arranges to open the credit and the date of actual payment, the buyer can arrange with the domestic bank at the time the letter of credit is opened to execute a forward exchange contract. Thus, the buyer knows the exact cost in dollars in time for the actual payment, and any exchange risk is assumed by its bank. In general, banks are better positioned to assume such risk as many have active foreign exchange management departments.

## HEDGING HINTS FOR SELLERS

If a seller receives a letter of credit in a foreign currency the seller may arrange with the local advising bank to sell the foreign currency to be realized upon payment. In this case, the risk of exchange is assumed by the seller, since the conversion of foreign currency into local currency will be made at the rate of exchange on the day the seller executes the exchange contract with its bank.

To avoid any risk of foreign currency devaluation on the date of transaction, the seller should consider borrowing the same foreign currency for the duration of the outstanding transaction and selling the loan proceeds at the current rate for the local currency. At the time of payment by the foreign bank, receipt of foreign currency will repay the borrowing. By immediately selling the loan proceeds at the outset for domestic currency and placing them on time deposit, the ensuring interest yield will reduce the gross borrowing expense.

CHAPTER 5

# Contract Basics

INTERNATIONAL BUSINESS TRANSACTIONS are complicated by the movement of goods and services between foreign jurisdictions with different legal systems. The drafting of a contract, performance or modification of contractual obligations, resolution of disputes, and enforcement of judgments or orders are relatively straightforward in domestic transactions, but they can be tortuous when you face international transactions subject to foreign laws and legal systems with which you are unfamiliar. In addition, many foreign governments actively take part in or become actual third parties to otherwise private contractual relationships.

Governments interfere with private contractual agreements for a variety of reasons. What may be consistent with or contrary to the public policy of a government may depend on current priorities for attracting technology or capital, balance of payments problems, or an unstable political regime. Foreign companies may even serve as convenient scapegoats to be expropriated or nationalized, despite previous contractual guarantees. Thus, in order to protect a company's commercial interests, contracts in countries with this type of instability should be drafted and negotiated by experienced international business managers and lawyers familiar with the country.

For a comprehensive view of international sales contracts for the nonattorney, refer to *A Short Course in International Contracts* by Karla C. Shippey, J.D., also by World Trade Press.

## Importance of Written Contracts

At the very least you should have a written contract whenever you pay for goods, especially when you do not take possession of them at the time of payment. Make sure you have documentation for the sale, even if it is just a simple description of goods, quantity, and price. This is usually sufficient for general merchandise if you take physical delivery and ship the goods yourself, rather than having the seller handle packaging and shipping.

## Know Your Jurisdiction

Wherever you are doing business you must keep in mind that international contracts must be prepared and negotiated in an entirely different context than domestic ones. A contract in international business is not merely a document setting forth quantity, price, and delivery schedule of the products (although it must surely include such information); it must also take into consideration the local legal system and political and currency risks in the countries involved.

The laws of some jurisdictions require certain contracts to be written in order to be enforceable; others do not. Some jurisdictions also require written contracts for the transfer of certain types of property, such as real (real estate) or immovable property. Observation of other formalities—such as notarization or signatures of witnesses—may be required. In some countries, an individual who works for a corporation may not be allowed to bind that company in a contract without a corporate resolution; in others, anybody who professes to speak for a company may irretrievably commit that company to perform.

## Anticipate Problems

For a contract that will be performed over time, such as a series of transactions, you should anticipate potential problems at the outset. Most people enter into an agreement to purchase and sell with the expectation that all will go smoothly and both parties will gain from the transaction. These positive expectations can be realized if your supplier and you provide for contingencies. Even with a simple sales contract, however, you must think about possible downstream problems, and provide for them in your agreement.

## What Your Contracts Should Include

When dealing internationally, you must consider the business practices and legal requirements of the countries where the buyer or seller are located. The laws of one or the other country may require specific terms or formats. In some transactions, the laws may even specify all or some of the contract terms. In other countries the contract must be in the local language.

Legal problems occur when you leave terms out of your contract because the gaps will be filled in by application of the law of one or the other country. The result will vary depending on which law is chosen. If terms are vague and open to interpretation, or if any aspect is left to implication or custom, you will have to rely on local law to determine your rights and obligations should a dispute arise. Disputes will be resolved according to the laws of the country with jurisdiction (the country designated in your contract, or the country where both parties have the most significant contacts, or sometimes simply the country whose courts will assume jurisdiction).

Accordingly, the best way to control the results of your contract is to clarify each party's responsibility in the agreement, and by paying close attention to each contract term. Always be specific. For instance, you may have an agreement that you will buy a certain quantity of a specific product, but how are you going to pick up the goods? Is someone going to box them? Do you want the entire order at once? When are they to be shipped?

## Basic Contract Provisions

Your primary objective will be to create a written agreement that clearly states the rights and responsibilities of both parties to the transaction. As such, you should always be certain to come to a definite understanding with the other party on four basic issues: the goods (including quantity, type, and quality); the time of delivery; the price; and the time and means of payment. In addition, you should include clauses on documentation, forum, governing law, damages, specific performance, and arbitration.

- GOODS This is where you describe what is being bought and sold. The description must include the number of units or quantity, the type (including model numbers if applicable and or any standard industry specifications), and quality. Quality cannot be stated subjectively, such as "good quality," but must be stated objectively using applicable industry standard designations.
- DELIVERY This can be either a ship date or a date of receipt. If it is a ship date, the buyer is advised to have some degree of control over the method of shipping. If it is a receipt date the seller should be in some control of the method of shipping.
- PRICE/CURRENCY The price may be a price per unit or a total price, but including both is preferable. The price should also state the currency of the transaction (such as US dollars, Korean won, etc.). The price should also state whether shipping (to a particular destination), insurance, taxes, customs duties, and other costs are to be included. The latter is an important issue and the subject of Chapter 6: Incoterms.
- PAYMENT This should state the means of payment—whether prepaid, 120 day credit terms, letter of credit, or any other payment instrument.
- DOCUMENTATION You must be certain that all documentation (bills of lading, invoices, certificates of origin, etc.) necessary for export from the country of origin and import into the country of destination is listed as a requirement of the contract and for payment.
- FORUM Forum refers to the place where any dispute will be settled. It is really a matter of convenience and is usually negotiable. When it is not feasible for you to go to the supplier's country, or vice versa, to settle a dispute, you can jointly designate a third country that would be more convenient to both.
- GOVERNING LAW The choice of law is critical. It determines not just where you can bring a suit or enforce a judgment, but what rules and procedures will govern the dispute settlement. Where and under what law you file suit will make a difference. Filing suit in your own country, with local counsel familiar with local commercial law and court procedures, will generally produce better results than being forced to rely on the court, counsel, and law of a foreign country.
- MEASURE OF DAMAGES IN BREACH OF CONTRACT ACTION The measure of damages in a breach of contract action varies from country to country and among legal systems. This can have a tremendous impact on your ability to recover your losses, and on the amount you may recover. Therefore, you should always specify which law, or measure of damages, will apply in such a case and ensure that all parties understand the consequences of this clause.
- SPECIFIC PERFORMANCE Specific performance is an alternative remedy to monetary damages, and some jurisdictions do not allow this recovery in some or any cases. Specific performance allows an injured party to request a court to compel the breaching party to fulfill the contract agreement. Thus, if you have a contract to buy goods, you can demand those specific goods rather than monetary compensation.

- ARBITRATION This clause establishes whether both parties agree to arbitration rather than legal action to resolve a dispute. There are advantages and disadvantages to arbitration for both the buyer and the seller. It should not be agreed to without thought.

## Don't Forget!

- Always include how, where, and in what language disputes will be resolved.
- Limit warranties or guarantees to conditions under your control.
- Structure a contract to offset political exposure and incorporate contingency exit strategies.
- "Boilerplate" or standard contract language should not be used.
- Some countries do not recognize choice of law and choice of method of dispute resolution in commercial contracts. Such a country may not even enforce a domestic judgment. Do your homework before signing.

## Going to Court

It is inevitable that disputes will arise in international transactions. While it is always best to try and resolve such disputes informally, if you are unable to do so you should take steps to protect your rights. There are essentially two types of disputes that can arise: those in which the buyer has a claim against the seller and those in which the seller has a claim against the buyer.

- BUYER'S CLAIMS AGAINST THE SELLER The goods may not be delivered, or delivery may be delayed. The wrong goods, or goods of a different quantity or quality may be delivered. Proper documentation might not accompany the goods. The goods might turn out to be defective after you have resold them. In all these cases, you will have a claim against the supplier in which you seek either performance or damages, or a combination of the two.
- SELLER'S CLAIMS AGAINST THE BUYER A supplier's claim against you will almost always be for nonpayment of all or part of the purchase price.

Different cultures have different ways of dealing with business disputes. In some countries, a lawsuit is viewed as a personal affront. Engaging in legal disputes, however, is almost always costly, and often results in a compromised outcome for both participants. The courts of many countries are biased in favor of their own nationals, and foreigners rarely, if ever, obtain satisfaction. As such, formal legal proceedings should be avoided if at all possible.

Even if a legal action is ultimately resolved in your favor there are major issues and pitfalls still to be confronted—most importantly, collection of the money awarded or specific performance of the contract terms. This is often impossible, and in any event can take several months or even years to accomplish. In most cases, the amount awarded will not adequately compensate you for the time and expense of litigation. As such it is important to protect yourself to the best extent possible in the initial stages of a business relationship.

## ARBITRATION

The parties to a commercial transaction may provide in their contract that any disputes over interpretation or performance of the agreement will be resolved through arbitration. Arbitration is where both parties to the dispute agree to have a third party resolve their differences. Arbitration offers neutrality (international arbitration allows each party to avoid the domestic courts of the other) and ease of enforcement (foreign awards can be easier to enforce than foreign court decisions).

Many organizations around the world provide arbitration services. Each arbitration association has its own rules of practice and procedure, but most are similar. For example, most arbitration rules provide that each party to a dispute choose one arbitrator, and that the two chosen arbitrators elect a third "neutral" arbitrator with the result decided by a majority (two out of three).

In an agreement to arbitrate, the parties have broad power to agree on many significant aspects of the arbitration. At a minimum, the arbitration agreement should contain these elements:

1. An agreement to arbitrate
2. The name of an arbitration organization to administer the arbitration. The International Chamber of Commerce (Paris), the American Arbitration Association (New York), and the Arbitration Institute of the Stockholm Chamber of Commerce (Sweden) are three such prominent institutions
3. The rules that will govern the arbitration, and the law that will govern procedural issues or the merits of the dispute
4. The location where the arbitration will be conducted, which may be a "neutral" site
5. Any limitations on the selection of arbitrators, for example, the exclusion of nationals from the countries of the disputing parties
6. The language in which the arbitration proceedings will be conducted
7. The effect of the arbitration decision—binding or nonbinding—on the parties

## COLLECTING AFTER AN AWARD

Enforcement of arbitration awards is more common than enforcement of court judgments, and most arbitration awards are not reviewed by foreign courts, unlike court judgments from other countries, which are carefully scrutinized. Most countries are now recognizing and enforcing domestic arbitration awards and many will allow cross-border enforcement of awards made in other countries. For example, more than eighty countries have ratified the UN Convention on the Recognition and Enforcement of Foreign Arbitral Awards. However, a foreign award that violates a country's laws or public policy is not likely to be recognized or enforced anywhere. Therefore, be aware of the rules governing such matters in both your and your counterpart's country.

CHAPTER 6

# Incoterms 2000

IN INTERNATIONAL BUSINESS transactions, you will use different methods of payment, and possibly a different currency, than you do in domestic transactions. In addition, while the terms of sale commonly used in international business transactions often sound similar to those used in domestic contracts, they often have different meanings in global transactions. Confusion over these terms can result in a lost sale or a financial loss on a sale. Thus, it is essential that you understand the various trade terms before you finalize a contract.

## Incoterms 2000 and the ICC

"Incoterms 2000" is a set of uniform rules codifying the interpretation of trade terms defining the rights and obligations of buyers and sellers in international transactions. Developed and issued by the International Chamber of Commerce (ICC) in Paris, the current version is publication No. 560a from 2000.

All international traders should be familiar with these terms and definitions. An excellent book describing obligations of buyers and sellers under Incoterms 2000 is available from: ICC Publishing, Inc; 156 Fifth Avenue; New York, NY 10010 USA; http://www.iccbooksusa.com

## Incoterms 2000[1]

1. Ex Works (EXW)
2. Free Carrier (FCA)
3. Free Alongside Ship (FAS)
4. Free On Board (FOB)
5. Cost and Freight (CFR)
6. Cost, Insurance and Freight (CIF)
7. Carriage Paid To (CPT)
8. Carriage and Insurance Paid To (CIP)
9. Delivered At Frontier (DAF)
10. Delivered Ex Ship (DES)
11. Delivered Ex Quay (DEQ)
12. Delivered Duty Unpaid (DDU)
13. Delivered Duty Paid (DDP)

## 1) EXW, Ex Works (...named place)

In Ex Works, the seller/exporter/manufacturer merely makes the goods available to the buyer at the seller's "named place" of business. This trade term places the greatest responsibility on the buyer and minimum obligations on the seller.

The seller does not clear the goods for export and does not load the goods onto a truck or other transport vehicle at the named place of departure.

The parties to the transaction, however, may stipulate that the seller be responsible for the costs and risks of loading the goods onto a transport vehicle. Such a stipulation must be made within the contract of sale.

If the buyer cannot handle export formalities the Ex Works term should not be used. In such a case Free Carrier (FCA) is recommended. The Ex Works term is often used when making an initial quotation for the sale of goods. It represents the cost of the goods without any other costs included. Normal payment terms for Ex Works transactions are generally cash in advance and open account.

## 2) FCA, Free Carrier (...named place)

In Free Carrier, the seller/exporter/manufacturer clears the goods for export and then delivers them to the carrier specified by the buyer at the named place.

If the named place is the seller's place of business, the seller is responsible for loading the goods onto the transport vehicle. If the named place is any other location, such as the loading dock of the carrier, the seller is not responsible for loading the goods onto the transport vehicle.

The Free Carrier term may be used for any mode of transport, including multimodal. The "named place" in Free Carrier and all "F" terms is domestic to the seller.

"Carrier" has a specific and somewhat expanded meaning. A carrier can be a shipping line, an airline, a trucking firm, or a railway. The carrier can also be an individual or firm who undertakes to procure carriage by any of the above methods of transport including multimodal. Therefore, a person, such as a freight forwarder, can act as a "carrier" under this term. In such a case, the buyer names the carrier or the individual who is to receive the goods.

The Free Carrier term is often used when making an initial quotation for the sale of goods. Normal payment terms for Free Carrier transactions are generally cash in advance and open account.

## 3) FAS, Free Alongside Ship (...named port of shipment)

In Free Alongside Ship, the seller/exporter/manufacturer clears the goods for export and then places them alongside the vessel at the "named port of shipment." [The seller's clearing the goods for export is new to Incoterms 2000.]

The parties to the transaction, however, may stipulate in their contract of sale that the buyer will clear the goods for export.

The Free Alongside Ship term is used only for ocean or inland waterway transport.

The "named place" in Free Alongside Ship and all "F" terms is domestic to the seller. The Free Alongside Ship term is commonly used in the sale of bulk commodity cargo such as oil, grains, and ore. Normal payment terms for Free Carrier transactions are generally cash in advance and open account, but letters of credit are also used.

### 4) FOB, Free On Board (...named port of shipment)

In Free On Board, the seller/exporter/manufacturer clears the goods for export and is responsible for the costs and risks of delivering the goods past the ship's rail at the named port of shipment. The Free On Board term is used only for ocean or inland waterway transport. The "named place" in Free On Board and all "F" terms is domestic to the seller. Normal payment terms for Free On Board transactions include cash in advance, open account, and letters of credit.

The Free On Board term is commonly used in the sale of bulk commodity cargo such as oil, grains, and ore where passing the ship's rail is important. However, it is also commonly used in shipping container loads of other goods.

The key document in FOB transactions is the "On Board Bill of Lading."

Sellers and buyers often confuse the Free On Board term with Free Carrier. Free On Board (FOB) does not mean loading the goods onto a truck at the seller's place of business. Free On Board is used only in reference to delivering the goods past a ship's rail in ocean or inland waterway transport. Free Carrier, on the other hand, is applicable to all modes of transport.

### 5) Cost and Freight (...named port of destination)

In Cost and Freight, the seller/exporter/manufacturer clears the goods for export and is responsible for delivering the goods past the ship's rail at the port of shipment (not destination).

The seller is also responsible for paying for the costs associated with transport of the goods to the named port of destination. However, once the goods pass the ship's rail at the port of shipment, the buyer assumes responsibility for risk of loss or damage as well as any additional transport costs.

The Cost and Freight term is used only for ocean or inland waterway transport.

The "named port of destination" in Cost and Freight and all "C" terms is domestic to the buyer. Normal payment terms for Cost and Freight transactions include cash in advance, open account, and letters of credit.

The Cost and Freight term is commonly used in the sale of oversize and overweight cargo that will not fit into an ocean freight container or exceeds weight limitations of such containers. The term is also used for LCL (less than container load) cargo and for the shipment of goods by rail in boxcars to the ocean carrier.

### 6) Cost, Insurance and Freight (...named port of destination)

In Cost, Insurance and Freight, the seller/exporter/manufacturer clears the goods for export and is responsible for delivering the goods past the ship's rail at the port of shipment (not destination).

The seller is responsible for paying for the costs associated with transport of the goods to the named port of destination. However, once the goods pass the ship's rail at the port of shipment, the buyer assumes responsibility for risk of loss or damage as well as any additional transport costs.

The seller is also responsible for procuring and paying for marine insurance in the buyer's name for the shipment. The Cost and Freight term is used only for ocean or inland waterway transport.

The "named port of destination" in Cost and Freight and all "C" terms is domestic to the buyer. Normal payment terms for Cost and Freight transactions include cash in advance, open account, and letters of credit.

## 7) Carriage Paid To (...named place of destination)

In Carriage Paid To, the seller/exporter/manufacturer clears the goods for export, delivers them to the carrier, and is responsible for paying for carriage to the named place of destination. However, once the seller delivers the goods to the carrier, the buyer becomes responsible for all additional costs.

In Incoterms 2000 the seller is also responsible for the costs of unloading, customs clearance, duties, and other costs if such costs are included in the cost of carriage such as in small package courier delivery. The seller is not responsible for procuring and paying for insurance cover. The CPT term is valid for any form of transport including multimodal The "named place of destination" in CPT and all "C" terms is domestic to the buyer, but is not necessarily the final delivery point.

The Carriage Paid To term is often used in sales where the shipment is by air freight, containerized ocean freight, courier shipments of small parcels, and in "ro-ro" (roll-on, roll-off) shipments of motor vehicles. A "carrier" can be a shipping line, airline, trucking firm, railway or also an individual or firm who undertakes to procure carriage by any of the above methods of transport including multimodal. Therefore, a person, such as a freight forwarder, can act as a "carrier" under this term. If subsequent carriers are used for the carriage to the agreed destination, the risk passes when the goods have been delivered to the first carrier.

## 8) Carriage and Insurance Paid To (...named place of destination)

In Carriage and Insurance Paid To, the seller/exporter clears the goods for export, delivers them to the carrier, and is responsible for paying for carriage and insurance to the named place of destination. However, once the goods are delivered to the carrier, the buyer is responsible for all additional costs.

In Incoterms 2000 the seller is also responsible for the costs of unloading, customs clearance, duties, and other costs if such costs are included in the cost of carriage such as in small package courier delivery. The seller is responsible for procuring and paying for insurance cover. The CIP term is valid for any form of transport including multimodal The "named place of destination" in CIP and all "C" terms is domestic to the buyer, but is not necessarily the final delivery point.

The Carriage and Insurance Paid To term is often used in sales where the shipment is by air freight, containerized ocean freight, courier shipments of small parcels, and in "ro-ro" (roll-on, roll-off) shipments of motor vehicles.

A "carrier" can be a shipping line, airline, trucking firm, railway or also an individual or firm who undertakes to procure carriage by any of the above methods of transport including multimodal. Therefore, a person, such as a freight forwarder, can act as a "carrier" under this term. If subsequent carriers are used for the carriage to the agreed destination, the risk passes when the goods have been delivered to the first carrier.

## 9) Delivered At Frontier (...named place)

In Delivered At Frontier, the seller/exporter/manufacturer clears the goods for export and is responsible for making them available to the buyer at the named point and place at the frontier, not unloaded, and not cleared for import.

In the DAF term, naming the precise point, place, and time of availability at the frontier is very important as the buyer must make arrangements to unload and secure the goods in a timely manner. Frontier can mean any frontier including the frontier of export. The DAF term is valid for any mode of shipment, so long as the final shipment to the named place at the frontier is by land. The seller is not responsible for procuring and paying for insurance cover.

### 10) Delivered Ex Ship (...named port of destination)

In Delivered Ex Ship, the seller/exporter/manufacturer clears the goods for export and is responsible for making them available to the buyer on board the ship at the named port of destination, not cleared for import.

The seller is thus responsible for all costs of getting the goods to the named port of destination prior to unloading.

The DES term is used only for shipments of goods by ocean or inland waterway or by multimodal transport where the final delivery is made on a vessel at the named port of destination. All forms of payment are used in DES transactions.

### 11) Delivered Ex Quay (...named port of destination)

In Delivered Ex Quay, the seller/exporter/manufacturer clears the goods for export and is responsible for making them available to the buyer on the quay (wharf) at the named port of destination, not cleared for import.

The buyer, therefore, assumes all responsibilities for import clearance, duties, and other costs upon import as well as transport to the final destination. This is new for Incoterms 2000. The DES term is used only for shipments of goods arriving at the port of destination by ocean or by inland waterway. All forms of payment are used in DEQ transactions.

### 12) Delivered Duty Unpaid (...named place of destination)

In Delivered Duty Unpaid, the seller/exporter/manufacturer clears the goods for export and is responsible for making them available to the buyer at the named place of destination, not cleared for import.

The seller, therefore, assumes all responsibilities for delivering the goods to the named place of destination, but the buyer assumes all responsibility for import clearance, duties, administrative costs, and any other costs upon import as well as transport to the final destination.

The DDU term can be used for any mode of transport. However, if the seller and buyer desire that delivery should take place on board a sea vessel or on a quay (wharf), the DES or DEQ terms are recommended. All forms of payment are used in DDU transactions. The DDU term is used when the named place of destination (point of delivery) is other than the seaport or airport.

### Delivered Duty Paid (...named place of destination)

In Delivered Duty Paid, the seller/exporter/manufacturer clears the goods for export and is responsible for making them available to the buyer at the named place of destination, cleared for import, but not unloaded from the transport vehicle. The seller, therefore, assumes all responsibilities for delivering the goods to the named place of destination, including all responsibility for import clearance, duties, and other costs payable upon import.

The DDP term can be used for any mode of transport. All forms of payment are used in DDP transactions. The DDP term is used when the named place of destination (point of delivery) is other than the seaport or airport.

CHAPTER 7

# Notes on Granting and Obtaining Credit

THE FINANCING OF TRADE is perhaps the greatest source of frustration for both buyers and sellers. Buyers universally wish for easy and long-term credit to give them time to resell products and make payment to the seller, while sellers universally wish for immediate payment so they can avoid credit risk and pay their own costs of production. The realities of business force many firms to grant credit terms to the buyer. Both the buyer and seller understand that credit terms can lead to increased sales and profits for both parties to the transaction. Granting credit, however, is a process fraught with risk.

This chapter outlines some of the opportunities, risks, and procedures for granting and obtaining credit.

## Granting Credit

Most principles of domestic credit management apply to export credit management as well. Exporters will grant credit terms only to those firms it deems able and willing to pay the full amount on time, as agreed. International transactions, however, add layers of uncertainty to the credit decision. Unknown firms, far away countries, different languages and cultures, foreign exchange risk, and political and economic risk all play a part in the decision.

Sellers should follow the same careful credit principles they follow for domestic customers. Some clients will be accepted for credit terms while others will not. The first step for sellers is to establish a written international credit policy and to adhere to it and to review it in light of actual experience.

The terms of payment granted in a given case will depend on the situation: the relationship between the seller and the buyer; the credit worthiness of the buyer; foreign exchange considerations; and the political, economic, and social stability of the buyer's country. Sales to an unfamiliar buyer in a developing country will call for prepayment or a confirmed letter of credit.

Sellers should also manage the credit period as a key cost of the transaction. If the buyer is not responsible for directly paying carrying costs, the seller should factor them into the selling price.

The credit policy should be appropriate for the individual company, the industry in which it operates, the size of sale contracts, the margin of profit on individual sales, the stability of the market, the stability of the customer, whether sales are one time only or repeat sales, frequency of sales to each customer, and minimum information upon which to base a decision.

### CREDIT PERIOD

A useful guide for determining the proper credit period is the normal commercial terms in the seller's industry for internationally traded products. Buyers generally expect to receive the benefits of such terms. With few exceptions, normal commercial terms range from 30 to 180 days for off-the-shelf items like consumer goods, chemicals, and other industrial raw materials, agricultural commodities, and spare parts and components. Custom-made or higher-value capital equipment, on the other hand, may warrant shorter or longer payment periods, depending on the situation. An allowance may have to be made for longer shipment times than are found in domestic trade, because foreign buyers are often unwilling to have the credit period start before receiving the goods.

### COMPETITIVE CONSIDERATIONS

Foreign buyers often press exporters for longer payment periods (and don't forget that liberal financing is a means of enhancing export competitiveness). The seller should recognize, however, that longer credit periods increase the risk of default for which the seller may be liable. Longer credit periods also cost the exporter money in financing costs. Thus the seller must exercise judgment in balancing competitiveness against considerations of cost and safety. Also, credit terms once extended to a buyer tend set the precedent for future sales, so the seller should carefully consider any credit terms extended to first-time buyers.

### CHARGING INTEREST

International customers are frequently charged interest on long-term credit (more than 180 days) but infrequently on short-term credit (up to 180 days). Most exporters absorb interest charges for the short-term unless the customer pays late.

Unless a domestic supplier agrees to grant the exporter more extended payment terms, or the foreign buyer agrees to make a cash advance (achievable in only a minor proportion of cases), or the seller has ready access to bank borrowing, a problem will exist.

### EXPORT FINANCING

There are a number of ways in which the exporter can manage the financial pressures inherent in export sales:

- **CONVERT EXPORT RECEIVABLES TO CASH** One option is to obtain immediate cash through receivables financing. This can be accomplished in several ways. The first is to use receivables as collateral to obtain a bank loan. Domestic banks are a bit skittish about such loans as they rarely have the experience to judge whether such receivables have value.

  Another method is to actually sell the receivables at a discount to a bank or financial institution that specializes in export finance. In this case the export finance company evaluates each receivable for company and country risk and term of payment to establish the discount. Although these firms deal in discounts against the original invoice, when expressed as interest,

  their rates factor as high as 20 to 50 percent annually. The deals can involve recourse or non-recourse to the seller. That is, if the buyer never pays, the finance company can have recourse to the seller up to the entire amount of the invoice value.

- **EXPAND CAPITAL RESOURCES** Another option is to expand working capital resources through traditional debt or equity vehicles.

- **BUYER CREDIT** When the purchase involves capital goods and the repayment period extends for a year or longer, a good method of obtaining immediate cash is to arrange for buyer credit. In this case, a lender makes a loan directly to the buyer for the project and the seller is paid immediately from the loan proceeds while the bank waits for payment and earns interest.
- **COUNTERTRADE** Another, less conventional method is countertrade. This is where the seller agrees to receive merchandise (usually from the home country of the buyer) in exchange for payment for goods. The advantage of this option is that the seller receives goods immediately that can then be sold in the sellers domestic market for, hopefully, shorter credit terms of perhaps 30 days.

The options that have been mentioned normally involve the payment of interest, fees, or others costs. Some options are more feasible when the amounts are in larger denominations, and sellers should always determine whether they incur financial liability should the buyer default.

### EXPORT GUARANTEES AND INSURANCE

Export trade promotion services of many nations have established programs that, under certain circumstances, guarantee or insure international receivables for companies operating within their jurisdiction. While many of these programs do not offer immediate payment for receivables they do guarantee payment. This guarantee may sometimes be used as leverage with domestic banks to obtain receivables financing more easily.

## Getting Credit

### DON'T OVERLOOK SOURCES OF FINANCE

Two generally underutilized sources of credit for buyer/importers are suppliers and export trade promotion services in the seller's country of origin. Although most official and quasiofficial trade facilitating organizations are concerned almost exclusively with promoting and financing exports from their domestic suppliers, this can really work to a buyer's benefit—after all, you are looking to buy what they have to sell.

### SELLER CREDIT

Don't be bashful about proposing imaginative financing alternatives to your supplier. One small-time importer making regular buying trips to the Far East was able to get favorable terms based on his presentation of himself as a reliable business partner. He paid with cash, using traveler's checks, on his first trip; by personal check on the second trip; by post-dated personal check on the third trip; got 60-day credit terms on the fourth trip; and got 120-day credit thereafter.

Eventually, several of his suppliers "fronted" larger quantities of merchandise for him to establish a distribution network in his own country without his having to finance the operation himself.

He succeeded by making his supplier comfortable with him. He (1) showed himself in person on a regular basis, (2) demonstrated knowledge of his industry, products, and domestic marketing channels, (3) studied the culture of his suppliers and presented himself as someone they could do business with, (4) established personal relationships with his suppliers, and (5) ALWAYS followed through on everything he said he was going to do. It is okay to be imaginative, but be sure you can deliver.

### EXPORT TRADE PROMOTION AGENCY CREDIT

With the support of the seller a buyer can sometimes obtain credit through an export trade promotion agency of the seller's country. This can be a complicated matter and is generally for medium- to larger-sized repetitive transactions. In some cases the export trade promotion agency offers a payment guarantee or insurance to the seller that the seller can use with their domestic bank to get receivables financing at reasonable rates.

For example, a US-based furniture chain obtained one-year financing on imports of leather furniture from a South American company because of the export insurance offered by an agency of the seller's government. In this case everyone was aware of the problems associated with maintaining inventory in the furniture business. It often took one month for the furniture to ship and arrive at the buyer's port of importation and another several months for it to sell through the distribution channels. The company was reliable but could not realistically expect to pay its invoices in 60, 90, or 120 days.

Ask your supplier if there is such a trade promotion agency in his country. You can also get information from a local commercial consulate of the seller's country in your area.

### CREDIT CARDS

In recent years, as working capital has become more difficult to obtain from traditional lenders, the use of credit cards as a payment mechanism has increased dramatically. It is not at all uncommon for an individual to have ten or more credit cards with credit limits of US$10,000 plus each. Many importers of low-value products purchased directly from the supplier can pay using credit cards. Many traders got their start by using credit cards to get an effective twenty-five to forty days free financing between the purchase and due dates. Some credit cards also offer mileage points for frequent flyer miles on airlines.

In some cases, the seller will want to add a surcharge to offset the charges that banks assess to the seller on the transaction. You should also realize that merchants are particularly resistant to accepting credit card payments in countries experiencing high inflation, which can heighten their risk between the time of the transaction and the time they actually get paid by the bank (regardless of when the buyer pays the charges). The several percentage points the seller demands may make it inadvisable to use your card unless you really need the credit or know you can turn the goods over quickly.

## International Credit Reports

It is always a good idea for both buyers and sellers to know who they are doing business with before committing to a transaction. Many business deals have gone sour when either the buyer or seller finds out that their counterpart is unable or unwilling to follow through on a transaction.

Sellers may be at risk even if they are using a relatively safe payment method or purchase credit risk insurance. Some well-known companies have horrible payment histories and policies. Buyers may also be at risk as goods shipped may not be what was ordered and paid for. Knowing the seller's reputation and ability and willingness to perform responsibilities under the terms of the contract is simply good business.

The following are a number of sources for company financial information:

## BANKS

Banks are often able to provide credit reports on foreign companies, either through their own foreign branches or through a correspondent bank. Banks can provide current information on the reputation, capabilities, and creditworthiness of firms and individuals in most countries.

## COMMERCIAL CONSULATES

Sometimes, the commercial consulate of your country can provide information on the reputation of a foreign seller or buyer. Alternatively you might try the local commercial consulate of the seller's or buyer's country for information. Information from the latter may well be prejudiced by their interest in aiding their domestic businesses, so be careful.

## PRIVATE CREDIT REPORTING SERVICES

Private credit reporting services also are available in most countries. Some firms offer credit reporting worldwide through affiliates. Several US companies compile financial information on foreign firms (especially larger companies) and make it available to subscribers. Many of these companies have extensive reporting services in foreign countries as well.

- **DUN & BRADSTREET (D&B)** Dun & Bradstreet is a major supplier of creditor information and offers three services to evaluate the risk of doing business with an overseas company: (1) The Business Information Report contains information such as payment experience, company summary, finances, history, operations, and corporate structure; (2) The Payment Analysis Report provides a comprehensive analysis of a company's payment habits; and (3) The Financial Profile provides detailed financial information on a company, plus key business ratios calculated for both the company and its industry. Dun & Bradstreet also has a full range of collection services to collect domestic and international past-due accounts. For more information, in the United States call (800) 234-DUNS.
- **UNITED STATES DEPARTMENT OF COMMERCE (US DOC)** The US DOC's International Company Profiles (ICP) provide useful information for credit checks. For a fee, an ICP may be requested on any foreign company. Although the ICP is itself not a credit report, it does contain financial information and identifies other local companies that do business with the reported firm. The trader may then contact those companies directly to find out about their payment experience.

---

**NOTE:** Be prepared to be underwhelmed by reports from some credit services. In some cases the information is so vague that it is impossible to make an educated credit decision.

---

### FOREIGN CREDIT REPORTING SOURCES

Credit evaluations can also be obtained from foreign services, many of which are listed in *The Exporter's Guide to Foreign Sources for Credit Information*, published by Trade Data Reports, Inc., 6 West 37th St., New York, NY 10018.

## International Debt Collection

In international trade, problems involving bad debt are more easily avoided than rectified. Presale credit and customer payment investigations can limit the risks. Nonetheless, just as in domestic business, international sellers occasionally encounter buyers who default on payments. Obtaining payment can be both difficult and expensive. Even when the seller has insurance to cover commercial credit risks, a default by a buyer requires time, effort, and cost. The trader must exhaust all reasonable means of obtaining payment before an insurance claim is honored, and there is often a significant delay before the insurance payment is made.

### WORK IT OUT WITH THE BUYER

The simplest and least costly solution is to negotiate with the buyer. With patience, understanding, and flexibility, a seller can often resolve conflicts to the satisfaction of both parties. This is especially true when a simple misunderstanding or technical problem is to blame and there is no question of bad faith. Even though the seller may be required to compromise on certain points—perhaps even on the price of the committed goods—the company may save a valuable customer and profit in the long run. Also, in some cultures, anything other than working it out with the buyer is considered such an insult that it may well be impossible to do business with the company ever again.

### DEBT COLLECTION AGENCIES

Most developed countries have established services that collect trade debt. The methods employed range from sending simple letters of request, to sending letters on the letterhead of an attorney, to full-blown litigation. These services usually charge a fee as a percentage of the invoice amount. This percentage fee is usually smaller as the invoice amount is larger. In difficult cases they will charge a non-refundable base fee plus a percentage. These services can be located through trade promotion agencies of your government, consulates and embassies of your country, and through advertisements in major trade journals.

### ARBITRATION

If negotiations fail and the sum involved is large enough to warrant the effort, and both parties agree, the dispute can be taken to an arbitration agency. This step may be preferable to legal action, since arbitration is often faster and less costly. On the other hand arbiters tend to "split the difference," which can be to your detriment if your case is strongest.

If arbitration is a viable option for you, be certain to include an arbitration clause in your contracts, either to arbitration with a specific arbitration agency, or to arbitration based upon the rules of a particular arbitration agency. Many US-based firms, for example, ask that arbitration be subject to the rules of the American Arbitration Association.

The International Chamber of Commerce (ICC) conducts many international arbitrations and is often acceptable to foreign companies because it is well known throughout the world and is not affiliated with any single country. This service, however, can be costly and is impractical for small sums.

Refer to Chapter 5: Contract Basics for more information on arbitration.

## GOING TO COURT

Going to court should be the last option. It is expensive, time consuming, and the outcome is far from certain. If you wish to take a foreign company to court in your own country they may simply not come. If you take them to court in their country they will probably have the upper hand in that they are closer to home, know their own legal system better, and most foreign legal systems are somewhat to extremely biased to nationals of their own country.

The first step is to obtain legal representation and review your options and the costs involved. You can find representation through referrals from domestic legal associations, your country's embassy or consulate in the subject country, or from referrals from other traders who have done business in the country of dispute. Finally, consider that even if you do win the case, collecting on the judgment may be difficult or impossible.

CHAPTER 8

# Drafts and Acceptances

IN DOCUMENTARY TRANSACTIONS sellers make a written demand upon either a bank or the buyer to pay for the shipment of goods. This demand accompanies the documentation package the seller presents to the bank. Such a formal written demand for payment is called a "draft."

## DRAFTS

The formal definition of draft is: An unconditional order in writing, signed by a person (drawer) such as a buyer, and addressed to another person (drawee), typically a bank, ordering the drawee to pay a stated sum of money to yet another person (payee), often the seller, on demand or at a fixed or determinable future time. The most common versions of drafts are: (1) Sight drafts which are payable when presented, and (2) Time drafts (also called usance drafts) which are payable at a future fixed (specific) date or determinable (e.g., 30, 60, 90 days) date.

## ACCEPTANCES

An acceptance is a time draft that has been accepted and signed by the drawee (the buyer or the bank) for payment at maturity. If a time draft is accepted by a buyer of merchandise, it is called a TRADE ACCEPTANCE. If a time draft is accepted by a bank it is called a BANKERS' ACCEPTANCE.

In most cases, obviously, a draft accepted by a bank enjoys higher credit standing than a draft accepted by a company or individual, since a bank is presumed to meet its obligation at maturity, and a company or individual in a foreign country may not as readily comply with its obligation.

## HOLDING OR DISCOUNTING ACCEPTANCES

In documentary transactions, the seller has two options, once the seller's time draft is accepted. The seller may either hold it until maturity and collect full face value, or discount the draft, most likely with the accepting bank, and take the net value in cash immediately. In these ways, trade and bankers' acceptances often represent the easiest, least expensive way for a seller to provide credit to a buyer, while enjoying the security provided by the documentary transaction.

## FINANCING TRANSACTIONS USING ACCEPTANCES

Thus, foreign buyers may indicate that they wish to provide a time documentary credit (rather than a sight documentary credit) but agree either to allow the seller to up the sales price slightly so as to offset the acceptance commission and discount costs or to absorb the acceptance commission and discount charges the bank will apply when discounting the draft at the request of the seller. In either case, the buyer and the buyer's bank will absorb the charges involved, and the seller will receive the full contract sales amount. Since the charges are usually lower than conventional financing charges, the buyer is still better off than if financing had been obtained through a bank loan.

SAMPLE DRAFT AND ACCEPTANCE

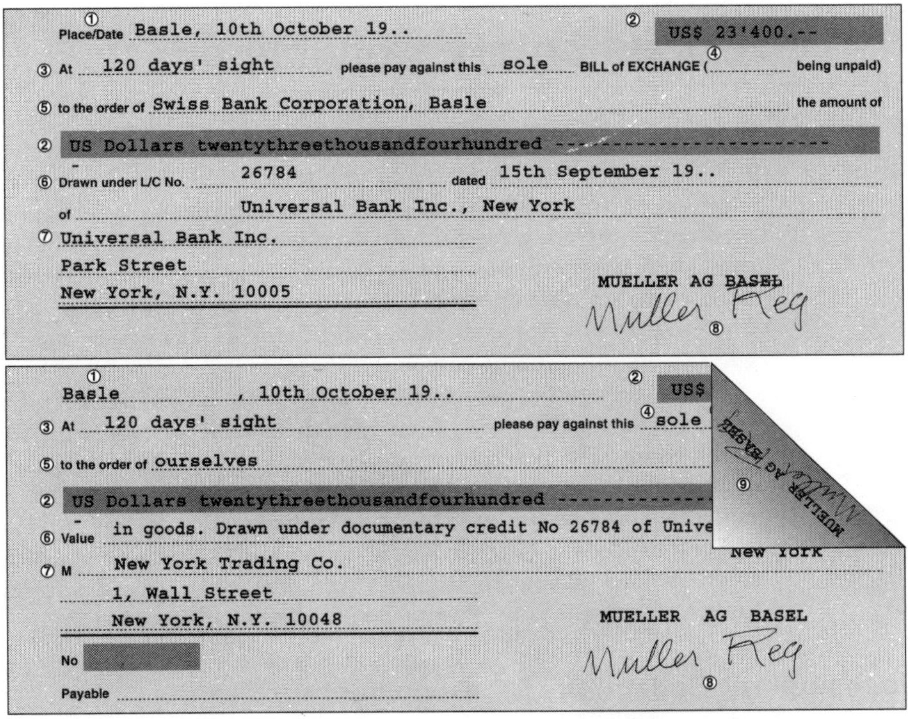
① Place/Date Basle, 10th October 19.. ② US$ 23'400.--

③ At 120 days' sight please pay against this sole BILL of EXCHANGE (④ being unpaid)

⑤ to the order of Swiss Bank Corporation, Basle the amount of

② US Dollars twentythreethousandfourhundred ---

⑥ Drawn under L/C No. 26784 dated 15th September 19..

of Universal Bank Inc., New York

⑦ Universal Bank Inc.
Park Street
New York, N.Y. 10005

MUELLER AG BASEL
Muller Reg ⑧

① Basle , 10th October 19.. ② US$

③ At 120 days' sight please pay against this ④ sole

⑤ to the order of ourselves

② US Dollars twentythreethousandfourhundred ---

⑥ Value in goods. Drawn under documentary credit No 26784 of Unive... New York

⑦ M New York Trading Co.
1, Wall Street
New York, N.Y. 10048

MUELLER AG BASEL
Muller Reg ⑧

No

Payable

⑨ MUELLER AG BASEL

① Place drawn and date
② Currency and amount in numbers and words
③ Validity period
④ Number of originals (sole or first/second)
⑤ If issued to own order: endorsement required
⑥ Reference to credit
⑦ Drawee
⑧ Drawer (handwritten signature)
⑨ Endorsement

## "CLEAN" ACCEPTANCES

A "clean" acceptance is one that does not have any notations attached that would compromise its value. In a trade acceptance the customer promises to pay the bank the full amount of the draft no later than the date of maturity, or upon demand of the bank. The accepted draft, when discounted, becomes a negotiable instrument that can be sold in the acceptance market, which is an over-the-counter market of brokers, dealers, and banks.

Bankers acceptances are generally short-term, that is up to 180 days. Bankers' acceptances become money market instruments once they are accepted by a major bank, which means that the bank has undertaken to honor this short-term note at its maturity. Because of this characteristic, bankers' acceptances often result in a lower financing costs. The difference can range from 1 to 3 percent depending on the transaction and the bank involved. Thus, they are important sources of financing.

CHAPTER 9

# Documentary Collections

THINK OF A DOCUMENTARY COLLECTION as an international COD (cash on delivery): the buyer pays for goods at delivery. A documentary collection, however, is distinguished from a typical COD transaction in two ways: (1) instead of an individual, shipping company, or postal service collecting the payment, a bank handles the transaction, and (2) instead of cash on delivery for goods it is cash on delivery for a title document (bill of lading) that is then used to claim the goods from the shipping company.

Banks, therefore, act as intermediaries to collect payment from the buyer in exchange for the transfer of documents that enable the holder to take possession of the goods. The procedure is easier than a documentary credit, and the bank charges are lower. The bank, however, does not act as surety of payment but rather only as collector of funds for documents.

For the seller and buyer, a documentary collection falls between a documentary credit and open account in its desirability. Advantages, disadvantages, and issues for both buyer and seller will be discussed in the following pages.

## Documentary Collections vs. Documentary Credits

In a documentary collection, the seller prepares and presents documents to the bank in much the same way as for a documentary letter of credit. However, there are two major differences between a documentary collection and a documentary credit: (1) the draft involved is not drawn by the seller (the "drawer") upon a bank for payment, but rather on the buyer itself (the "drawee"), and (2) the seller's bank has no obligation to pay upon presentation but, more simply, acts as a collecting or remitting bank on behalf of the seller, thus earning a commission for its services.

## The Uniform Rules for Collections (URC)

Although documentary collections, in one form or another, have been in use for a long time, questions arose about how to effect transactions in a practical, fair, and uniform manner.

The Uniform Rules for Collections (URC) is the internationally recognized codification of rules unifying banking practice regarding collection operations for drafts and for documentary collections. The URC was developed by the International Chamber of Commerce (ICC) in Paris. It is revised and updated from time-to-time; the current valid version is ICC publication No. 322.

## Introducing the Parties to a Documentary Collection

There are four main parties to a documentary collection transaction. Note below that each party has several names. This is because businesspeople and banks each have their own way of thinking about and naming each party to the transaction. For example, as far as businesspeople are concerned there are just buyers and sellers and the buyer's bank and the seller's bank. Banks, however, are not concerned with buying and selling. They are concerned with remitting (sending) documents from the principal (seller) and presenting drafts (orders to pay) to the drawee (buyer) for payment. The four main parties are

### THE PRINCIPAL (SELLER/EXPORTER/DRAWER)

The principal is generally the seller/exporter as well as the party that prepares documentation (collection documents) and submits (remits) them to his bank (remitting bank) with a collection order for payment from the buyer (drawee). The principal is also sometimes called the remitter.

### THE REMITTING (PRINCIPAL'S/SELLER'S/EXPORTER'S) BANK

The remitting bank receives documentation (collection documents) from the seller (principal) for forwarding (remitting) to the buyer's bank (collecting/presenting bank) along with instructions for payment.

### THE COLLECTING OR PRESENTING (BUYER'S) BANK

This is the bank that presents the documents to the buyer and collects cash payment (payment of a bank draft) or a promise to pay in the future (a bill of exchange) from the buyer (drawee of the draft) in exchange for the documents.

### THE DRAWEE (BUYER/IMPORTER)

The drawee (buyer/importer) is the party that makes cash payment or signs a draft according to the terms of the collection order in exchange for the documents from the presenting/collecting bank and takes possession of the goods. The drawee is the one on whom a draft is drawn and who owes the indicated amount.

## Basic Documentary Collection Procedure

The documentary collection procedure involves the step-by-step exchange of documents giving title to goods for either cash or a contracted promise to pay at a later time. Refer to the diagram on the opposite page for each numbered step.

### BUYER AND SELLER

The buyer and seller agree on the terms of sale of goods: (a) specifying a documentary collection as the means of payment, (b) naming a collecting/presenting bank (usually the buyer's bank), and (c) listing required documents.

### PRINCIPAL (SELLER)

1. The seller (principal) ships the goods to the buyer (drawee) and obtains a negotiable transport document (bill of lading) from the shipping firm/agent.
2. The seller (principal) prepares and presents (remits) a document package to his bank (the remitting bank) consisting of (a) a collection order specifying the terms and conditions under which the bank is to hand over documents to the buyer and receive payment, (b) the negotiable transport document (bill of lading), and (c) other documents (e.g., insurance document, certificate of origin, inspection certificate, etc.) as required by the buyer.

### REMITTING BANK

3. The remitting bank sends the documentation package by mail or by courier to the designated collecting/presenting bank in the buyer's country with instructions to present them to the drawee (buyer) and collect payment.

### COLLECTING BANK

4. The presenting (collecting) bank (a) reviews the documents making certain they are in conformity with the collection order, (b) notifies the buyer (drawee) about the terms and conditions of the collection order, and (c) releases the documents once the payment conditions have been met.

### BUYER/DRAWEE

5. The buyer (drawee) (a) makes a cash payment (signing the draft), or if the collection order allows, signs an acceptance (promise to pay at a future date) and (b) receives the documents and takes possession of the shipment.

### COLLECTING BANK

6. The collecting bank pays the remitting bank either with an immediate payment or, at the maturity date of the accepted bill of exchange.

### REMITTING BANK

7. The remitting bank then pays the seller (principal).

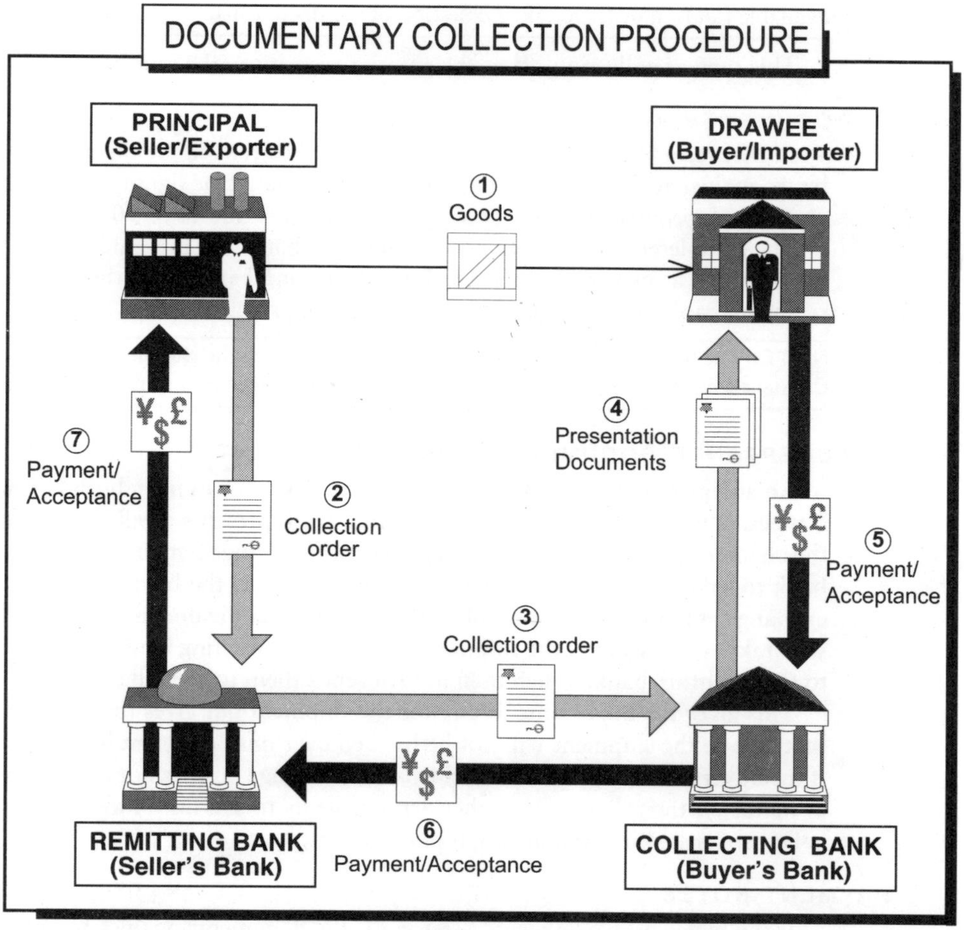


### A NOTE CONCERNING CORRESPONDENT BANKS

The remitting bank may find it necessary or desirable to use an intermediary bank (called a correspondent bank) rather than sending the collection order and documents directly to the collecting bank. For example, the collecting bank may be very small or may not have an established relationship with the remitting bank.

## Three Types of Collections

There are three types of documentary collections and each relates to a buyer option for payment for the documents at presentation. The second and third, however, are dependent upon the seller's willingness to accept the option and his specific instructions in the collection order. The three types are

### 1. DOCUMENTS AGAINST PAYMENT (D/P)

In D/P terms, the collecting bank releases the documents to the buyer only upon full and immediate cash payment. D/P terms most closely resemble a traditional cash-on-delivery transaction.

---

NOTE: The buyer must pay the presenting/collecting bank the full payment in freely available funds in order to take possession of the documents.

---

This type of collection offers the greatest security to the seller.

### 2. DOCUMENTS AGAINST ACCEPTANCE (D/A)

In D/A terms the collecting bank is permitted to release the documents to the buyer against acceptance (signing) of a bill of exchange or signing of a time draft at the bank promising to pay at a later date (usually 30, 60 or 90 days).

The completed draft is held by the collecting bank and presented to the buyer for payment at maturity, after which the collecting bank sends the funds to the remitting bank, which in turn sends them to the principal/seller.

---

NOTE: The seller should be aware that he gives up title to the shipment in exchange for the signed bill of exchange that now represents his only security in the transaction.

---

### 3. ACCEPTANCE DOCUMENTS AGAINST PAYMENT

An acceptance documents against payment has features from both D/P and D/P types. It works like this: (a) the collecting bank presents a bill of exchange to the buyer for acceptance, (b) the accepted bill of exchange remains at the collecting bank together with the documents up to maturity, (c) the buyer pays the bill of exchange at maturity, (d) the collecting bank releases the documents to the buyer who takes possession of the shipment, and (e) the collecting bank sends the funds to the remitting bank, which then in turn sends them to the seller.

This gives the buyer time to pay for the shipment but gives the seller security that title to the shipment will not be handed over until payment has been made. If the buyer refuses acceptance of the bill of exchange or does not honor payment at maturity, the seller makes other arrangements to sell his goods. This type of collection is seldom used in actual practice.

### PAYMENT NOTES

If the buyer draws (takes possession of) the documents against acceptance of a bill of exchange, the collecting bank sends the acceptance back to the remitting bank or retains it on a fiduciary basis up to maturity. On maturity, the collecting bank collects the bill and transfers the proceeds to the remitting bank for crediting to the seller.

## General Notes and Cautions

Specific notes and cautions for sellers, buyers, and banks involved in documentary collection transactions are listed at the end of this chapter. Listed below are notes and cautions that are fundamental to the process and of importance to all parties to the transaction.

- The banks involved in a documentary collection do not guarantee payment or assume any credit risk, as they do in documentary credit transactions. The banks act merely as intermediaries to facilitate payment for a shipment.
- If the shipper/seller sends goods directly to the buyer's address, the shipment will be handed over without the buyer first making payment. The seller, therefore, will usually address the shipment to his agent in the buyer's country or to the collecting bank if it is known to him and prior agreement has been obtained to do so.
- Goods are transported, stored, and insured at the expense and risk of the seller until payment or acceptance occurs. Generally, banks are under no obligation to protect the goods. Banks are also not responsible if the shipment is seized by customs or confiscated to cover any accrued storage costs.
- Documentary collections have one additional safeguard over transactions conducted on an open-account basis. The existence of the draft itself, which has been duly presented and accepted through a bank in the buyer's country, is an acknowledged evidence of debt. However, this may not be of great value against a purchaser who is determined not to pay.
- In D/P terms the buyer may refuse to pay, in which case the seller maintains title to the shipment. The seller may decide to negotiate new terms with the buyer, locate another buyer, or have the goods returned, incurring the cost of shipping, insurance, and bank fees. If the goods are perishable, the seller may be in a difficult position to find a new buyer quickly.
- In D/A terms the buyer may refuse to accept the draft, in which case the seller is in the same position as in D/P terms where the buyer refuses to pay the draft. (See the preceding item for details.)
- In D/A terms the buyer may accept (sign) the draft, take possession of the goods, but then refuse to pay the draft at maturity. In this case the seller has neither payment nor the goods. The seller's options are effectively reduced to trying to enforce the buyer's obligation to pay the draft through banking channels or legal action, both of which involve additional costs.
- Since the banks are under no obligation to authenticate documents, it is possible that the seller will send a short shipment, the incorrect goods, or inferior goods. The only recourse available to the buyer is through direct contact with the seller or legal action.

## Transaction Documents

The documents required under a documentary collection are fundamentally the same as those in a documentary letter of credit transaction. In the original agreement between buyer and seller the buyer specifies documents that (1) make it possible to secure the shipment from the shipping company (bill of lading), (2) secure release from the customs authority (certificates of origin, commercial invoice, etc.), and (3) offer some guarantee of quality and count (inspection certificates).

Refer to Chapter 16: Documents for a full description of documents used in both documentary collection and documentary credit transactions.

## The Collection Order

The collection order is the key document prepared by the seller specifying the terms and conditions of the documentary collection. It must be prepared with great care and precision as the banks are only permitted to act upon the instructions given in the order and not on instructions from past transactions or verbal understandings. On the following page is a sample collection order and below are notes for key provisions of the document.

1. The payment period as agreed with the buyer
2. The name and address of the buyer
3. The buyer's bank
4. Instructions, if any, about what to do with the accepted bill of exchange
5. Notation concerning payment of charges for the documentary collection
6. Notation/instructions for the lodging of a protest in the event of nonacceptance or nonpayment
7. Instructions for notification of agent or representative in the buyer's country

## SAMPLE COLLECTION ORDER

Sender:

Müller Ltd.
Tellstrase 26

4053 Basle

**Documentary collection**

Basle, 12th August 19..
Place / Date

**Our Reference** AK/83

We send you herewith the following documents for collection:

Registered

**Swiss Bank Corporation**
**Schweizerischer Bankverein**

Documentary collections
P.O. Box

4002 Basle

| Amount | Maturity | Drawee (2) |
|---|---|---|
| US$ 14'300.-- | 90 days sight (1) | Maxwell Hammerton Inc.<br>12, Broadway<br>New York, N.Y. 10014 |
| | | Drawee's bank: Commercial Credit Bank (3)<br>New York |

| Draft/ Receipt | Invoice: com-mercial | Invoice: cust.-/ consul. | Insur.-Cert. | Certif. of Orig. | Weight/ Packing List | Bill of Lading | Waybill | Postal-/ Forw.-Receipt | other documents | |
|---|---|---|---|---|---|---|---|---|---|---|
| 1 | | 4 | 2 | | 2 | | | | 2 | analysis certificates |
| 3/3 | | | | | | | | | | |

Goods: 100 barrels "Chemical products - harmless"

by: s/s CAP SAN GIORGIO from: Le Havre to: New York on: 31.7.19..

Please follow the instructions marked «x»

| | Documents/goods to be delivered against | | | | | | Draft (4) | | State the exact due-date | | |
|---|---|---|---|---|---|---|---|---|---|---|---|
| | payment (1) | X | acceptance | | | | to be sent back after acceptance | | to be collected on due-date | | |
| (5) X | Your charges for drawee's account; if refused | | | | | X | waive charges | | do not deliver documents | | |
| X | Your correspondent's charges are for drawee's account; if refused | | | | | | waive charges | X | do not deliver documents | | |
| (6) X | Protest in case of | X | non-payment | | non-acceptance | X | Do not protest in case of | | non-payment | X | non-acceptance |
| X | Advise | X | non-payment | | non-acceptance | | by airmail | X | by cable | X | giving reasons |

Please credit the proceeds as follows:

☒ to our SFr account Nr. 10-326'791.0

☐ remit to

(7) Remarks:

In case of difficulties, the collecting bank is requested to inform our representatives: Messrs. Beach & Co. Inc., Broad Street 485, New York 34, who will be of assistance but who are not allowed to alter the above instructions.

Müller Ltd

Signature: ______________

Enclosures

E 6851 N 1/2 4.80 5000

The execution of this order is subject to the «Uniform rules for collections» issued by the International Chamber of Commerce

## Important Principles Regarding the Role of Banks

It is important to note that documentary collection procedures are not infallible. Things can and do go wrong. (Refer to the list of issues for sellers, buyers, and banks on the pages that follow.) Since banks act as intermediaries between buyers and sellers, both look to the banks as protectors of their interests. However, while banks have clear cut responsibilities, they are also shielded from certain problems deemed to be out of their control or responsibility. Several instances:

1. Banks act upon specific instructions given by the principal (seller) in the collection order. Seller's instructions left out of the collection order by mistake or omitted because "we've always done it that way" don't count. The principal, therefore, should take great care in preparing the collection order so that it gives complete and clear instructions.

2. Banks are required to act in good faith and exercise reasonable care to verify that the documents submitted APPEAR to be as listed in the collection order. They are, however, under no obligation to confirm the authenticity of the documents submitted.

3. Banks are not liable nor can they be held accountable for the acts of third parties. Third parties include freight forwarders, forwarding agents, customs authorities, insurance companies and other banks. Specifically, they are not responsible for delays or consequences resulting from Acts of God (floods, earthquakes, etc.), riots, wars, civil commotions, strikes, lockouts, or other causes beyond their control.

4. Banks also assume no liability or responsibility for loss arising out of delays or loss in transit of messages, letters, documents, etc.

5. Banks assume no responsibility regarding the quantity or quality of goods shipped. They are only concerned that documents presented appear on their face to be consistent with the instructions in the collection order. Any dispute as to quality or quantity of goods delivered must be settled between the buyer and the seller.

6. Without explicit instructions, the collecting bank takes no steps to store or insure the goods. This, of course, can be a problem for both the seller and the buyer. If the seller has not received payment he still has ownership and an insurable interest in the goods.

7. If a collection remains unpaid or a bill of exchange is not accepted and the collecting bank receives no new instructions within 90 days, it may return the documents to the bank from which it received the collection order.

If there are any conclusions to be made from the above they are: first, that the buyer and seller should know each other and have at least some basis of trust to be doing business in the first place and second, that all parties to the transaction should take responsibility to follow through on their responsibilities carefully.

## Notes, Tips, and Cautions For Sellers

1. A seller should only agree to a documentary collection payment if
   a) The seller does not doubt the buyer's ability and willingness to pay for the goods;
   b) The buyer's country is politically, economically, and legally stable;
   c) There are no foreign exchange restrictions in the buyer's country, or all licenses for foreign exchange have already been obtained; and
   d) The shipped goods are easily remarketable.
2. The seller should check on the buyer's creditworthiness and reputation before consenting to a documentary collection, especially D/A terms.
3. The seller should find out from the buyer what documents are required for customs clearance in the buyer's country. The seller should then assemble the documents carefully and make sure they are in the required form and endorsed or authenticated as necessary.
4. If the buyer does not get the required documents he may refuse the collection altogether, or in D/A terms he may unknowingly sign the acceptance and then find that he cannot clear the goods through customs. Although he is legally responsible for payment, he may be unable to pay because he never received the goods. Either leaves the seller in a compromised situation.
5. As a rule, the remitting (seller's) bank will not review the documents before forwarding them to the presenting/collecting (buyer's) bank. Review of the documentation is the primary responsibility of the buyer.
6. Because goods may be refused, the seller should only ship goods that are readily marketable to other buyers.
7. Risks to the seller center around the fact that payment is not made until after the goods are shipped.
8. The seller assumes liability for shipping, insurance, and storage while the goods are in transit and before payment is made. If the buyer does not pay the draft the seller is still responsible for these costs.
9. If the buyer refuses payment (in D/P terms) or acceptance (in D/A terms) the seller retains ownership of the shipment. The seller may have the goods shipped back or try to sell them to another buyer. If the buyer takes no action, customs may seize the goods and auction or otherwise dispose of them.
10. In D/A terms if the buyer signs the acceptance, takes possession of the goods, and then refuses to pay the bill of exchange at maturity the seller has given up title to the shipment and the only recourse is to the buyer, not the banks.

## Notes, Tips, and Cautions For Buyers

1. A buyer should only agree to documentary collection payment terms if there is trust that the seller will ship the goods as specified in accordance with the agreement between buyer and seller.
2. The buyer should be aware of any documentation, certifications, or authorizations that may be required for customs clearance or for eventual sale of the goods in his own country.
3. The buyer should specify all documentation required of the seller in his agreement with the seller.
4. Upon presentation by the presenting bank the buyer must carefully inspect the documents to make certain they meet all specifications for customs clearance and for eventual sale of the goods in his own country.
5. As a special favor, the collecting bank may allow the buyer to take temporary possession of the documents for inspection before payment. The collecting bank, however, assumes responsibility for the documents until redemption.
6. In the above case, the buyer should immediately return the entire set of documents to the collecting bank if he is unwilling or unable to meet the agreed upon payment procedure.
7. In a documentary collection the buyer is generally in a secure position because ownership or responsibility for goods does not have to be assumed until documents have been paid for or a time draft signed.
8. The buyer may not sample or inspect the goods before accepting and paying for the documents unless authorized to do so by the seller. The buyer may, however, specify a certificate of inspection from a reliable third party as part of the required documentation package.
9. Unless bound by a separate contract, the buyer assumes no liability for goods if he refuses to take possession of the documents.
10. Partial payment in exchange for the documents is not allowed unless specifically authorized in the seller's collection order.
11. With D/A terms, the buyer may receive the goods and resell them for profit before the time draft matures, thereby using the proceeds of the sale to pay for the goods. The buyer is responsible for payment, however, even if the goods cannot be sold.
12. The main risk for buyers is that goods shipped might not conform to the goods specified. Because banks deal only in documents and not in goods, the buyer's only recourse is with the seller.

## Notes, Tips, and Cautions For Banks

1. Documents sent for collection must be accompanied by a collection order giving the principal's complete and precise instructions.
2. Banks are only permitted to act upon the specific instructions given by the principal in the collection order.
3. If a remitting, collecting, or presenting bank cannot comply with the instructions in the principal's collection order, it must immediately advise the party from whom it received the order.
4. Banks have the responsibility to verify that documents received with a collection order appear on their face to be as specified in the collection order, but do not have the responsibility to authenticate individual documents.
5. If it appears that documents are missing from the document package (as determined by those listed in the collection order) the bank must immediately notify the party from whom the documents were received.
6. If the principal names a specific collecting bank the remitting bank is to use such bank as the collecting bank.
7. If the principal does not name a collecting bank the remitting bank is free to make its own choice as to the collecting bank in the country of payment.
8. Collection documents may be sent directly to the collecting/presenting bank or through an intermediary bank called a correspondent bank.
9. The drawee is to be presented the documents in the form in which they were received from the principal. However, the remitting and collecting banks may affix stamps or rubber stamps, make endorsements, or attach a cover letter to the document package.
10. If an incomplete or incorrect address of the drawee is shown on the collection order, the collecting bank may, without obligation or responsibility, attempt to find the correct address.
11. The banks must make presentation of documents without delay.
12. If the documents call for payment in a specific currency, the banks must, unless otherwise instructed, collect payment for documents in that currency.
13. The collecting bank may not accept partial payments from the drawee unless otherwise instructed in the collection order.
14. If a collection remains unpaid or a bill of exchange is not accepted and the collecting bank receives no new instructions within 90 days, it may return the documents to the bank from which it received the collection order.

CHAPTER 10

# Documentary Credits, Part 1

## Basic Procedure

A DOCUMENTARY CREDIT is the written promise of a bank, undertaken on behalf of a buyer, to pay a seller the amount specified in the credit provided the seller complies with the terms and conditions set forth in the credit. The terms and conditions of a documentary credit revolve around two issues: (1) the presentation of documents that evidence title to goods shipped by the seller, and (2) payment.

In simple terms, banks act as intermediaries to collect payment from the buyer in exchange for the transfer of documents that enable the holder to take possession of the goods.

Documentary credits provide a high level of protection and security to both buyers and sellers engaged in international trade. The seller is assured that payment will be made by a party independent of the buyer so long as the terms and conditions of the credit are met. The buyer is assured that payment will be released to the seller only after the bank has received the title documents called for in the credit.

Documentary credits are so named because of the importance of documents in the transaction. Letter of credit (L/C) is the historic and popular term used for a documentary credit because such credits were and are transmitted in the form of a letter from the buyer's bank. Both "documentary credit" and "letter of credit" will be used for our discussions.

## Types of Credits

There are a number of different types of standard and special documentary credits. Each type contains a variety of features designed to meet the different needs of buyers, sellers, or the banks involved.

For example, standard documentary credits can be either revocable (may be cancelled by the buyer), or irrevocable (noncancellable by the buyer), or confirmed (a second bank, in addition to the buyer's bank, guarantees payment) or unconfirmed (payment guaranteed only by the issuing bank). The most popular variation for sellers is the irrevocable confirmed credit because it cannot be cancelled by the buyer, and a second bank (usually the seller's bank) adds its guarantee of payment to that of the buyer's bank. Standard credits are discussed in Chapter 12: Standard Credits.

Specialized credits include revolving credits, red clause credits, standby credits, transferable credits, and back-to-back credits. These are discussed in Chapter 13: Special Letters of Credit.

This chapter describes basic procedures. Subsequent chapters must be read to understand fully how to use both standard and special types of credits.

## Limitations of Documentary Credits

Although documentary credits provide good protection and are the preferred means of payment in many international transactions, they do have limitations. They do not, for example, ensure that the goods actually shipped are as ordered nor do they insulate buyers and sellers from other disagreements or complaints arising from their relationship. It is up to the parties to settle questions of this nature between themselves.

Advantages, disadvantages, and issues for both buyer and seller will be discussed in detail later in this chapter and in subsequent chapters. Please note that these issues can have a significant impact on a given transaction. An incomplete understanding of the subject can be more dangerous than no knowledge at all.

## Role of Banks

It is important to note, and not for the last time, that a fundamental principle of documentary credits is that banks deal in documents and not goods. Banks are responsible for issues relating to documents and the specific wording of the documentary credit as opposed to issues relating to the goods themselves.

Therefore, banks are not concerned if a shipment is in conformity with the documents, only that the documents are in conformity to the wording of the credit. This principle will be explained in detail in this and other chapters.

## The Uniform Customs and Practice

Although documentary credits, in one form or another, have been in use for a long time, questions arose about how to effect transactions in a practical, fair, and uniform manner.

The Uniform Customs and Practice for Documentary Credits (UCP) is the internationally recognized codification of rules unifying banking practice regarding documentary credits. The UCP was developed by a working committee attached to the International Chamber of Commerce (ICC) in Paris. It is revised and updated from time to time; the current valid version is ICC publication No. 500. Information regarding ICC publications including No. 500 can be found in Chapter 20: Resources.

## Parties to the Transaction

There are four main parties to a basic documentary letter of credit transaction. They are introduced below and described in detail in the following pages. Note that each party has multiple names. The name used for each party to the transaction depends upon who is speaking. Businesspeople like to use the names buyer, seller, buyer's bank and seller's bank. The banks prefer to use the names applicant, beneficiary, issuing bank, and advising bank. The four parties are:

### THE BUYER (APPLICANT/IMPORTER)

The buyer initiates the documentary credit process by applying to his bank to open a documentary credit naming the seller as the beneficiary. The buyer, therefore, may be called the buyer in commercial terms, the importer in economic terms, and the applicant in banking terms. They are all one and the same.

### THE ISSUING (BUYER'S) BANK

Upon instructions from the buyer, the issuing bank (typically the buyer's regular business bank) issues a documentary credit naming the seller as the beneficiary and sends it to the advising bank (typically the seller's bank).

### THE ADVISING (SELLER'S) BANK

Upon instructions from the issuing bank and the buyer, the advising bank (typically the seller's bank) advises the seller of the credit. The advising bank is typically the seller's regular business bank and is in the seller's country.

### THE SELLER (BENEFICIARY/EXPORTER)

The seller receives notification (advice) of the credit from the advising bank, complies with the terms and conditions of the credit, and gets paid. The seller is the beneficiary of the documentary credit. The seller, therefore, may be called the seller in commercial terms, the exporter in economic terms, and the beneficiary in banking terms. They are all one and the same.

## Basic Documentary Credit Procedure

The documentary credit procedure involves the step-by-step exchange of documents giving title to the goods for either cash or a contracted promise to pay at a later time. There are four basic groupings of steps in the procedure.

#### ISSUANCE

Issuance describes the process of the buyer's applying for and opening a documentary credit at the issuing bank and the issuing bank's formal notification of the seller through the advising bank.

#### AMENDMENT

Amendment describes the process whereby the terms and conditions of a documentary credit may be modified after the credit has been issued.

#### UTILIZATION

Utilization describes the procedure for the seller's shipping of the goods, the transfer of documents from the seller to the buyer through the banks, and the transfer of the payment from the buyer to the seller through the banks (settlement).

#### SETTLEMENT

Settlement (a subpart of utilization) describes the different ways in which payment may be effected to the seller from the buyer through the banks. Settlement is discussed in Chapter 11: Settlement.

---

NOTE: Issues relating to applying for a documentary credit, confirmed vs. unconfirmed credits, special types of credits, settlement, correspondent and confirming banks will be discussed after the basic procedure is explained.

---

## Issuance

### PROCEDURE

Refer to the diagram on the facing page for each numbered step.

#### BUYER AND SELLER

1. The buyer and seller agree on the terms of sale: (a) specifying a documentary credit as the means of payment, (b) naming an advising bank (usually the seller's bank), and (c) listing required documents.

#### BUYER (APPLICANT/IMPORTER)

2. The buyer applies to his bank (issuing bank) and opens a documentary credit naming the seller as beneficiary based on specific terms and conditions that are listed in the credit.

#### ISSUING (BUYER'S) BANK

3. The issuing bank sends the documentary credit to the advising bank named in the credit.

#### ADVISING (SELLER'S) BANK

4. The advising bank informs (advises) the seller of the documentary credit.

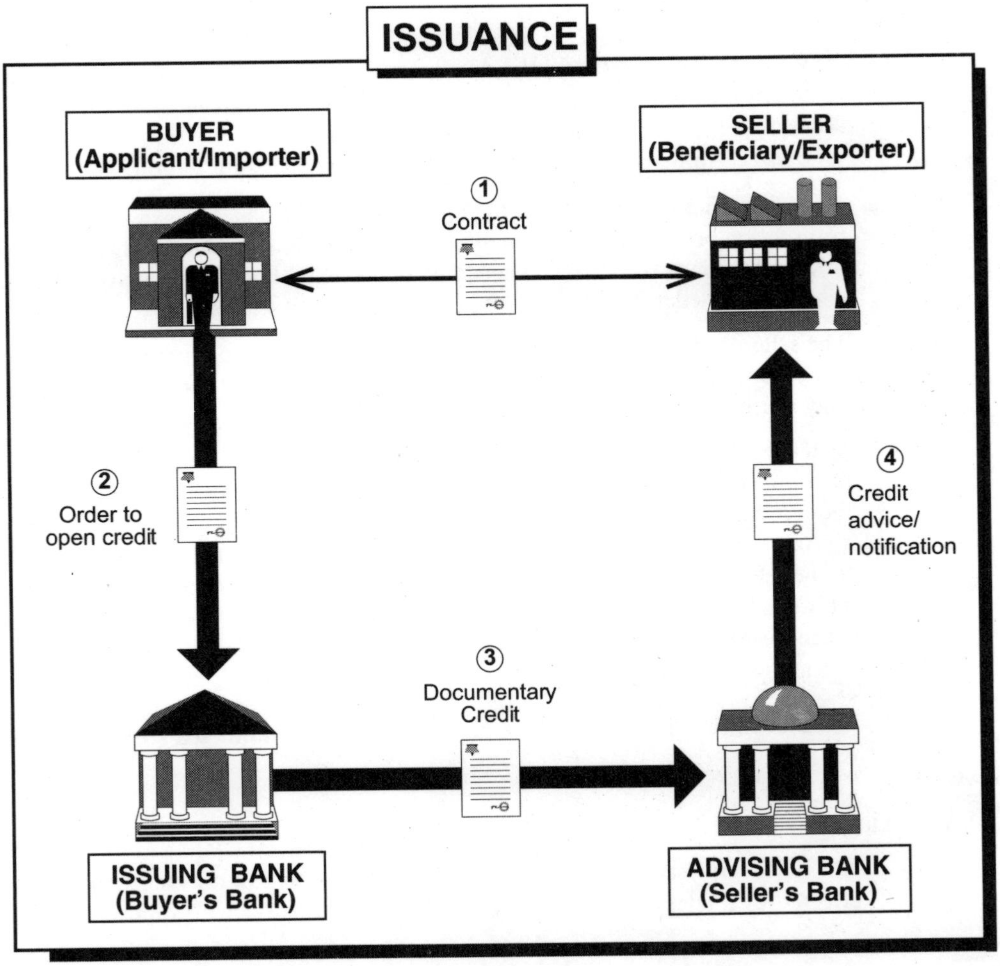
ISSUANCE
BUYER
(Applicant/Importer)
SELLER
(Beneficiary/Exporter)
1
Contract
2
Order to
open credit
4
Credit
advice/
notification
3
Documentary
Credit
ISSUING BANK
(Buyer's Bank)
ADVISING BANK
(Seller's Bank)

## Amendment

When the seller receives the documentary credit it must be examined closely to determine if the terms and conditions (1) reflect the agreement of the buyer and seller, and (2) can be met within the time stipulated.

Upon examination, the seller may find problems. Some examples:

- The seller might disagree with the terms and conditions. For example, the transaction price listed in the credit may be lower than the originally agreed upon price, or perhaps the seller has specified that the total price is to include shipping, whereas the seller originally quoted a price without shipping.
- The seller might find himself unable to meet specific requirements of the credit. For example, the time may be too short to effect shipment, or certain documents may not be available.

If the buyer still wants to proceed with the transaction, but with modification to the terms of the credit, he or she should contact the buyer immediately and request an amendment.

Amendments must be authorized by the buyer and issued by the issuing bank to the seller through the same channel as the original documentary letter of credit. This can be an involved undertaking so any amendments should be initiated only when necessary and as soon as a problem is identified.

### PROCEDURE

Refer to the diagram on the facing page for each numbered step.

### SELLER

1. The seller requests that the buyer make an amendment to the credit. This can be effected by a telephone call, a fax letter, or by face-to-face negotiation.

### BUYER

2. If the buyer agrees, the buyer orders the issuing bank to issue the amendment.

### ISSUING BANK

3. The issuing bank amends the credit and notifies the advising bank of the amendment.

### ADVISING BANK

4. The advising bank notifies seller of the amendment.

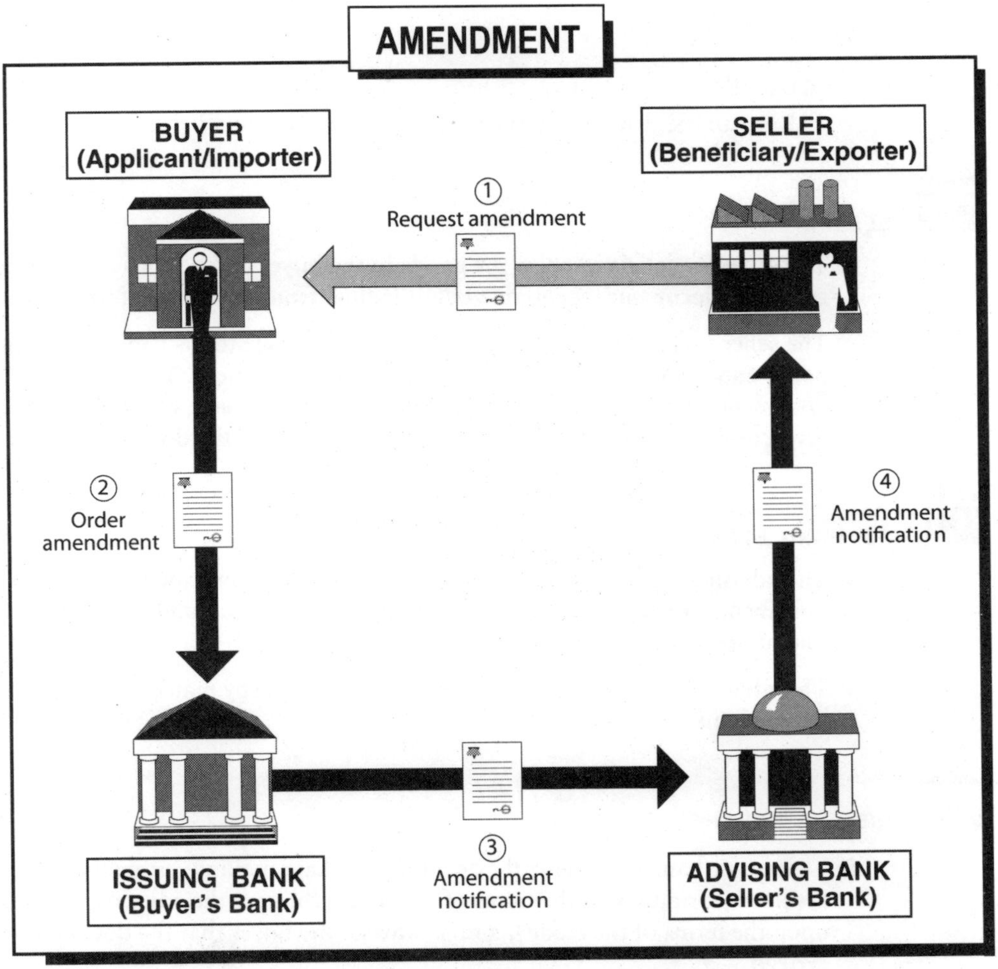
AMENDMENT
BUYER
(Applicant/Importer)
SELLER
(Beneficiary/Exporter)
① Request amendment
② Order amendment
③ Amendment notification
④ Amendment notification
ISSUING BANK
(Buyer's Bank)
ADVISING BANK
(Seller's Bank)

## Utilization

### PROCEDURE

Refer to the diagram on the facing page for each numbered step.

### SELLER

1. The seller (beneficiary) ships the goods to the buyer and obtains a negotiable transport document (negotiable bill of lading) from the shipping firm/agent.

2. The seller prepares and presents a document package to his bank (the advising bank) consisting of (a) the negotiable transport document, and (b) other documents (e.g., commercial invoice, insurance document, certificate of origin, inspection certificate, etc.) as required by the buyer in the documentary credit.

### ADVISING BANK

3. The advising bank (a) reviews the document package making certain the documents are in conformity with the terms of the credit and (b) pays the seller (based upon the terms of the credit).

4. The advising bank sends the documentation package by mail or by courier to the issuing bank.

### ISSUING BANK

5. The issuing bank (1) reviews the document package making certain the documents are in conformity with the terms of the credit, (b) pays the advising bank (based upon the terms of the credit), and (c) advises the buyer that the documents have arrived.

### BUYER

6. The buyer (a) reviews the document package making certain the documents are in conformity with the terms of the credit, and (b) makes a cash payment (signs a sight draft) to the issuing bank, or if the collection order allows, signs an acceptance (promise to pay at a future date).

### ISSUING BANK

7. The issuing bank sends the document package by mail or courier to the buyer who then takes possession of the shipment.

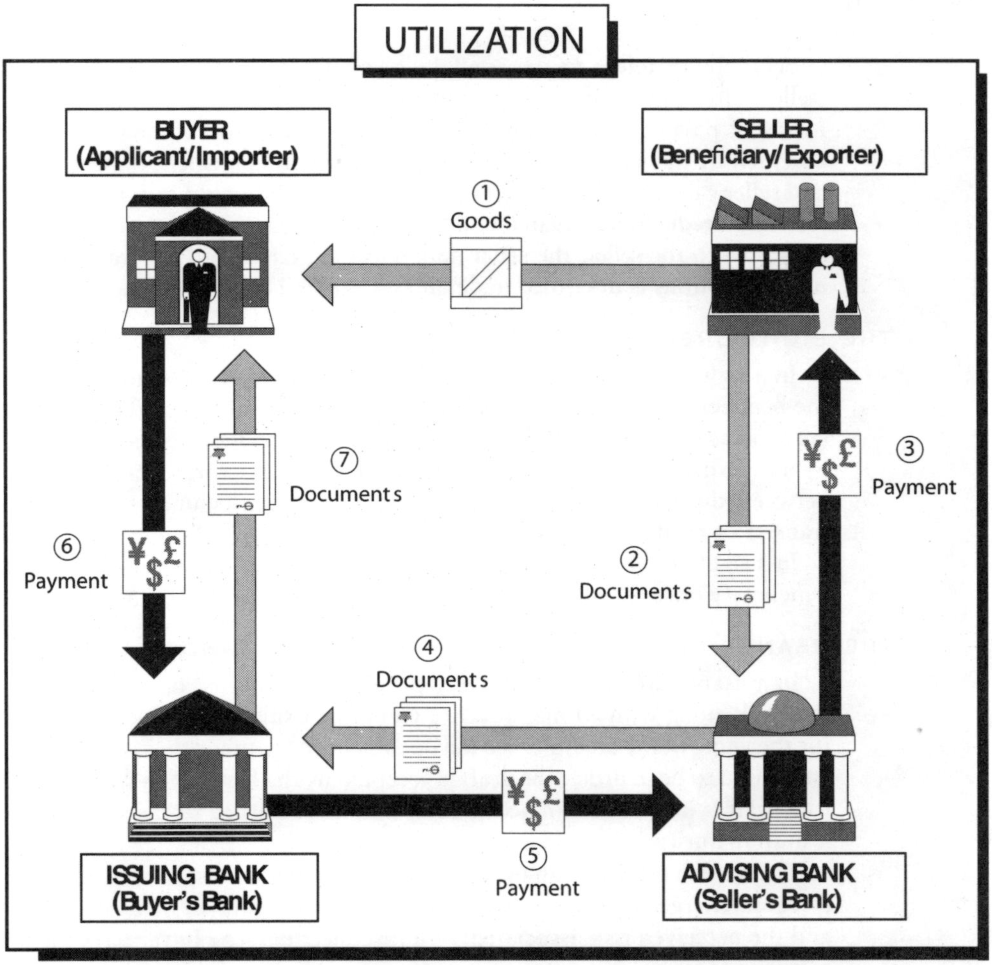


NOTE: There are important variations on this basic procedure that have to do with confirmation of the credit and payment. Please refer to "Availability" on the following page, Chapter 11: Settlement, Chapter 12: Basic Credits, and Chapter 13: Special Letters of Credit for complete information.

## Availability

Availability refers to the availability of proceeds (funds) to the beneficiary (seller) after presentation of documents under the credit. Each of the following forms of payment availability must be specified in the original credit, and be accepted by the seller. For example, if the original agreement between the buyer and seller calls for a sight credit (immediate availability of funds to the seller) and a usance credit (funds available in 30, 60 or 90 days) is prescribed in the credit presented to the seller, the seller may reject the credit and the transaction. Each of these options is described in detail in Chapter 11: Settlement.

### THE SIGHT CREDIT (SETTLEMENT BY PAYMENT)

In a sight credit (confirmed sight credit) the value of the credit is available to the beneficiary as soon as the terms and conditions of the credit have been met (as soon as the prescribed document package has been presented to and checked by the confirming bank). When foreign exchange is at issue, several days may pass between the time of beneficiary's presentation of documents and the actual transfer of funds to the beneficiary's account.

In a sight credit (unconfirmed), the value of the credit is made available to the beneficiary once the advising bank has received the funds from the issuing bank.

### THE USANCE CREDIT (SETTLEMENT BY ACCEPTANCE)

In a usance credit the beneficiary presents the required document package to the bank along with a time draft drawn on the issuing, advising, or a third bank for the value of the credit. Once the documents have made their way to the buyer and found to be in order, the draft is accepted by the bank upon which it is drawn (the draft is now called an acceptance) and it is returned to the seller who holds it until maturity.

The seller has the option of selling the acceptance by discounting its value. The discount charged will be in some proportion to the time to maturity of the draft and the perceived risk associated with its collection. The buyer pays the draft at maturity to its holder.

### THE DEFERRED PAYMENT CREDIT (SETTLEMENT BY NEGOTIATION)

In a deferred payment credit the buyer accepts the documents and agrees to pay the bank after a set period of time. Essentially, this gives the buyer time (a grace period) between delivery of the goods and payment. The issuing bank makes the payment at the specified time, when the terms and conditions of the credit have been met.

Deferred payment credits are often used in transactions involving food or drugs that require inspection prior to import and approval by a government agency. In this case the bank will release the documents to the importer/buyer against a trust receipt. The bank holds the title documents to the goods and still owns the merchandise. Once the goods have been approved by the government agency, the bank transfers the titles documents to the buyer, charges the buyer's account, and pays the seller.

---

NOTE: See Chapter 11: Settlement, for details concerning the different ways in which payment may be effected to the seller from the buyer through the banks.

---

## Opening a Documentary Credit

### INTRODUCTION

The success or failure of a documentary credit transaction can turn upon the wording of the documentary credit itself. As such, the buyer (whose responsibility it is to open the credit) should adhere to the greatest extent possible to the terms and conditions of the original contractual agreement, keeping the specifications clear and concise and as simple as possible.

### REFER TO DOCUMENTS

The buyer's instructions to the issuing bank should be given in clear, professional wording, and should pertain only to documentation, not to the goods themselves. It is very important to demand documents in the credit that clearly reflect the agreements reached.

EXAMPLE 1: Require confirmation that goods are shipped by Conference vessel no more than twenty years old, rather than that the goods be shipped by Conference vessel no more than twenty years old.

EXAMPLE 2: Require confirmation that the goods were packaged in double-strength, waterproof containers, rather than requiring that the goods be packaged in double-strength, waterproof containers.

EXAMPLE 3: Require proof of notification to buyer (such as a copy of the cable or telex) that goods were shipped, rather than requiring that the buyer be notified that the goods were shipped.

Remember, the banks are concerned only with the documents presented, not with whether a party has complied with the contract clauses when they check compliance with the documentary credit terms.

### BE CLEAR AND CONCISE

The wording in a documentary credit should be simple but specific. The more detailed the documentary credit is, the more likely the seller will reject it as too difficult to fulfill. It is also more likely that the banks will find a discrepancy in the details, thus voiding the credit, even though simpler terms might have been found to be in compliance with the credit.

The buyer should, however, completely and precisely set forth the details of the agreement as it relates to credit terms and conditions and the presentation of documents.

### DO NOT SPECIFY IMPOSSIBLE DOCUMENTATION

The documentary credit should not require documents that the seller cannot obtain; nor should it call for details in a document that are beyond the knowledge of the issuer of the document. The documents specified should be limited to those required to smoothly and completely conclude an international sale of goods.

## Documentary Credit Application

PROCEDURE

Refer to the application form on the facing page for each numbered step.

BUYER

1. BENEFICIARY Always write the seller's company name and address completely and correctly. A simple mistake here may result in the seller preparing inconsistent or improper documentation on the other end.
2. AMOUNT State the actual amount of the credit. You may state a maximum amount in a situation where actual count or quantity is in question. You also may use the words APPROXIMATE, CIRCA, or ABOUT to indicate an acceptable 10 percent plus or minus amount from the stated amount. If you use such wording, you will need to be consistent and use it also in connection with the quantity as well.
3. VALIDITY PERIOD The validity and period for presentation of the documents following shipment of the goods should be sufficiently long to allow the exporter time to prepare the necessary documents and send them to the bank.
4. BENEFICIARY'S BANK Either leave blank to indicate that the issuing bank may freely select the correspondent bank or name the seller's bank.
5. TYPE OF PAYMENT AVAILABILITY Sight drafts, time drafts, or deferred payment may be used, as previously agreed to by the seller and buyer.
6. DESIRED DOCUMENTS The buyer specifies which documents are needed. Buyer can list, for example, a bill of lading, a commercial invoice, a certificate of origin, certificates of analysis, and so on.
7. NOTIFY ADDRESS An address is given for notification of the imminent arrival of goods at the port or airport of destination. This address can also be used for notification of damage to the shipment while en route. The buyer's business or shipping agent is most often used.
8. MERCHANDISE DESCRIPTION A short, precise description of the goods is given, along with quantity. Note the comments in number two above concerning approximate amounts.
9. CONFIRMATION ORDER If the foreign beneficiary (exporter) insists on having the credit confirmed by a bank in his or her country it will be so noted in this space.

## SAMPLE DOCUMENTARY CREDIT APPLICATION FORM

Sender
Argentine Trading Company
Lavalle 1716, Piso 2
1048 Buenos Aires
Argentina

Our reference AB/02

**Instructions to open a Documentary Credit**

Buenos Aires, 30th September 19..
Place / Date

**Argentine Bank Corporation**
Documentary Credits
P.O. Box 1040
Buenos Aires, Argentina

Please open the following

☒ irrevocable ☐ revocable documentary credit

Beneficiary
① American Import-Export Co., Inc.
123 Main Street
San Francisco, California
USA

Beneficiary's bank (if known)
④ US Domestic Bank
525 Main Street
San Francisco, CA 94105
USA

Amount
② US$1,250,000.--

Please advise this bank
☐ by letter
☒ by letter, cabling main details in advance
☐ by telex / telegram with full text of credit

Date and place of expiry
③ 25th November 19.. in San Francisco

Partial shipments ☒ allowed ☐ not allowed
Transhipment ☐ allowed ☒ not allowed

Terms of shipment (FOB, C & F, CIF)
CIF Buenos Aires

Despatch from / Taking in charge at: Oakland
For transportation to: Buenos Aires

Latest date of shipment: 10th Nov. 19.. ③
Documents must be presented not later than 15 days after date of despatch

**Beneficiary may dispose of the credit amount as follows** ⑤
☒ at sight upon presentation of documents
☐ after ..........days, calculated from date of ..........

☐ by a draft due ..........
drawn on ☐ you ☐ your correspondents
which you / your correspondents will please accept

**against surrender of the following documents** ⑥
☒ invoice (...3...copies)

Shipping document
☒ sea: bill of lading, to order, endorsed in blank
☐ rail: dublicate waybill
☐ air: air consignment note
☐

☒ insurance policy, certificte covering the following risks: (.......... copies)
"all risks" including war up to final destination in Argentina
☐ Additional documents
☒ Confirmation of the carrier that the ship is not more than 15 years old
☒ packing list (3 copies)

Notify address in bill of lading / goods addressed to
Argentine Trading Company ⑦
Lavalle 1716, Piso 2
1048 Buenos Aires Argentina

Goods insured by ☐ us ☒ seller

Goods ⑧
1,000 "Computers model 486 as per pro forma invoice no. 74/1853 dd 10th September 19.."

at US$1,250.00 per unit

Your correspondents to advise beneficiary ☐ adding their confirmation ☒ without adding their confirmation ⑨
Payments to be debited to our U.S. Dollars account no 10-32679150

This credit is subject to the «Uniform customs and practice for documentary credits» fixed by the International Chamber of Commerce. It is understood that you do not assume any responsibility neither for the correctness, validity or genuineness of the documents which [illegible] remitted to you nor for the description, quality, quantity and weight of the goods thereby represented.

NB. The applicable text is marked by ☒

Argentine Trading Company

Signature ____________________

For mailing please see overleaf

## Details on Parties and Procedures

### THE BUYER (IMPORTER/APPLICANT)

Since a documentary credit is a pledge by the bank to make payment to the seller, the bank will want to evaluate the creditworthiness of the buyer. If the buyer's credit and relationship with the bank is excellent, the bank will issue a credit for the full value. If the buyer's relationship is good, but perhaps not excellent, the bank will require that the buyer pledge a percentage of the value of the documentary credit in cash funds. If the buyer's relationship with the bank is less established, the bank will require that they buyer pledge 100 percent of the value of the documentary credit in cash funds in advance.

It is essential that the application for the documentary credit be in conformity with the underlying sales contract between the buyer and the seller. The buyer's instructions to the issuing bank must be clear with respect to the type of credit, the amount, duration, required documents, shipping date, expiration date, and beneficiary.

### THE ISSUING (BUYER'S) BANK

Upon receiving the buyer's application, the opening bank checks the credit of the applicant, determines whether cash security is necessary, and scrutinizes the contents of the application to see whether they generally are consistent with national and international banking and legal requirements. If the application is satisfactory to the bank, the buyer and the opening bank will sign an agreement to open a documentary credit. The credit must be written and signed by an authorized person of the issuing bank.

The issuing bank usually sends the original documentary credit to the seller (called the beneficiary) through an advising bank, which may be a branch or correspondent bank of the issuing (opening) bank. The seller may request that a particular bank be the advising bank, or the buyer's bank may select one of its correspondent banks in the seller's country.

### THE ADVISING (SELLER'S) BANK

Upon receipt of the credit from the issuing bank, the advising bank informs the seller that the credit has been issued.

The advising bank will examine the credit upon receipt. The advising bank, however, examines the terms of the credit itself; it does not determine whether the terms of the credit are consistent with those of the contract between the buyer and seller, or whether the description of goods is correctly stated in accordance with the contract. The advising bank then forwards the credit to the seller.

If the advising bank is simply "advising the credit," it is under no obligation or commitment to make payment, and it will so advise the seller. In some cases the advising bank confirms (adds its guarantee to pay) the seller. In this case it becomes the confirming bank. (Details on confirmed documentary credit are discussed in detail in Chapter 12: Standard Credits.)

If the advising bank confirms the credit it must pay without recourse to the seller when the documents are presented, provided they are in order and the credit requirements are met.

### SELLER/EXPORTER/BENEFICIARY

In addition to assessing the reputation of the buyer prior to signing a sales contract, the seller should also assess the reputation of the buyer's (issuing) bank before agreeing to rely upon that bank for payment in a documentary credit. It is not unknown for sellers to receive fictitious documentary credits from non-existent banks and to realize their mistake after shipment.

The seller must carefully review all conditions the buyer has stipulated in the documentary credit. If the seller cannot comply with one or more of the provisions, or if the terms of the credit are not in accordance with those of the contract, the buyer should be notified immediately and asked to make an amendment to the credit.

The seller should also scrutinize the credit to make certain that it does not contain provisions that specify documents such as acceptance reports, progress reports, etc. that have to be signed or approved by the buyer. By refusing to sign such documents, the buyer can block payment.

After reaching agreement, the seller is well-advised to provide the buyer with a sample of the final product specified in the credit for confirmation of quality, suitability, etc.

## Complying With the Documentary Credit

### SELLER/EXPORTER/BENEFICIARY

Upon receipt of the documentary credit, the seller should immediately and carefully examine it to ensure it conforms with the original sales contract with the buyer and that all the conditions stated in the credit can be met. If any of its conditions have to be amended, which can be time-consuming, the seller should immediately contact the buyer.

### EXAMINING THE DOCUMENTARY CREDIT

The following is a checklist for the seller's examination of the credit:

1. The buyer's and seller's names and addresses are correct. ☐
2. The amount of the credit is in accordance with the contract, including unit prices, shipping charges, handling costs, and total invoice amounts. ☐
3. The merchandise description is consistent with the sales contract. ☐
4. The credit's payment availability agrees with the contract conditions. ☐
5. The shipping, expiration, and presentation dates allow sufficient time for processing the order, shipping the merchandise, and preparing the documents for presentation to the bank. ☐
6. Partial or transshipments are specified correctly. ☐
7. The point of dispatch, taking charge of the goods, loading on board, or of discharge at final destination are as agreed. ☐
8. Insurance coverage and party to pay charges are as agreed.
9. Instructions on whom the drafts are to be drawn, and in what tenor (maturity dates), are correct. ☐
10. The credit is confirmed or unconfirmed as agreed. See Chapter 12: Standard Credits. ☐
11. There are no unacceptable conditions. ☐
12. The specified documents can be obtained in the form required. ☐
13. The issuing (or confirming) bank is known to the seller. ☐

CHAPTER 11

# Documentary Credits, Part 2

## SETTLEMENT (MAKING PAYMENT)

SETTLEMENT REFERS to the process of payment of the beneficiary(ies) to the credit after presentation of documents under the credit. Utilization, availability of payment and settlement are all closely related and often the terms are used interchangeably.

Utilization is the process of the seller shipping the goods, presenting documentation and getting paid. Availability and settlement are part of the same process, but refer more specifically to the seller getting paid.

There are three primary means of settlement: settlement by payment, settlement by acceptance, and settlement by negotiation. Each is described briefly below and in greater detail in the pages which follow.

### SETTLEMENT BY PAYMENT

If the credit is an irrevocable, confirmed credit, the value of the credit is available to the beneficiary as soon as the terms and conditions of the credit have been met (as soon as the prescribed document package has been presented to and checked by the confirming bank). In an unconfirmed credit the value of the credit is made available to the beneficiary once the advising bank has received the funds from the issuing bank. See the following chapter for information on confirmed and unconfirmed credits.

### SETTLEMENT BY ACCEPTANCE

In settlement by acceptance the beneficiary presents the required documentation package to the bank along with a time draft drawn on the issuing, advising, or a third bank for the value of the credit. Once the documents have made their way to the buyer and found to be in order, the draft is accepted by the bank upon which it is drawn (the draft is now called a bank acceptance) and it is returned to the seller who holds it until maturity.

### SETTLEMENT BY NEGOTIATION

In settlement by negotiation the buyer accepts the documents and agrees to pay the bank after a set period of time. Essentially, this gives the buyer time (a grace period) between delivery of the goods and payment. The issuing bank makes the payment at the specified time, when the terms and conditions of the credit have been met.

## Settlement by Payment

### PROCEDURE

Refer to the diagram on the facing page for each numbered step.

### SELLER

1. The seller (beneficiary) ships the goods to the buyer and obtains a negotiable transport document (negotiable bill of lading) from the shipping firm/agent.
2. The seller prepares and presents a document package to the advising/confirming bank consisting of (a) the negotiable transport document, and (b) other documents (e.g., commercial invoice, insurance document, certificate of origin, inspection certificate, etc.) as required by the buyer in the documentary credit.

### ADVISING/CONFIRMING BANK

3. The advising/confirming bank (a) reviews the document package making certain the documents are in conformity with the terms of the credit, and **(b) pays the seller.**
4. The advising/confirming bank then sends the documentation package by mail or by courier to the issuing bank.

### ISSUING BANK

5. The issuing bank (a) reviews the document package making certain the documents are in conformity with the terms of the credit and (b) pays or reimburses the advising/confirming bank as previously agreed (in the documentary credit).
6. Sends the document package by mail or courier to the buyer.

### BUYER

7. The buyer pays or reimburses the issuing bank as previously agreed.

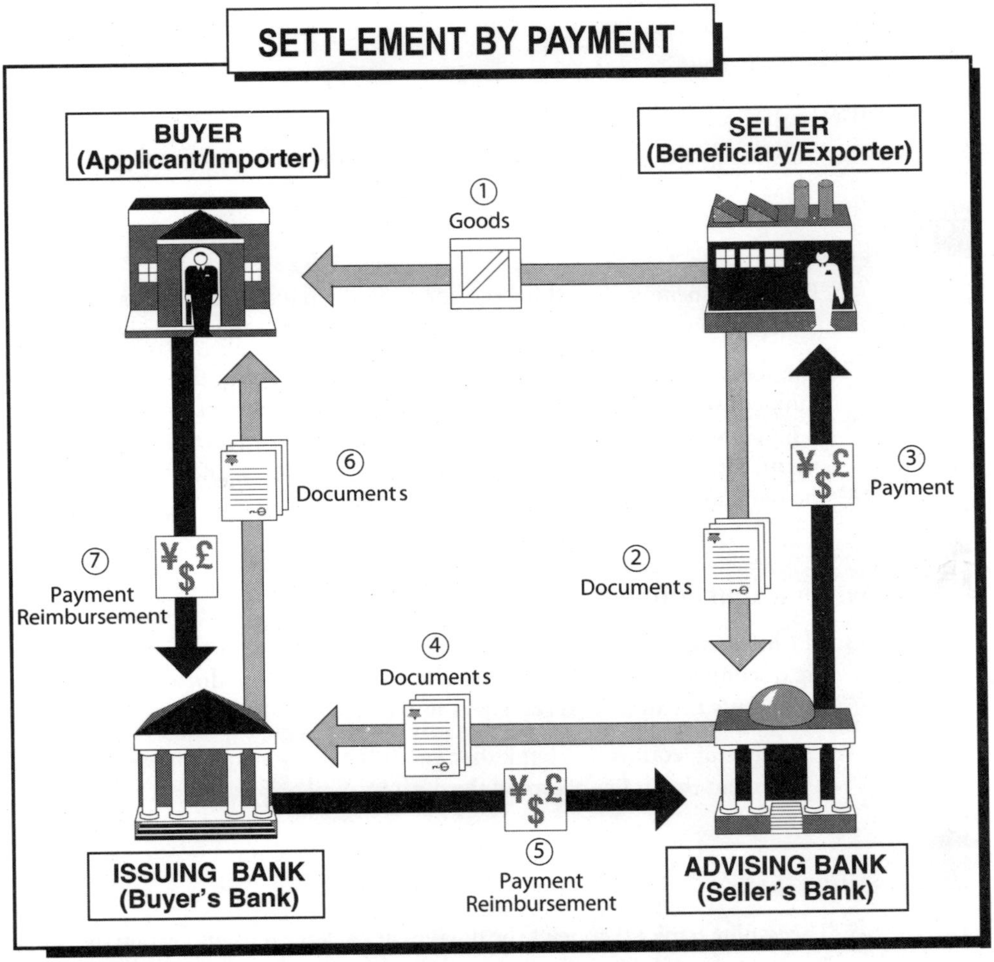
SETTLEMENT BY PAYMENT
BUYER
(Applicant/Importer)
SELLER
(Beneficiary/Exporter)
① Goods
② Documents
③ Payment
④ Documents
⑤ Payment Reimbursement
⑥ Documents
⑦ Payment Reimbursement
ISSUING BANK
(Buyer's Bank)
ADVISING BANK
(Seller's Bank)

## Settlement by Acceptance

### PROCEDURE

Refer to the diagram on the facing page for each numbered step.

### SELLER

1. The seller (beneficiary) ships the goods to the buyer and obtains a negotiable transport document (negotiable bill of lading) from the shipping firm/agent.
2. The seller prepares and presents a document package to the advising/confirming bank consisting of (a) the negotiable transport document, (b) other documents (e.g., commercial invoice, insurance document, certificate of origin, inspection certificate, etc.) as required by the buyer in the credit, and **(c) a draft drawn on the bank at the specified tenor** (maturity date).

### ADVISING/CONFIRMING BANK

3. The advising/confirming bank (a) reviews the document package making certain the documents are in conformity with the terms of the documentary credit, and **(b) accepts the draft and returns it to the seller.**
4. The advising/confirming bank then sends the documentation package **along with a statement that it has accepted the draft** by mail or by courier to the issuing bank.

### ISSUING BANK

5. The issuing bank (a) reviews the document package making certain the documents are in conformity with the terms of the documentary credit and **(b) at maturity of the draft pays or reimburses the advising/confirming bank as previously agreed (in the documentary credit).**
6. Sends the document package by mail or courier to the buyer.

### BUYER

7. The buyer pays or reimburses the issuing bank as previously agreed (in the documentary credit).

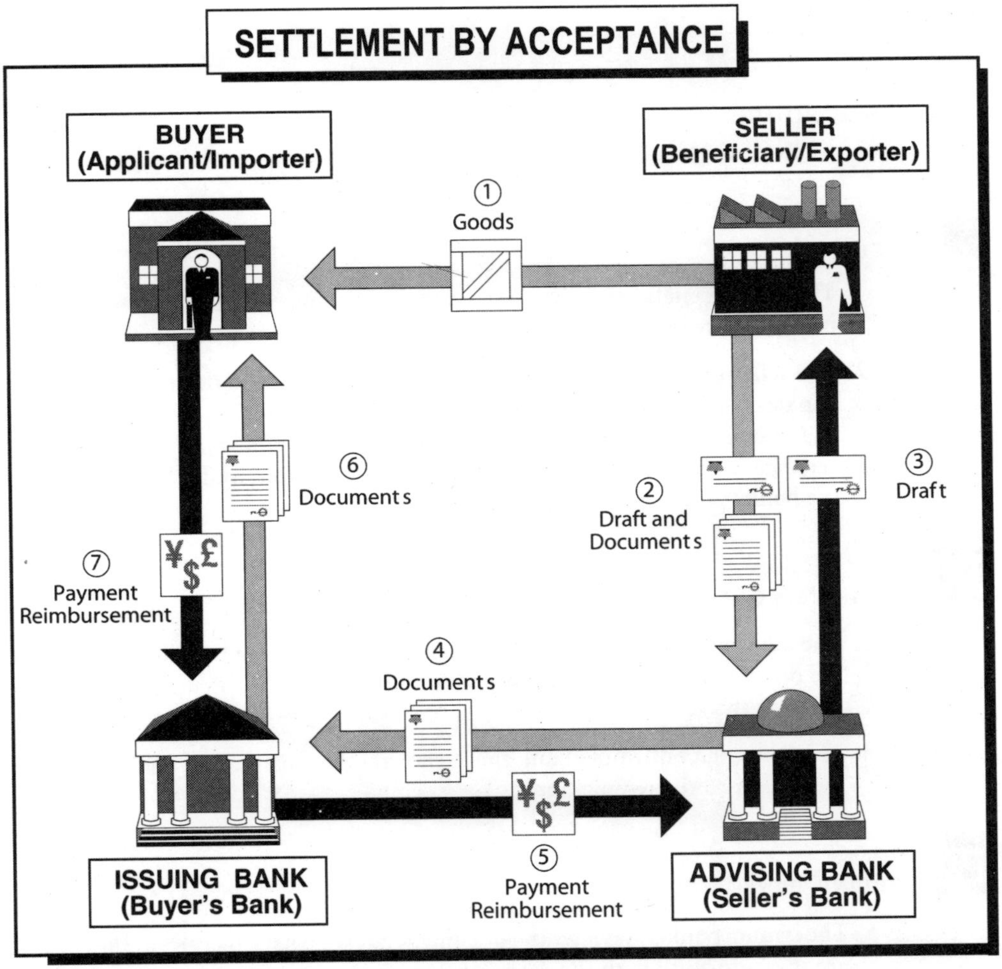
SETTLEMENT BY ACCEPTANCE
BUYER
(Applicant/Importer)
SELLER
(Beneficiary/Exporter)
① Goods
② Draft and Documents
③ Draft
④ Documents
⑤ Payment Reimbursement
⑥ Documents
⑦ Payment Reimbursement
ISSUING BANK
(Buyer's Bank)
ADVISING BANK
(Seller's Bank)

## Settlement by Negotiation

### PROCEDURE

Refer to the diagram on the facing page for each numbered step.

### SELLER

1. The seller (beneficiary) ships the goods to the buyer and obtains a negotiable transport document (negotiable bill of lading) from the shipping firm/agent.
2. The seller prepares and presents a document package to the advising/confirming bank consisting of (a) the negotiable transport document, (b) other documents (e.g., commercial invoice, insurance document, certificate of origin, inspection certificate, etc.) as required by the buyer in the credit, and **(c) a draft drawn on the bank.**

### ADVISING/CONFIRMING BANK

3. The advising/confirming bank (a) reviews the document package making certain the documents are in conformity with the terms of the documentary credit, and **(b) pays the seller.**
4. The advising/confirming bank then sends the documentation package by mail or by courier to the issuing bank.

### ISSUING BANK

5. The issuing bank a) reviews the document package making certain the documents are in conformity with the terms of the documentary credit and **b) pays or reimburses the advising/confirming bank as previously agreed** (in the documentary credit).
6. Sends the document package by mail or courier to the buyer.

### BUYER

7. The buyer pays or reimburses the issuing bank as previously agreed (in the documentary credit).

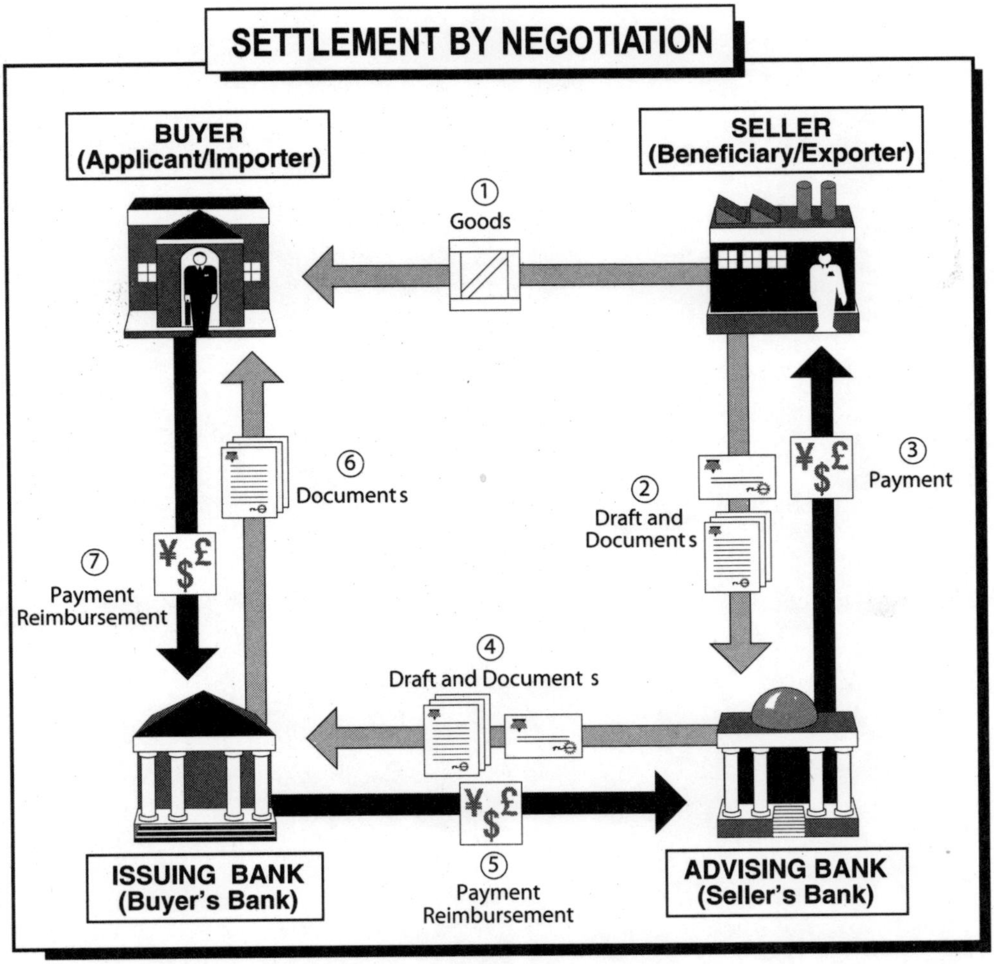
SETTLEMENT BY NEGOTIATION
BUYER
(Applicant/Importer)
SELLER
(Beneficiary/Exporter)
① Goods
② Draft and Documents
③ Payment
④ Draft and Documents
⑤ Payment Reimbursement
⑥ Documents
⑦ Payment Reimbursement
ISSUING BANK
(Buyer's Bank)
ADVISING BANK
(Seller's Bank)

CHAPTER 12

# Documentary Credits, Part 3

## STANDARD CREDITS

## Revocable vs. Irrevocable Documentary Credits

Documentary credits may be issued by the buyer and issuing bank as revocable or irrevocable. (The buyer must indicate either revocable or irrevocable on the application form to the issuing bank.) Each has a distinct advantage for buyers and sellers.

### REVOCABLE CREDIT

A revocable documentary credit gives the buyer and/or issuing bank the ability to amend or cancel the credit at any time right up to the moment of intended payment without approval by, or notice to, the seller. Revocable credits are, therefore, of great advantage to the buyer.

Revocable credits are, conversely, of great disadvantage to the seller as the credit may be canceled at any time, even while the goods are in transit, giving the seller no security whatsoever. Although revocable credits are sometimes used between affiliated firms, sellers are advised never to accept a revocable credit as a payment method.

### IRREVOCABLE CREDIT

An irrevocable documentary credit constitutes a firm contractual obligation on the part of the issuing bank to honor the terms of payment of the credit as issued. The buyer and issuing bank cannot amend or cancel the credit without the express approval of the seller.

Irrevocable credits are of advantage to the seller. As long as the seller complies with the terms of the credit, payment will be made by the issuing bank. Virtually all documentary credits issued today are irrevocable and so state on their face (on the face of the documentary credit itself). Sellers are advised to insist upon an irrevocable credit from the buyer.

## Confirmed vs. Unconfirmed Documentary Credits

Payment under an irrevocable documentary credit is guaranteed by the issuing bank. However, from the seller's perspective, this guarantee may have limited value as the issuing bank may be (1) in a foreign country, (2) beholden to the buyer, (3) small and unknown to the seller, or (4) subject to unknown foreign exchange control restrictions. The seller, therefore, might wish that another, more local bank add its guarantee (confirmation) of payment to that of the issuing bank.

Within the category of irrevocable credits there are two further options for the buyer and seller. These are the irrevocable unconfirmed credit and the irrevocable confirmed credit. Once again, each has a distinct advantage for buyers and sellers.

## UNCONFIRMED (OR ADVISED) DOCUMENTARY CREDIT

Under an unconfirmed documentary credit only the issuing bank assumes the undertaking to pay, thus payment is the sole responsibility of the issuing bank. An unconfirmed documentary credit will be communicated (advised) to the seller through a bank most likely located in the seller's country, and the related shipping and other documents will usually be presented to that bank for eventual payment. However, the final responsibility for payment rests with the issuing bank alone. The advising bank may or may not negotiate the seller's draft depending on the degree of political and financial risk anticipated in the issuing bank's country, as well as the credit standing of the issuing bank.

In dealing with a readily identifiable issuing bank in a developed country, an unconfirmed documentary credit is very probably an acceptable, safe instrument for most sellers. If you have any doubt about the issuing bank and its standing, you can check the name through a local bank with an international department.

---

NOTE: Some countries (most notably China) do not permit confirmation of letters of credit issued by their banks, deeming that the credit of their national financial institutions should not be questioned by others.

---

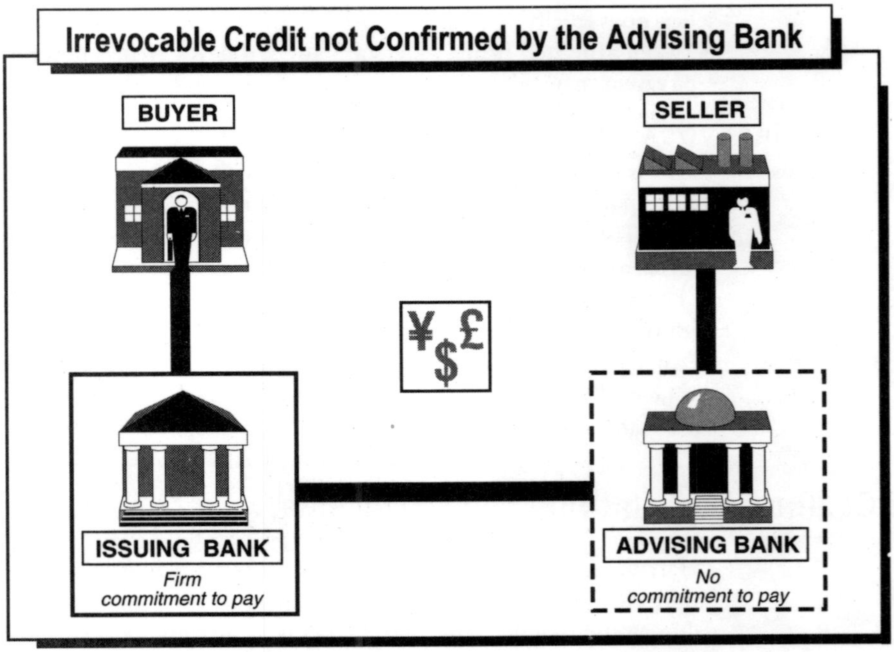

## CONFIRMED DOCUMENTARY CREDIT

Confirmed letters of credit carry the commitment to pay of both the issuing and the advising banks. The advising bank adds its undertaking to pay to that of the issuing bank, and its commitment is independent of that of the issuing bank. Therefore, when documents conforming to the requirements of the confirmed documentary credit are presented in a timely manner, the payment from the advising bank to the seller is final in all respects as far as the seller is concerned.

Confirmed, irrevocable letters of credit give the seller the greatest protection, since sellers can rely on the commitment of two banks to make payment. The confirming bank will pay even if the issuing bank cannot or will not honor the draft for any reason whatever. In accordance with the additional risk assumed by the banks, however, confirmed, irrevocable letters of credit are more expensive than unconfirmed letters of credit.

NOTE: Confirmed, irrevocable letters of credit are used most frequently in transactions involving buyers in developing countries.

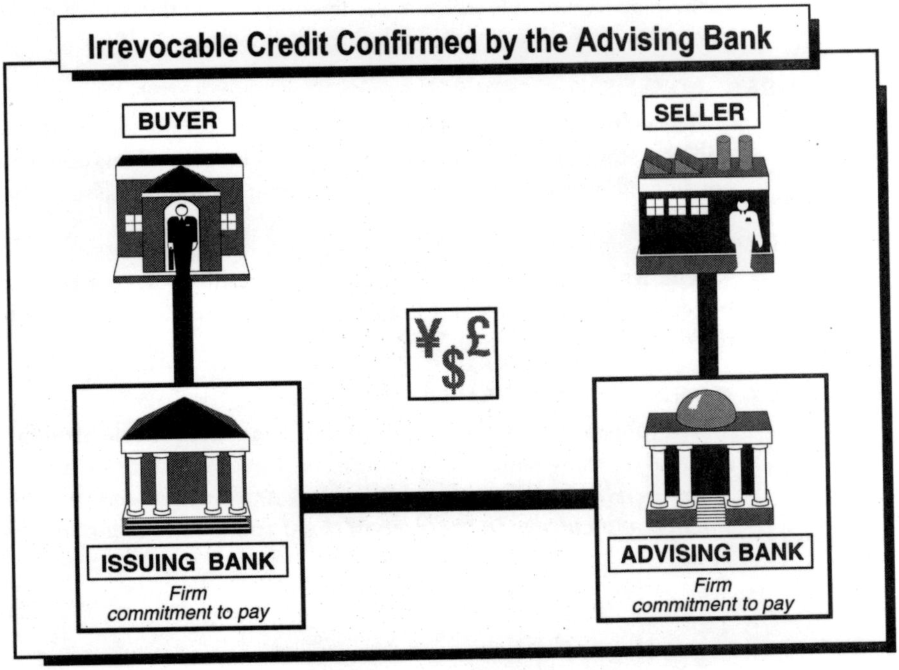


NOTE: Examples of irrevocable confirmed and unconfirmed documentary credits can be found later in this chapter.

## Irrevocable Straight Documentary Credit

### DEFINITION

An irrevocable straight documentary credit conveys a commitment by the issuing bank to only honor drafts or documents as presented by the beneficiary of the credit.

### EXPLANATION

This means that the beneficiary of the documentary credit (the seller) is supposed to deal directly with the issuing bank in presenting drafts and documents under the terms of the credit.

It is quite normal for banks and other financial institutions to purchase the drafts and documents of a beneficiary at a discount. For example, a seller may possess a draft obligating the issuing bank to pay a stated sum in 90 days. If the seller needs the money he may wish to sell it to his bank at a discount for immediate cash. In an irrevocable straight documentary credit the issuing bank has no formal obligation to such a purchaser/holder of the draft.

### USES

The irrevocable straight documentary credit is typically used in domestic trade and for standby credits, both situations where confirmation or negotiation is considered unnecessary because of the reputation of the issuing bank.

### ADVANTAGES/DISADVANTAGES

The irrevocable straight documentary credit is of greatest advantage to the buyer who does not incur a liability to pay the seller until his own bank reviews the documents.

### KEY WORDING/ENGAGEMENT CLAUSE

The obligation of the issuing bank in an irrevocable straight documentary credit is typically stated in the credit itself with wording such as:

*We hereby engage with you that each draft drawn and presented to us under and in compliance with the terms of this documentary credit will be duly honored by us.*

## SAMPLE IRREVOCABLE STRAIGHT DOCUMENTARY CREDIT

The Trade Bank
525 Market Street, 25th Floor
San Francisco, CA 94105

Date of Issue: May 15, 20XX

We hereby issue our irrevocable documentary credit
No. 1234567

Date of expiry August 15, 20XX
Place of expiry: At our counter

Applicant:
US Buying Company
125 Main Street
San Francisco, California

Beneficiary:
US Selling Company
987 Broadway
New York, New York

Amount: US$100,000, One hundred thousand US dollars

Credit available with The Trade Bank, San Francisco by payment of Beneficiary's draft at sight drawn on The Trade Bank for 100 percent of invoice value accompanied by the documents detailed herein.

Partial shipments: Allowed
Transshipments: Not Allowed

Taking in charge at: Hong Kong
Not later than June 5, 20XX
For transportation to San Francisco, California USA

Documents to be presented:
Original and three signed copies of commercial invoice
Clean ocean port-to-port bill of lading consigned to Applicant marked freight collect, notify applicant.

Covering: merchandise as per Proforma Invoice No. 1234, FOB Hong Kong

Insurance effected by the Applicant

Documents must be presented at place of expiration no later than 10 days after date of shipment and within documentary credit validity.

Documents must be forwarded to us in one parcel and be mailed to The Trade Bank, 525 Market Street, 25th Floor, San Francisco, California 94105 USA.

Draft(s) must indicate the number and date of this credit.

Each draft presented hereunder must be accompanied by this original credit for our endorsement thereon of the amount of such draft.

This credit is subject to the Uniform Customs and Practice for Documentary Credits (1993 Revision), International Chamber of Commerce, Publication Number 500.

We hereby engage with you that each draft drawn and presented to us under and in compliance with the terms of this documentary credit will be duly honored by us.

The Trade Bank

## Irrevocable Negotiation Documentary Credit

### DEFINITION

An irrevocable negotiation documentary credit conveys a commitment by the issuing bank to honor drafts or documents as presented by the beneficiary or any third parties who might negotiate or purchase the beneficiary's drafts or documents as presented under the documentary credit.

### EXPLANATION

This means that the beneficiary of the documentary credit (the seller) may ask a third party bank or financial institution to negotiate or purchase and resell drafts and documents as presented under the documentary credit. The issuing bank commits to honoring drafts and documents held by third parties so long as the beneficiary and third parties comply with the terms and conditions of the documentary credit.

### USES

The great majority of documentary credits are freely negotiable. They are common in international trade as a foreign seller typically wants to be able to obtain payment for a shipment immediately from his local bank.

### ADVANTAGES/DISADVANTAGES

This form of credit is of advantage to the seller in that he does not have to wait until the buyer's bank reviews the documents to get paid the proceeds of the credit.

### KEY WORDING/ENGAGEMENT CLAUSE

The obligation of the issuing bank in an irrevocable negotiation documentary credit is typically stated in the credit itself with wording such as:

*Credit available with any bank, by negotiation for payment of beneficiary's draft at sight . . .*

and

*This credit is subject to the Uniform Customs and Practice for Documentary Credits (1993 Revision), International Chamber of Commerce, Publication Number 500, and engages us in accordance with the terms thereof.*

## SAMPLE IRREVOCABLE NEGOTIATION DOCUMENTARY

The Trade Bank
525 Market Street, 25th Floor
San Francisco, California USA

To: Indonesia Export Bank

Jakarta, Indonesia

We hereby issue our irrevocable documentary credit No. 1234567

Date of Issue: May 15, 20XX
Date of expiry: July 7, 20XX
Place of expiry: Indonesia

Applicant:
US Coffee Importer
San Francisco, California USA

Beneficiary:
ABC Coffee Exporter
Jakarta, Indonesia

Amount: US$65,000, Sixty-five thousand US dollars

Credit available with any bank, by negotiation for payment of beneficiary's draft at sight drawn on The Trade Bank for 100 percent of invoice value.

Partial shipments: Not allowed
Transshipments: Allowed
Shipment from Indonesia no later than June 16, 2002 to San Francisco, California USA

Goods: Fifteen metric tons of 60-kilo bags of new crop Sumatra Mandheling Arabica Grade 1 green coffee as per buyer's purchase order No. 1234, To be shipped in one ocean container.

CIF San Francisco, California USA

Documents required

1. Original and four copies of signed commercial invoice
2. Negotiable insurance policy or certificate and 02 copies for at least 110 percent of invoice value, covering marine risks and all risks, indicating loss, if any, payable in the United States in U.S. dollars.
3. Full set of clean "on board" ocean bill of lading to the order of shipper blank endorsed marked "freight prepaid" showing "notify John Smith & Company 123 Main Street San Francisco, CA 94123"

Draft(s) must indicate the number and date of this credit.

The amount of each draft negotiated under this credit must be endorsed on the reverse of this credit and the presentation of any such draft to us shall be a warranty by the presenting bank, that such endorsement has been made.

Documents must be forwarded to us by courier in one parcel and may be mailed to The Trade Bank, 525 Market Street, San Francisco, CA USA.

This credit is subject to the Uniform Customs and Practice for Documentary Credits (1993 Revision), International Chamber of Commerce, Publication Number 500, and engages us in accordance with the terms thereof.

Charges: All charges of banks other than ours are for beneficiary's account. However, our out of pocket expenses incurred in effecting any payment(s) hereunder are also for beneficiary's account.

Period for presentation: Documents must be presented at place of expiration no later than 21 days after date of shipment and within documentary credit validity.

Confirmation instructions: Without

The Trade Bank

## Irrevocable Unconfirmed Documentary Credit

### DEFINITION

An irrevocable unconfirmed documentary credit conveys a commitment by the issuing bank to honor drafts or documents as presented by the beneficiary of the credit. Such a credit is advised (notification to the beneficiary) through an advising bank.

### EXPLANATION

The advising bank is often the seller's bank in the seller's country and acts as an agent of the issuing bank. The advising bank's responsibility is limited to a reasonable review of the documents forwarded by the issuing bank prior to their being passed on to the beneficiary of the credit.

The advising bank specifically does not confirm (add its guarantee of) payment of the credit. This means that the beneficiary of the documentary credit (the seller) will be paid by and has recourse to the issuing bank only.

### USES

The irrevocable unconfirmed documentary credit is used when the reputation of the issuing bank is strong enough to give confidence to the seller that he will get paid.

### ADVANTAGES/DISADVANTAGES

There is a slight advantage to the buyer as the buyer is typically responsible for paying the documentary credit fees. Since confirmation incurs a fee, the buyer would have a small savings.

### KEY WORDING/ENGAGEMENT CLAUSE

The obligation of the issuing bank in an irrevocable unconfirmed documentary credit is typically stated in the credit itself with wording such as:

*Confirmation instructions: Without.*

and

*This credit is subject to the Uniform Customs and Practice for Documentary Credits (1993 Revision), International Chamber of Commerce, Publication Number 500, and engages us in accordance with the terms thereof.*

### ADVICE WORDING

The advising bank passes on the issuing bank's documentary credit to the beneficiary and adds wording such as:

*The enclosed advice is sent to you without confirmation.*

## SAMPLE IRREVOCABLE UNCONFIRMED DOCUMENTARY

Korean Export/Import Bank
Seoul, Korea

To: The Trade Bank, San Francisco, California USA

We hereby issue our irrevocable documentary credit No. 2345678

Date of Issue: June 15, 20XX
Date of expiry: August 10, 20XX
Place of expiry: USA

Applicant:
Korean Electronic Importer
Seoul, Korea

Beneficiary:
American Electronics Exporter
San Jose, California USA

Amount: US$15,000, Fifteen thousand US dollars

Credit available with any bank, by negotiation.
Drafts payable at sight.

Drawee Korean Export/Import Bank, Seoul, Korea

Partial shipments: Allowed
Transhipments: Prohibited
Loading on board San Francisco International Airport, For transportation to Kimpo Airport Seoul Korea.

Latest day of shipment: July 20, 20XX

Description of goods: DRAM chips Model Number MP164Ft12 per proforma invoice dated May 29, 2002.

Quantity: 3,000

Unit price: US$5.00; Unit: Each Amount: US$15,000.00

Terms of price: EXW

Country of origin: U.S.A./Taiwan/Singapore/Philippines

Documents required
1. Signed commercial invoice in triplicate
2. Airway bill consigned to Korean Export/Import Bank marked "freight collect" and "notify"
3. Packing list in triplicate

Additional conditions: Notify party on commercial invoice and air waybill must show Korean Electronics Importer Seoul Korea
Air freight should be effected by Emery Airfreight

Charges: All banking commissions and charges, including reinbursement charges and postage outside Korea are for account of beneficiary.

Period for presentation: Documents must be presented within 021 days after the date of shipment.

Confirmation instructions: Without.

Reinbursement bank: Korean Export/Import Bank, Los Angeles, CA USA.

Instructions to the Paying/Accepting/Negotiating Bank: The amount of each negotiation (draft) must be endorsed on the reverse of this credit by the negotiating bank.
All documents must be forwarded directly by courier service in one lot to Korean Export/Import Bank Seoul Korea.
If documents are presented with discrepancies, a discrepancy fee of US$40.00 or equivalent should (will) be deducted from the reimbursement claim.

This credit is subject to the Uniform Customs and Practice for Documentary Credits (1993 Revision), International Chamber of Commerce, Publication Number 500, and engages us in accordance with the terms thereof.

Korean Export/Import Bank

## Irrevocable Confirmed Documentary Credit

### DEFINITION

An irrevocable confirmed documentary credit is one that contains a guarantee on the part of both the issuing and advising banks of payment to the beneficiary (seller) so long as the terms and conditions of the credit are met.

### EXPLANATION

Confirmation is only added to an irrevocable credit at the request of the issuing bank. Confirmation of an irrevocable documentary credit adds the guarantee of a second bank (usually the seller's bank in the seller's country) to the credit. This means that the beneficiary of the irrevocable confirmed documentary credit (the seller) will be paid by the confirming bank once the terms and conditions of the credit have been met.

### USES

A confirmed credit is used when the seller does not have confidence that the buyer's bank can effectively guarantee payment. It is also used when the seller fears economic, political, or legal risk in the buyer's country.

### ADVANTAGES/DISADVANTAGES

This is the most secure credit for the seller as it adds the guarantee of a second (and usually local) bank to that of the issuing bank.

Confirmation by a second bank is the equivalent of added insurance, and insurance costs money, so this form of credit is more costly.

### KEY WORDING/ENGAGEMENT CLAUSE

The obligation of the issuing bank in an irrevocable confirmed documentary credit is typically stated in the credit itself with wording such as:

*Confirmation instructions: With, Confirm, or Confirmed*

and

*This credit is subject to the Uniform Customs and Practice for Documentary Credits (1993 Revision), International Chamber of Commerce, Publication Number 500, and engages us in accordance with the terms thereof.*

## Silent Confirmation

If a documentary credit does not contain a confirmation request by the issuing bank, in certain circumstances the possibility exists of confirming the credit by silent confirmation (without the issuing bank's knowledge). In this case the beneficiary and the advising bank make an independent agreement that adds the advising bank's confirmation to the credit for a fee.

## SAMPLE IRREVOCABLE CONFIRMED DOCUMENTARY CREDIT

Turkish Export/Import Bank
Ankara, Turkey

To: The Trade Bank, 525 Market Street, 25th Floor, San Francisco, CA USA

We hereby issue our irrevocable documentary credit No. 3456789

Date of Issue: July 15, 20XX
Date of expiry October 12,20XX
Place of expiry: USA

| Applicant: | Beneficiary: |
|---|---|
| Turkey Medical Equipment Importer | American Medical Equipment Exporter |
| Ankara, Turkey | Houston, Texas, USA |

Amount: US$12,000, Twelve thousand US dollars

Credit available at sight with The Trade Bank, 525 Market Street, San Francisco, California USA, by payment.

Partial shipments: Allowed
Transhipments: Allowed
Shipment from any USA airport, for transportation to Esenboga Airport, Ankara Turkey by plane.

Latest day of shipment: September 20, 20XX

Description of goods: Blood plasa machine per proforma invoice No. 123.

Quantity: 1 (one)

Unit price: US$12,000.00, Total price US$12,000.00.

Terms of price: FOB Texas

Documents required

1. Signed commercial invoice in original and 02 copies certifying that merchandise is in strict conformity with proforma invoice and indicating quality, quantity and unit price
2. Certificate of origin, legalized by local chamber of commerce in 02 copies indicating that the goods are of U.S.A. origin.
3. Copy of fax sent to us on shipment date about expedition details as description, value, loaded quantity of merchandise and characteristics of transport vehicle (flight no.) our fax No.: 0-312-1234567.
4. Clean air waybill, in 3 copies consigned to Turkish Export/Import Bank and mark notify applicant and freight collect.
5. Beneficiary's written statement showing that 01 original invoice, 01 certificate of origin legalized by local chamber of commerce, 01 original clean air waybill have been sent together with the goods.

Additional conditions: Insurance will be covered by applicant
Original documents will be sent to us by courier "DHL"
All documents should bear our and the negotiating/presenting bank's reference numbers.

Charges: All charges outside Turkey are for beneficiary's account.

Period for presentation: Documents to be presented within 021 days after shipment date.

Confirmation instructions: Confirm.

Reinbursement bank: New York Bank, New York, NY USA.

If presented documents contain discrepancies, US$ 100. or equivalent in the documentary credit currency will be deducted from proceeds as additional processing fees.

Advise through bank: The Trade Bank, San Francisco, California USA

This credit is subject to the Uniform Customs and Practice for Documentary Credits (1993 Revision), International Chamber of Commerce, Publication Number 500, and engages us in accordance with the terms thereof.

Turkish Export/Import Bank

CHAPTER 13

# Documentary Credits, Part 4

## SPECIAL LETTERS OF CREDIT

THERE ARE SEVERAL special credits designed to meet the specific needs of buyers, suppliers, and intermediaries. Special credits involve increased participation by banks, so financing and service charges are higher. Each of the credits listed below is explained in greater detail in the pages that follow.

### STANDBY CREDIT

Standby credits are often called nonperforming letters of credit because they are only used if the collection on a primary payment method is past due. Standby credits can be used to guarantee repayment of loans, fulfillment by subcontractors, and securing the payment for goods delivered by third parties.

### REVOLVING CREDIT

This is a commitment on the part of the issuing bank to restore the credit to the original amount after it has been used or drawn down. This credit is used in cases where a buyer wishes to have certain quantities of the ordered goods delivered at specified intervals, such as in a multiple delivery contract.

### RED CLAUSE CREDIT

A red clause credit has a special clause (red clause) that authorizes the confirming bank to make advances to the beneficiary (seller) prior to the presentation of the shipping documents. In this credit the buyer, in essence, extends financing to the seller and incurs ultimate risk for all sums advanced under the credit.

### TRANSFERABLE CREDIT

A transferable credit is one where the original beneficiary transfers all or part of the proceeds of an existing credit to another party (typically the ultimate supplier of the goods). It is normally used by middlemen as a financing tool.

### BACK-TO-BACK CREDIT

This is a new credit opened on the basis of an already existing, nontransferable credit. It is used by traders to make payment to the ultimate supplier. A trader receives a documentary credit from the buyer and then opens another documentary credit in favor of the ultimate supplier. The first documentary credit is used as collateral for the second credit. The second credit makes price adjustments from which comes the trader's profit.

## Standby Credit

### DEFINITION

A standby documentary credit is an obligation on the part of an issuing bank to pay a beneficiary in the case of the nonperformance of the applicant.

### EXPLANATION

In a standard commercial documentary credit the issuing bank has an obligation to pay the beneficiary based on the performance of the beneficiary (the beneficiary's fulfillment of the terms and conditions of the credit). In a standby documentary credit the issuing bank is obligated to pay the beneficiary based on the nonperformance of the applicant.

Standby documentary credits are, therefore, also called "nonperforming letters of credit," because they are only used as a backup payment method if the collection on a primary payment method is past due.

A standby documentary credit is generally obtained and held in reserve or paid out only as a result of noncompliance with some underlying contract between the parties involved.

Exporters may be asked to provide a standby documentary credit as a requirement of working on complicated infrastructure projects abroad or as an assurance under a contractual obligation that they will perform as agreed. If the goods are provided, or the service performed, as agreed, the standby documentary credit will expire unused. The exporter must also be certain that the documents submitted are exactly as required in the documentary credit.

Standby credits are often used in the United States as a legal form of bank guarantee (US law prohibits banks from making certain types of guarantees).

### USES

Standby letters of credit can be used to guarantee the following types of payments and performance:

1. Repayment of loans
2. Fulfillment by contractors and subcontractors
3. Securing payment for goods or services delivered by third parties

### ADVANTAGES/DISADVANTAGES

Since the beneficiary (typically the seller) of a standby documentary credit can draw from it on demand the buyer assumes added risk.

## Revolving Credit

### DEFINITION

A revolving documentary credit is an obligation on the part of an issuing bank to restore a credit to the original amount after it has been utilized, without the need for amendment. A revolving documentary credit can be revocable or irrevocable, cumulative or noncumulative, and can "revolve" in number, time, or value.

### EXPLANATION

A revolving credit is designed to facilitate ongoing relationships between buyers and sellers where buyers wish to purchase either (1) a set maximum value of product per period of time, (2) a certain maximum value of product, or (3) as much product as the seller can produce or supply.

- NUMBER/TIME In this form, the credit may be available for a set value for a set number of times—for example, US$10,000 per month for twelve months. Each month the seller may draw up to US$10,000 and the issuing bank will automatically reinstate it for another US$10,000 for twelve months. This form of credit may be cumulative or noncumulative.
- CUMULATIVE In a cumulative revolving credit any sum not utilized by the beneficiary during an installment period may be carried over and added to a subsequent installment period. Using the above example, if the beneficiary only utilizes US$8,000 the first month, the value of the credit the following month increases to US$12,000. With a total value (or from the banker's perspective liability) of US$120,000, this cumulative revolving credit can be utilized for a cumulative total of up to US$10,000 the first month, US$20,000 the second month, etc.
- NONCUMULATIVE In this credit any value not utilized during an installment period may not be carried over and added to a subsequent installment period.
- VALUE In this form, the credit amount is reinstated after utilization for a potentially infinite number of times during the validity period of the credit.

### USES

Revolving documentary credits are used in situations where a buyer and seller agree that goods will be shipped on a continuing basis and where the parties to the credit wish to establish one credit to handle all the shipments rather than to establish individual letters of credit for each shipment.

NOTE: A credit for the full value of the goods to be shipped but requiring specific quantities to be shipped weekly or monthly and allowing part-shipments is not a revolving credit. It is a credit available by installments.

### ADVANTAGES/DISADVANTAGES

Unless limited to a maximum value or a maximum number of revolutions, a revolving credit can obligate the issuing bank and the applicant/buyer to potentially limitless liability.

## Red Clause Credit

### DEFINITION

A red clause documentary credit is an obligation on the part of an issuing bank to guarantee advance payments made by a confirming (or any other nominated bank) to the beneficiary prior to presentation of documents.

### EXPLANATION

A red clause documentary credit is a mechanism for providing funding to the seller prior to the shipment of goods. It is often used to assist manufacturers in paying for labor and materials used in manufacturing or to middlemen who need financing to conclude a transaction. Ultimately, it is a form of financing provided by the buyer to the seller.

A red clause credit is so named because the clause authorizing advance payment is traditionally written in red ink. The clause states the amount(s) of the authorized advances and any terms and conditions of the advance(s). The authorized advance may be for up to the full amount of the credit.

---

EXAMPLE: A furniture manufacturer in Taiwan (the buyer/importer) through an issuing bank in Taiwan opens a red clause documentary credit naming a hardwood lumber dealer in Indonesia as beneficiary, with the dealer's Indonesian bank as the confirming bank. The hardwood dealer draws against the red clause credit, obtaining funds from the bank to pay his suppliers as he finds lumber that meets the needs of the furniture manufacturer in Taiwan.

If the hardwood dealer is unable to ship the lumber according to the terms and conditions of the original credit, the confirming bank in Indonesia has recourse to the issuing bank in Taiwan, which also has recourse to the beneficiary (seller/hardwood dealer) in Indonesia.

---

### ADVANTAGES/DISADVANTAGES

A red clause credit is useful to the buyer in situations where the supplier is trusted and the difficulty of obtaining the raw materials/goods directly is high. The disadvantage to the buyer is that the seller may not perform and the buyer may totally lose the paid advances. The advantage to the seller is that another party is providing financing for the transaction. The disadvantage to the seller is that he still maintains responsibility for ultimate delivery of goods, and he is liable for repayment of the full amount of the credit, plus costs, if unable to perform.

## Transferable Credit

### DEFINITION

A transferable documentary credit is one where the beneficiary may request that part of the proceeds (payment) of the credit be transferred to one or more other parties who become second beneficiaries.

### EXPLANATION

A transferable credit is used by a "middleman" who acts as an intermediary between a buyer and a seller to earn a profit for structuring the transaction.

The buyer opens a documentary credit naming the intermediary as the beneficiary. The intermediary then transfers both the obligation to supply the goods and part of the proceeds of the credit to the actual supplier.

In the process, the intermediary commits little or no funds to the transaction. This form of payment is often used in situations where the intermediary does not wish the buyer and the actual supplier to know each other's identity.

### DETAILS

- At the time of opening the credit the buyer must request that it be made transferable.
- The credit itself, as issued, must be clearly marked as "transferable." Terms such as "divisible," "fractionally," "assignable," or "transmissible" do not make the credit transferable.
- Transferable credits can be transferred once. A second beneficiary cannot transfer to a third beneficiary.
- Transferable credits can be transferred in whole or in part.
- The fewer the documents specified and the simpler the terms stipulated in the original credit, the smoother the transaction can be handled.

### PARTIAL QUANTITIES/MULTIPLE SUPPLIERS

The transfer of partial quantities by multiple sellers to the buyer is possible but only if the credit permits partial deliveries. Fulfillment of the original contract with the buyer through partial quantities by multiple suppliers is more expensive as banks charge fees and/or commissions for each transfer.

The "middleman" may substitute his own invoices and drafts on the buyer, for those presented to the bank by the seller (second beneficiary). The bank has the responsibility, however, of reviewing such invoices and drafts against other documents to make certain they all conform with the terms and conditions of the original credit.

## PERMITTED CHANGES TO THE CREDIT

A transferable credit can be transferred only under the terms stated in the original credit. However, the intermediary may transfer the credit with the following changes:

1. The name and address of the intermediary may be substituted for that of the original buyer (applicant of the credit).
2. Unit prices and the total amount of the credit may be reduced to enable the intermediary an allowance for profit.
3. The expiration date, the final shipment date, and the final date for presentation of documents may all be shortened to allow the intermediary time to meet obligations under the original credit.
4. Insurance coverage may be increased in order to provide the percentage amount of cover stipulated in the original credit.

## AMENDMENTS TO A TRANSFERABLE CREDIT

Since the ultimate buyer and the actual seller/supplier are separated by the intermediary there is the question of how to deal with amendments. Do amendments by the buyer get sent (advised) to the second beneficiary?

The intermediary, therefore, must establish, irrevocably, at the time of the request for transfer of the credit, and prior to the actual transfer of the credit, whether the transferring bank may advise amendments to the seller (second beneficiary).

Options for transfer rights on amendments include full or partial transfer of the credit with

1. Retainment of rights on amendments
2. Partial waiver of rights on amendments
3. Waiver of rights on amendments

If the transferring bank agrees to the transfer, it must advise the seller (second beneficiary) of the intermediary's amendment instructions.

## USES

Transferable documentary credits are used as a financing tool in transactions where the buyer trusts the intermediary.

## ADVANTAGES/DISADVANTAGES

Since the transferable credit must be clearly marked "transferable," the buyer knows that the first beneficiary is not the ultimate supplier and is relying upon the credit as the financing instrument. This credit is generally for use only by more sophisticated traders.

In this form of credit both the buyer and ultimate supplier may feel at a disadvantage not knowing each other and placing their trust in an intermediary who did not have the financing to conclude the transaction on his own. The more paperwork and the more parties to the transaction, the greater the opportunity for problems.

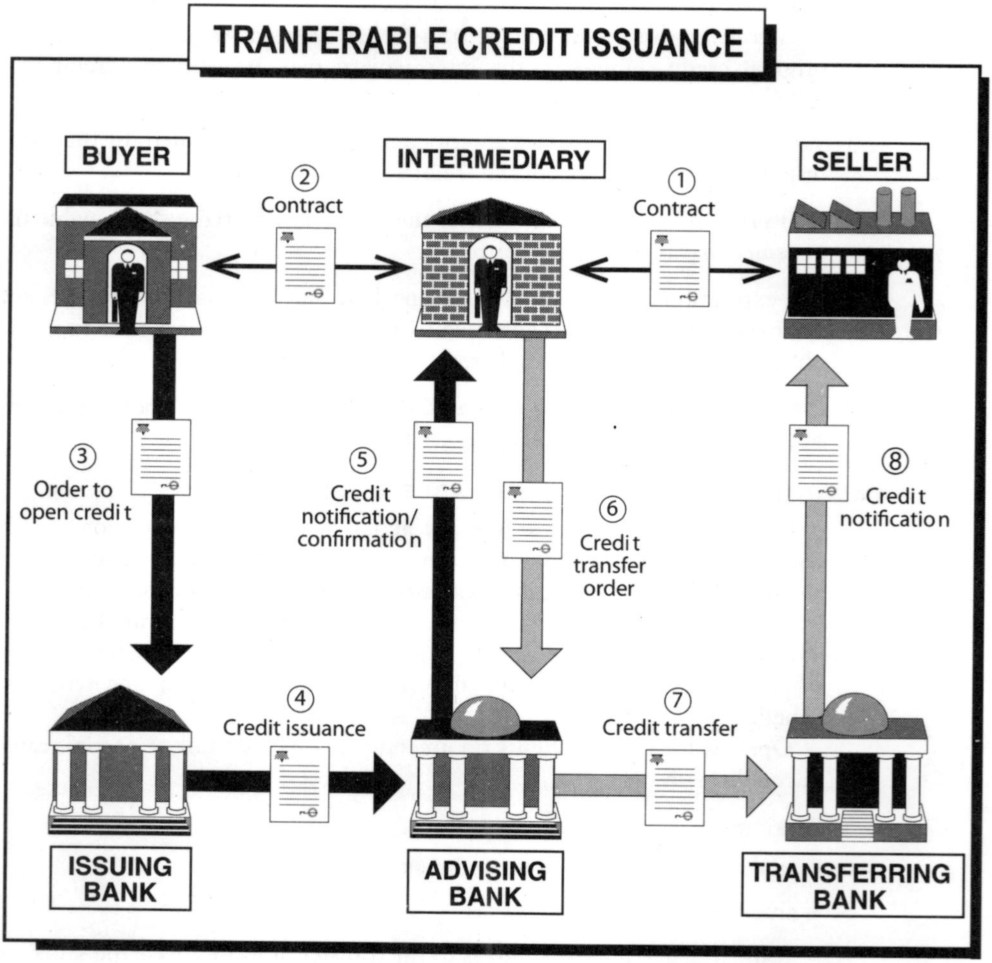


TRANSFERABLE CREDIT ISSUANCE PROCEDURE

1. Intermediary (first beneficiary) contracts with seller (second beneficiary) to purchase goods.
2. Intermediary contracts to sell goods to buyer. (Or steps 1 and 2 are reversed.)
3. Buyer applies for and opens a documentary credit with issuing bank.
4. Issuing bank issues the documentary credit and forwards it to advising bank.
5. Advising bank notifies intermediary of documentary credit.
6. Intermediary orders transfer of documentary credit to seller (second beneficiary).
7. Advising bank transfers credit in care of transferring (seller's) bank.
8. Transferring bank notifies seller (second beneficiary) of documentary credit.

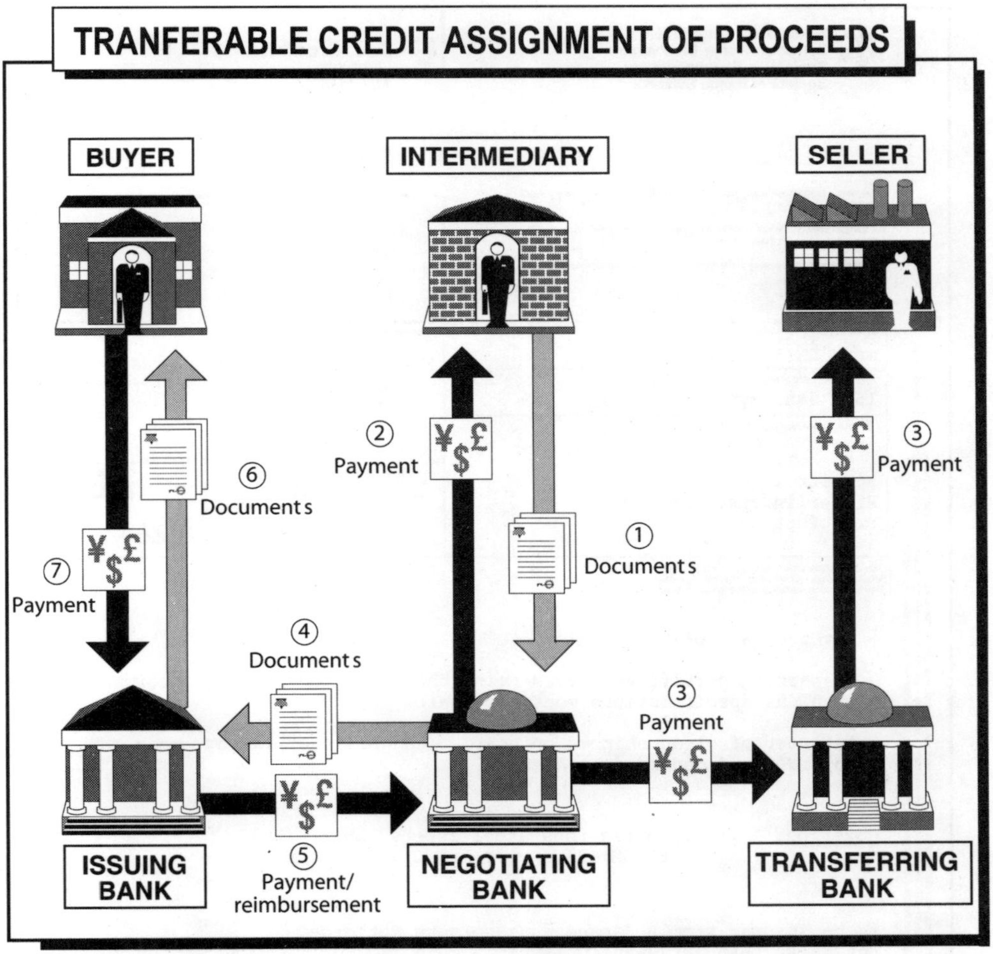


TRANSFERABLE CREDIT ASSIGNMENT OF PROCEEDS PROCEDURE

1. Intermediary (first beneficiary) presents documents to the negotiating bank.
2. Negotiating bank pays intermediary any funds not assigned to the seller (second beneficiary).
3. Negotiating bank pays transferring bank who then in turn pays the seller (second beneficiary) the assigned funds.
4. Negotiating bank presents documents to the issuing bank.
5. Issuing bank pays/reimburses the negotiating bank in accordance with the terms of the credit.
6. Issuing bank presents documents to the buyer.
7. Buyer pays/reimburses the issuing bank in accordance with the terms of the credit.

## SAMPLE TRANSFERABLE DOCUMENTARY CREDIT

**Swiss Bank Corporation**
**Schweizerischer Bankverein**
**Société de Banque Suisse**
**Società di Banca Svizzera**

Notre / Unsere / Our **Doc. Credit No** 173'896

4002 Basle, 20th October 19..
Lieu/Date Ort/Datum Luogo/Data

Nous vous informons de l'ouverture du crédit documentaire irrévocable suivant en votre faveur:

Wir benachrichtigen Sie von der Eröffnung des folgenden unwiderruflichen Dokumentarkredites zu ihren Gunsten:

We inform you of the opening of the following irrevocable documentary credit in your favour:

REGISTERED
TRANSITO LTD.
Rheinallee 183

4002 B a s e l

| | |
|---|---|
| Montant / Betrag / Amount<br>max. DM 386'000.-- | Banque émettrice / Eröffnende Bank / Issuing bank<br>Bank for Trade and Industry<br>P.O. Box 1283<br><br>D-6000 Frankfurt 30 |
| Validité / Gültigkeit / Validity<br>15th January 19.. | |
| Donneur d'ordre / Auftraggeber / Applicant<br>Schmitt & Co. Ltd.<br>Hinterlindenstrasse 47<br>Frankfurt 34 | No de réf. de notre correspondant / Ref.-Nr. unseres Korrespondenten / Ref. no of our correspondent: LC/539284<br>Ordre du / Auftrag vom / Order dated: 19.10.19.. |

Utilisable contre remise des documents suivants:
Benützbar gegen Einreichung folgender Dokumente:
Available against surrender of the following documents:

- invoice, 3 copies
- inspection certificate, evidencing that the goods are in accordance with the specifications mentioned below
- full set of clean shipped on board ocean bills of lading, made out to order and endorsed in blank

covering: 1'000 metric tons steel sheets DIN 456/243 at DM 386.-- per mt, C & F Rotterdam

to be shipped from a Japanese seaport to Rotterdam not later than 1st January 19..
Partial deliveries are permitted. Transshipment not allowed.
Documents to be presented not later than 15 days after date of shipment.

This documentary credit is transferable.

We confirm this documentary credit to you as irrevocably valid until 15th January 19..

Yours faithfully

Swiss Bank Corporation

Ce credit est soumis aux • Règles et usances uniformes relatives aux crédits documentaires • approuvées par la Chambre de Commerce Internationale.
Dieser Kredit unterliegt den • Einheitlichen Richtlinien und Gebräuchen für Dokumenten-Akkreditive • wie sie von der Internationalen Handelskammer gutgeheissen worden sind.
This credit is subject to the • Uniform customs and practice for documentary credits • fixed by the International Chamber of Commerce.

F 6804N 1/8 2.82 10000

## SAMPLE ORDER OF ASSIGNMENT

**MÜLLER AG**

**Postfach 10283, 4087 Basel**
**Telefon: (061) 247 86 86**
**Telex: 247 86 86 mulag ch**

Basle, 20th October 19..

Swiss Bank Corporation
Documentary Credits
P.O. Box

4002 B a s l e

Documentary credit no. 204356 in our favour, for SFr. 65'000.--, covering 200 tons of fertilizer

Dear Sirs,

In accordance with article 164 et seq. of the Swiss Law of Contract we hereby assign from the above documentary credit an amount of SFr. 300.-- per delivered ton of fertilizer, total SFr. 60'000.--, to Dünger Ltd., Feldmeilenstrasse 21, 8002 Zurich.

Would you kindly inform Dünger Ltd., Zurich, that you have taken note of this assignment and that the amount due will be transferred to them once the credit has been negotiated and the funds are freely available.

Yours faithfully

M ü l l e r Ltd.

Müller Frey

## SAMPLE FORWARDING OF ASSIGNMENT BY THE BANK

**Swiss Bank Corporation**
**Schweizerischer Bankverein**
**Société de Banque Suisse**
**Società di Banca Svizzera**

Dünger Ltd.
Feldmeilenstrasse 21

8002 Zurich

| Your ref. | Our dept./ref. | Through dialing (061) | **4002 Basle,** 21st October 19.. |
|---|---|---|---|
| | DOK/BU | 20 20 20 | |

Documentary credit no. 204356 in favour
Müller AG, Basel

Dear Sirs,

By order of Müller AG, Basle, we received the following assignment:

In accordance with article 164 et seq. of the Swiss Law of Contract we hereby assign from the above documentary credit an amount of SFr. 300.-- per delivered ton of fertilizer, total SFr. 60'000.-- to Dünger Ltd., Feldmeilenstrasse 21, 8002 Zurich.

At the request of Müller AG, Basle, we confirm that we have duly taken note of this assignment. We undertake to hold at your disposal an amount up to SFr. 60'000.--. The amount due will be transferred to you as soon as the credit has been negotiated and the funds are freely available.

Yours faithfully,

Swiss Bank Corporation

E 90001 S

## SAMPLE TRANSFERABLE CREDIT ORDER

**TRANSITO AG**
**Import - Export - Kommission**
**Rheinallee 183, 4087 Basel**
**Telefon: (061) 251 87 87**

Basle, 21st October 19..

Swiss Bank Corporation
Documentary Credits
P.O. Box

4002 B a s l e

Documentary credit no. 173896 - DM 386'000.--, opened by Handels- und Industriebank, Frankfurt, by order of Schmitt & Co. KG, Frankfurt, confirmed by yourselves

Dear Sirs,

Would you please transfer the above-mentioned documentary credit as follows:

| | |
|---|---|
| New beneficiaries : | Handels GmbH<br>Sendlauerstrasse 28<br>Vienna 28 |
| to be advised by : | Overseas Bank Ltd., Vienna |
| amount : | DM 350'000.-- |
| validity : | 5th January 19.., |
| price : | DM 350.-- per mt C & F Rotterdam |

All other conditions remain unchanged. Please credit the balance of funds in our favour to our DM account with yourselves.

We appreciate your assistance in this matter and look forward to receiving your advice of execution.

Yours faithfully

TRANSITO LTD.

Baumann

## Back-to-Back Credit

### DEFINITION

A back-to-back documentary credit is a new documentary credit opened in favor of another beneficiary on the basis of an already existing, irrevocable, non-transferable documentary credit.

### EXPLANATION

As the name implies, a back-to-back documentary credit is actually two distinct documentary credits:

1. A documentary credit opened by the buyer naming the seller as the beneficiary, and
2. A second documentary credit opened by the seller naming the actual supplier of the goods as the beneficiary.

A back-to-back credit is used in situations where the original credit is not transferable and where the bank is willing to open the second credit at the request of the seller, using the first credit as collateral or support for the second credit.

The bank, however, is under no obligation to issue the second credit. In fact, most banks will refuse to open such a credit unless they have extreme confidence in the seller's creditworthiness and ability to perform. Because of the complexity of the transaction, banks see the first credit less as collateral than as an item of support for issuance of the second credit.

Since the seller is the applicant for the second credit, the seller is responsible to the bank for payment regardless of whether or not he himself is paid under the first credit.

The second credit must be carefully worded to require all the documents (except for the commercial invoice) as required under the first credit. Also, since there is a time lag between issuance of the first credit and the second credit, the second credit must be worded to require that documents be presented in time to satisfy the requirements of the first credit.

### USES

The uses of a back-to-back documentary credit are similar to those of a transferable credit. The seller/intermediary uses the financial strength of the buyer to effect the transaction.

### ADVANTAGES/DISADVANTAGES

Since the first credit names the seller as the beneficiary the buyer is unaware that there is a supplier other than the seller. This credit is generally for use only by more sophisticated traders. The more paperwork and the more parties to the transaction, the greater the opportunity for problems.

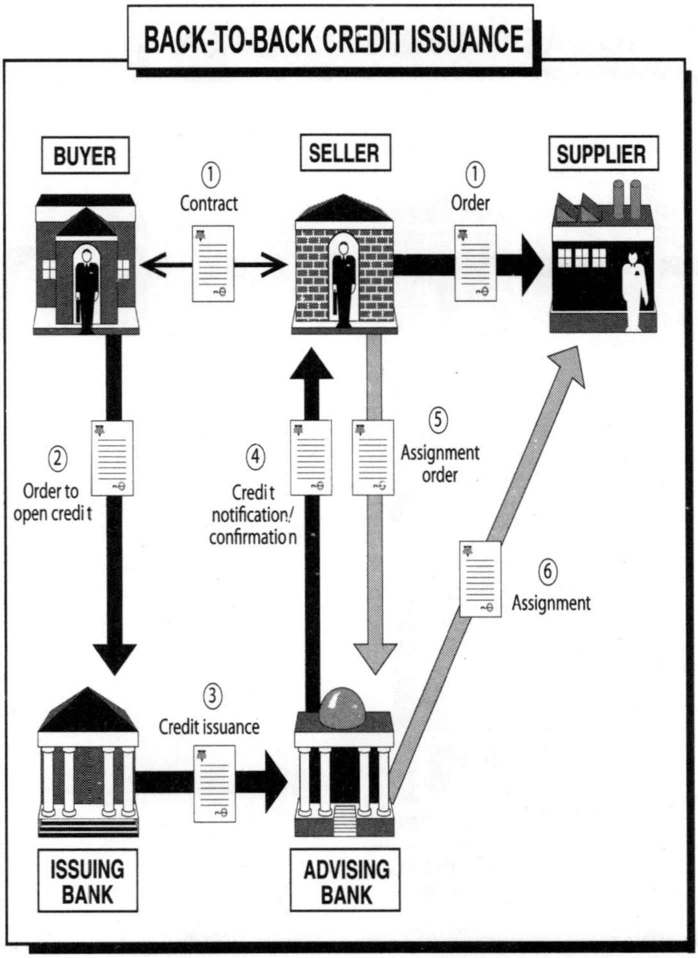


BACK-TO-BACK CREDIT ISSUANCE PROCEDURE

1. Buyer and seller negotiate a contract. Seller places order with supplier.
2. Buyer applies for and opens a documentary credit with issuing bank.
3. Issuing bank issues the documentary credit and forwards it to advising bank.
4. Advising bank notifies seller of documentary credit.
5. Seller orders assignment of credit to supplier.
6. Advising bank assigns credit to supplier.

NOTE: At step 6 the advising bank may transfer the credit to a second advising or confirming bank. This step is left out for the sake of simplicity.

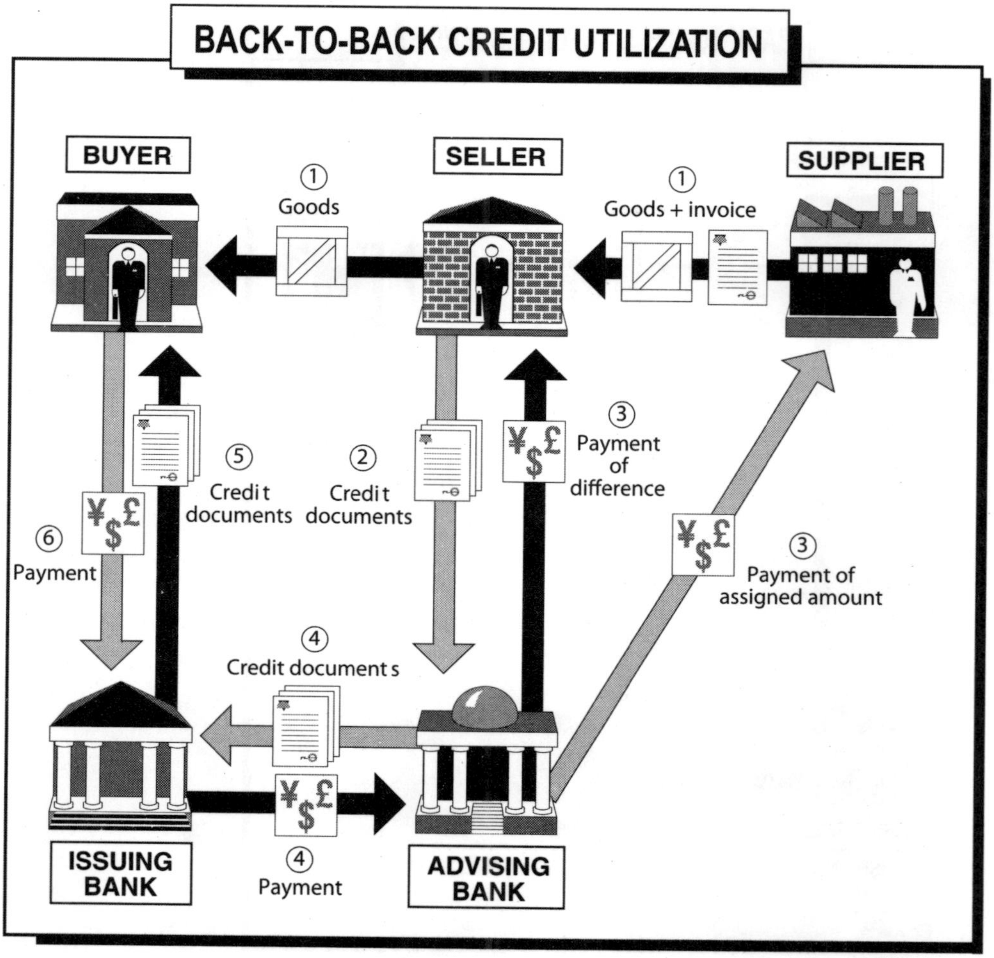


BACK-TO-BACK CREDIT UTILIZATION PROCEDURE

1. Ultimate supplier ships goods and invoice to seller who in turn ships the goods to the buyer.
2. Seller forwards documents to advising bank.
3. a) Advising bank pays the supplier the amount designated in seller's assignment order.
   b) Advising bank pays the seller the difference between the original credit amount and the amount assigned to the supplier.
4. a) Advising bank forwards documents to the issuing bank.
   b) Issuing bank pays advising bank.
5. Issuing bank forwards documents to buyer.
6. Buyer pays issuing bank.

CHAPTER 14

# Documentary Credits, Part 5

## Issues and Checklists

### Regarding the Role of Banks

It is important to note that documentary credit procedures are not infallible. Things can and do go wrong. Since banks act as intermediaries between the buyer and seller, both look to the banks as protectors of their interests. However, while banks have clear cut responsibilities, they are also shielded from certain problems deemed to be out of their control or responsibility. Several instances:

1. Banks act upon specific instructions given by the applicant (buyer) in the documentary credit. Buyer's instructions left out of the credit by mistake or omitted because "we've always done it that way" don't count. The buyer, therefore, should take great care in preparing the application so that it gives complete and clear instructions.

2. Banks are required to act in good faith and exercise reasonable care to verify that the documents submitted *appear* to be as listed in the credit. They are, however, under no obligation to confirm the authenticity of the documents submitted.

3. Banks are not liable nor can they be held accountable for the acts of third parties. Third parties include freight forwarders, forwarding agents, customs authorities, insurance companies, and other banks. Specifically, they are not responsible for delays or consequences resulting from Acts of God (floods, earthquakes, etc.) riots, wars, civil commotions, strikes, lockouts, or other causes beyond their control.

4. Banks also assume no liability or responsibility for loss arising out of delays or loss in transit of messages, letters, documents, etc.

5. Because banks deal in documents and not goods, they assume no responsibility regarding the quantity or quality of goods shipped. They are only concerned that documents presented appear on their face to be consistent with the terms and conditions of the documentary credit. Any dispute as to quality or quantity of goods delivered must be settled between the buyer and the seller.

6. So long as the documents presented to the banks appear on their face to comply with the terms and conditions of the credit, banks may accept them and initiate the payment process as stipulated in the documentary credit.

If there are any conclusions to be made from the above they are: first, that the buyer and seller should know each other and have at least some basis of trust to be doing business in the first place, and second, that all parties to the transaction should take responsibility to follow through on their part carefully.

## Common Problems with Documentary Credits

Despite the protections offered by a documentary credit, problems can and do arise. Most problems have to do with the ability of the seller to fulfill the obligations established by the buyer in the original documentary credit, or with discrepancies in the documents presented by the seller under the documentary credit.

Some of the common problems sellers have with documentary credits are

1. Shipment schedule stipulated in the documentary credit cannot be met.
2. Stipulations concerning freight costs are deemed unacceptable.
3. Price is insufficient due to changes in exchange rates.
4. Quantity of product ordered is not the expected amount.
5. Description of product to be shipped is either insufficient or too detailed.
6. Documents stipulated in the documentary credit are difficult or impossible to obtain.

## Discrepancies with Documents

Perhaps the greatest problem associated with documentary credits is discrepancies with documents as they are prepared, presented, and reviewed by sellers, buyers, and the banks. All parties have the obligation to check the documentation to make certain it is in order and all parties are at risk for failing to do so properly.

The buyer can introduce problems to the process by specifying documents that are difficult or impossible to obtain. The seller can introduce problems by incorrectly preparing and presenting the document package to his bank.

Advising, confirming, and issuing banks can introduce problems by incorrectly reviewing (negotiating in bank language) the documents provided by the seller against the requirements of the documentary credit.

### CONFORMITY WITH THE DOCUMENTARY CREDIT

The key issue is that the documents presented by the seller must be in conformity with the specifications of the documentary credit. Once again, banks deal in documents, not goods. The banks, therefore, are seeking conformity of the documentation to the wording of the credit and not of the goods to the documents.

The bottom line is that if the seller's documents are not prepared in accordance with the terms and conditions of the credit, the bank is under no obligation to pay the seller for the shipment. (Note the seller's document presentation checklist on the pages that follow.)

### BANK OPTIONS

Banks have up to seven banking days following the receipt of documents to examine and notify the party from which it received the documents of their acceptance or nonacceptance. If a bank involved in the transaction finds discrepancies in the documents, it has several options:

1. The advising or confirming bank can refuse to accept the documents and return them to the seller (beneficiary) so that they can be corrected or replaced.
2. The issuing bank, if it feels the discrepancy is not material to the transaction, can ask the buyer (applicant) for a waiver for the specific discrepancy, but must do so within seven banking days.
3. The advising or confirming bank can remit the documents under approval to the issuing bank for settlement.
4. The issuing or confirming bank can return the incorrect document(s) directly to the seller for correction or replacement and eventual return directly to the issuing or confirming bank.
5. The bank can proceed with payment to the seller but require a guarantee from the seller to reimburse the bank if the issuing bank does not honor the documents as presented.

If there is a discrepancy, the buyer and seller must communicate directly and then inform the banks of their decision. In the case of serious discrepancies, an amendment to the credit may be necessary.

The seller may request the opening bank to present the documents to the buyer on a collection basis. However, the buyer may refuse to accept the merchandise and be responsible for shipping and insurance costs.

## Electronic Applications for Documentary Credits

Electronic application for documentary credits is becoming more and more common. Buyers install software in their office PCs that enable them to fill out an application and send it via modem to the bank processing center. Security is provided using a special password system. Electronic applications enable the repeat letter of credit applicant faster turnaround and cut paperwork for the bank.

## Fraud

As has been repeatedly stated, documentary credits are not foolproof. There are layers of protection for both the buyer and the seller, but opportunities for fraud do exist. Many of the opportunities for fraud center around the fact that banks deal in documents and not goods, and therefore the seller has the opportunity for presenting fraudulent documents. Obviously, the seller will have difficulty doing this more than once or twice as no bank will repeatedly accept documents from a supplier accused of such practices. Also, most every country has criminal statutes against fraud and the seller will eventually get caught, but perhaps only after *you* have been defrauded.

As a reminder, it is always best to know your counterpart and the banks involved and to exercise caution and common sense in making decisions.

The situations listed below are extremely uncommon, but do exist.

1. Sellers have reported receiving an advice or a confirmation of a documentary credit from nonexisting banks. The perpetrator of the fraud attempts to get the seller to ship goods and present documents for payment to a bank that does not exist. By the time the seller is aware of the fraud, the "buyer" has received the goods.
2. Buyers have reported receiving empty crates or crates filled with sand instead of the merchandise they ordered. By the time they received the shipment the banks had already paid the "supplier."
3. Buyers have reported receiving defective merchandise from sellers. While there may be some latitude for interpretation of what constitutes "defective," it is clear that some suppliers have purposefully shipped incorrect or substandard goods.
4. Buyers have reported being short-shipped. In some cases buyers have ordered a valuable commodity sold by weight and were shortchanged by being charged for the gross weight rather than the net weight. They were charged the commodity price per kilogram for the packing materials.
5. Buyers of commodities, especially gray market goods, have reported being defrauded by the seller's providing fraudulent shipping documents, evidencing shipment on a nonexistent ship.

## Contract Provision

When a buyer and seller agree to use a documentary credit for payment in the purchase/sale of goods, they are well-advised to insert a payment provision in their contract to that effect. The following is a sample contract provision.

- PAYMENT: To secure payment, the BUYER NAME shall have ISSUING BANK NAME open an IRREVOCABLE documentary credit naming SELLER as beneficiary.
  The documentary credit is to be CONFIRMED by CONFIRMING BANK NAME.
  The documentary credit must remain valid for NUMBER OF MONTHS after issuance and be available AT SIGHT against presentation of the following documents:
  1. . . .
  2. . . .
  3. etc.

  The cost of the credit is to be paid by BUYER NAME.
  The credit shall be subject to the Uniform Customs and Practice for Documentary Credits (1993 Revision), International Chamber of Commerce, Publication Number 500.

The items in small capital letters are the variables. As with all legal matters it is best to consult with an experienced attorney for exact wording to best reflect your individual transaction.

## Notes on Insurance

1. If the documentary credit stipulates CIF (Cost Insurance and Freight) or CIP (Cost and Insurance Paid) terms the seller is responsible for providing insurance against damage or loss to the shipment. More specifically, the seller is responsible for presenting an insurance document with the document package that evidences insurance cover.
2. The credit should name the specific type of insurance coverage required and any additional risks that are to be covered. The terms "usual risks" or "customary risks" should not be used as they will be ignored by the banks. The buyer should be specific as to what insurance document is required, the dates of coverage, and the amount of coverage.
3. The insurance document is typically issued in duplicate and, if so, both originals must be presented with the document package.
4. The insurance document must be issued by an insurance company or its agent. Cover notes issued by brokers are not acceptable unless authorized in the credit. Banks will, unless otherwise stated in the credit, accept an insurance certificate under an open insurance cover which is presigned by the insurance company or underwriter.
5. The insurance document must indicate that the cover is effective at the latest from the date of loading of the goods on board a transport vessel or the taking in charge of the goods by the carrier, as indicated by the transport document (bill of lading, etc.).
6. The insurance document must specify coverage for at least 110 percent of either: (a) the CIF or CIP value of the shipment, if such can be determined from the various documents on their face, otherwise, (b) the amount of the payment, acceptance, or negotiation specified in the documentary credit, or (c) the gross amount of the invoice.
7. The insurance currency (e.g., US dollars, Japanese yen, etc.) should be consistent with the currency of the documentary credit.
8. Even if the buyer has responsibility under the contract to insure the shipment, the seller still may wish to take out contingency coverage to cover the possibility that the insurance steps taken by the buyer are inadequate.
9. If a documentary credit calls for an insurance document specifying "insurance against all risks," the banks will accept an insurance document containing any "all risks" notation or clause, even if the document indicates that certain risks are excluded.

## Notes for the Buyer

1. Before opening a documentary credit, the buyer should reach agreement with the seller on all particulars including description of the goods, quantities, unit price and total price, terms of sale (FOB, CIF, etc.), shipment schedule, and documents to be presented by the seller.
2. When choosing the type of documentary credit to be used, the buyer should take into account standard payment methods in the country of the seller.
3. When opening a documentary credit, the buyer should keep the requirements and required documentation to a minimum.
4. Documents specified in the documentary credit should include all those the buyer requires for customs clearance.
5. The buyer should be prepared to amend or renegotiate terms of the credit with the seller. This is a common procedure in international trade. On irrevocable letters of credit amendments may be made only if all parties involved in the documentary credit agree.
6. The buyer should use a bank experienced in foreign trade as the issuing bank.
7. The validation time stated on the documentary credit should give the seller adequate time to produce the goods or to pull them from stock.
8. The buyer should be aware that documentary credits are not fail-safe. Banks are responsible only for the documents exchanged and not the goods shipped. Documents in conformity with documentary credit specifications cannot be rejected on grounds that the goods were not delivered as specified in the contract. The goods shipped may not in fact be the goods ordered and paid for.
9. Purchase contracts and other agreements pertaining to the sale between the buyer and seller are not the concern of the issuing bank. Only the terms of the documentary credit are binding on the bank.

## Notes for the Seller—1

1. Before signing a contract, the seller should make inquiries about the buyer's creditworthiness and business practices. The seller's bank will generally assist in this investigation.
2. The seller should confirm the good standing of the buyer's bank if the credit is unconfirmed.
3. For a confirmed credit, it is preferable that the seller's regular commercial bank make the confirmation.
4. The seller should carefully review the documentary credit to make sure its conditions can be met, particularly schedules of shipment, type of goods to be sent, packaging, and documentation. All aspects of the documentary credit must be in conformance with the terms agreed upon, including the seller's name and address, the amount to be paid, and the prescribed transport route.
5. The seller must comply with every detail of the documentary credit specifications; otherwise the security given by the credit is lost.
6. The seller should ensure that the documentary credit is irrevocable.
7. If conditions of the credit have to be modified, the seller should contact the buyer immediately so the buyer can instruct the issuing bank to make the necessary amendments.
8. The seller should confirm with the insurance company that it can provide the coverage specified in the credit and that insurance charges in the documentary credit are correct. Typical insurance coverage is for CIF (cost, insurance, freight), often the value of the goods plus 10 percent.
9. The seller must ensure that the details of the goods being sent comply with the description in the documentary credit and that their description in the invoice matches that on the documentary credit.
10. The seller should be familiar with foreign exchange limitations in the buyer's country that could hinder payment procedures.

## Notes for the Seller—2

DOCUMENT CHECKLIST PRIOR TO SUBMISSION TO THE BANK

1. Do all the documents refer to the same order and the same credit? ❑
2. Are the documents present in the correct number and in complete sets? ❑
3. Is the name and address of the shipper correct? ❑
4. Is the name and address of the buyer/consignee correct? ❑
5. Is the issuer name and address correct? ❑
6. Does the description of the goods, unit price, and total price match the description in the credit? ❑
7. Is the description of the goods, unit price, and total price consistent from document to document? ❑
8. Does the invoice total not exceed the amount available in the credit? ❑
9. Is the country of origin of the goods listed and as specified in the documentary credit? ❑
10. Is the country of destination of the goods listed and as specified in the documentary credit? ❑
11. Do all the dimensions, weights, number of units, and markings agree on all documents? ❑
12. Have all the necessary documents been certified or legalized? ❑
13. Are the invoice numbers and documentary credit numbers correct and listed in the proper places? ❑
14. Is the bill of exchange legally signed? ❑
15. Does the bill of exchange have to be endorsed? ❑
16. Does the insurance document cover all the risks specified in the credit? ❑
17. Has the insurance document been properly endorsed? ❑
18. Are the documents being presented within the validity period? ❑
19. Is the bill of lading "clean," without notations? ❑
20. If the bill of lading has an "on deck" notation, does the credit allow for it? ❑
21. If the bill of lading is a charter party bill, does the credit allow for it? ❑
22. Is the notify address in the bill of lading correct? ❑
23. Is the bill of lading endorsed? ❑
24. Are corrections properly initialed by their originator? ❑

CHAPTER 15

# Sample Bank Fees

BANK FEES FOR DOCUMENTARY credits and documentary collections vary from country to country and from market to market within a country. Fees also vary depending upon the relationship a company has with its bank.

EXAMPLE: Bank fees in Hong Kong are low because of the widespread use of such payment methods there. On the other hand, they are quite high in Europe where such payment methods are not in as much favor. Prices in the United States are about in the middle.

Within large and geographically diverse markets like the United States, however, there is a great variance in bank fees. These are dependent on local market considerations. For example, in some markets documentary credits are considered to be "commodity services" meaning that customers generally know what they are buying, consider it to be virtually the same from every source, and buy based on price rather than service.

Finally, larger commercial banking customers who use documentary credits and collections on a regular basis will pay less than small firms who only use them infrequently. In our survey of bank fees, several bankers reported that processing a single documentary credit for a first-time customer results in a loss to the bank; so much time is spent educating a customer who may be using a documentary credit for the first and last time.

Bank fees for documentary credits and documentary collections are not charged on a package basis, but rather on an individual, or "à la carte," basis. Everything you order adds to the bill. The fees listed on the following pages will give you a range of typical charges. The examples will give you a more concrete idea of what individual transactions cost.

## DISCLAIMER

It is always awkward to list sample fees in a book with international distribution. Fees vary wildly from market to market and change from time to time within given markets. The structure of a bank's rates may vary as well. Although bankers and traders from several countries were interviewed, your company situation, banking market, and local government regulation may produce rates different from those listed below.

## Import Documentary Credit Fees

The range of banking fees listed below relate to importers. Lowest fees are generally for electronic issuance.

All figures are expressed in US dollars,
min = minimum, qtr = quarter, mo = month, ba = by arrangement.

| | LOW | HIGH |
|---|---|---|
| Issuance | 1/8%, $50 min/qtr | 1/4%, $105 min/qtr |
| Amendment to Increase Value | $40 | 1/4%, $80 min/qtr |
| Amendment w/out Increase in Value | $40 | $80 |
| Negotiation | 1/8%, $60 min | 1/4%, $100 min |
| Acceptance | 2% per annum, $90 min | 2% per annum, $100 min |
| Deferred Payment | ba, $90 min | ba, $100 min |
| Transfer | 1/4%, $100 min | 1/4%, $150 min |
| Assignment | 1/8%, $85 min | 1/4%, $200 min |
| Discrepancy | $40 | $60 |
| Steamship Guarantee | $75/qtr | $100/mo |
| Air Waybill | $50 | $75 |
| Expiry/ Amount Unused | $30 | $40 |
| Cancellation | $50 | $75 |

EXAMPLE 1: An import documentary credit issued for US$10,000 with one amendment and one document discrepancy might be subject to the following fees:
1) Issuance fee (minimum charge) US$100.00
2) Cable charge 50.00
3) Negotiation fee (minimum charge) 100.00
4) Amendment fee 70.00
5) Discrepancy fee60.00
TOTAL US$380.00

EXAMPLE 2: An import documentary credit issued for US$100,000 with two amendments might be subject to the following fees:
1) Issuance fee (1/8%) US$125.00
2) Cable charge 70.00
3) Negotiation fee (1/8%) 125.00
4) Amendment fee, 2 @ 70.00140.00
TOTAL US$460.00

Obviously, the smaller the credit issued the greater the total fees as a percentage of the total credit.

## Export Documentary Credit Fees

All figures are expressed in US dollars,
min = minimum, qtr = quarter, mo = month, ba = by arrangement.

| | Low | High |
|---|---|---|
| Pre-advice | $30 | $50 |
| Advice | $35 | $100 |
| Confirmation | 1/10%/qtr, $100 min | 1/4%/qtr, $100 min |
| Amendment | $45 | $75 |
| Amendment–confirmed DC | 1/8%/qtr, $85 min | 1.5%/annum, $125 min |
| Negotiation to same bank account | 1/8%/qtr, $85 min | 1/2%/qtr, $165 min |
| Negotiation to other account | 1/8%/qtr, $85 min | 1/8%/qtr, $115 min |
| Documents sent unexamined | $65 | $115 |
| Acceptance | ba, $90 min | 3%/annum, $125 min |
| Reimbursement | $65 | $70 |
| Deferred payment/confirmed DC | 2% annum, $75 min | 3% annum, $90 min |
| Deferred payment/unconfirmed DC | $50 | $75 |
| Discrepancy | $40 | $60 |
| Transfer | 1/4%/qtr, $100 min | 1/2%, $200 min |
| Assignment–pay proceeds | 1/4%, $150 min | 1/2%, 150 min |

EXAMPLE 3: An export documentary credit issued for US$50,000 might be subject to the following fees:
1) Advice fee (minimum charge) US$60.00
2) Confirmation 125.00
3) Negotiation fee 115.00
4) Amendment fee 70.00
TOTAL US$370.00

## Sample Documentary Collection Fees

The range of banking fees listed below relate to both importers and exporters using documentary collections (D/A and D/P terms).

All figures are expressed in US dollars,
min = minimum, qtr = quarter, mo = month, ba = by arrangement.

| | Low | High |
|---|---|---|
| Usance | $80 | $105 |
| Sight | $60 | $80 |
| Direct Collection Letter | $40 | $50 |
| Amendment | $20 | $30 |
| Tracer | $15 | $25 |
| Maintenance | 30 days free, $25/mo. | |
| Protest | $25 | $250 plus expenses |
| Bill of Lading Guarantee | 1/4%/qtr, $60 min | |
| Air Waybill Release | $50 | $75/qtr |

## Miscellaneous Fees

All figures are expressed in US dollars, min = minimum, qtr = quarter, mo = month, ba = by arrangement.

| | Low | High |
|---|---|---|
| Short Telex/SWIFT | $30 | $40 |
| Long Telex/SWIFT | $65 | $70 |
| Fedwire | $20 | $25 |
| Mail Domestic | $5 min | $10 min |
| Courier Domestic | $20 | |
| Courier International | $35 min | $40 min |
| Fax Domestic | no charge | $5/document |
| Fax International | $10/document | $15/document |
| Wire Remittances | | |
| —Inward | | |
| Credit to account holder | Free | $20 |
| Payment to non-account holder | $20 | $50 |
| —Outward | | |
| Domestic | $10 | $20 |
| Overseas | $30 | $35 |
| Tracer/Cancellation/Stop Payment | $20 | |
| Credit Reference Inquires | $30 plus foreign charges | $50 plus foreign charges |

CHAPTER 16

# Documents

THIS CHAPTER DEALS with issues related to the documents used in international payments. By extension, these are also the most common documents used in international trade. Each document will be defined, key elements listed, and cautions offered concerning important issues and common problems associated with each.

It is important to once again mention that the technical name for letters of credit is *documentary credits* and, along with *documentary collections*, that *documents* are at the heart of all forms of international payment.

As with all matters involving money and payments, the form and content of these documents is of great importance to all parties to the transaction. Subtle differences between forms and subtle changes in wording can mean the difference between a successful and an unsuccessful transaction.

The documents called for by a payment type will differ somewhat according to the nature of the goods and the countries of export and import. Some documents, however, such as the commercial invoice and a bill of lading, are specified in all transactions.

Before specifying the required documents the buyer should ensure that the seller is willing and able to provide the documents called for and that they can be provided in the form and with the details stipulated.

## Consistency Among Documents

One of the major issues in the preparation, presentation, and verification of documentation by sellers, buyers, and banks in payment transactions is consistency among documents. All parties have the obligation to check the documentation to make certain it is in order.

---

EXAMPLE: In examining the documentation for a transaction involving the sale of five pieces of machinery, the buyer noticed that the commercial invoice listed the net weight as 12,140 kilograms and the gross weight as 12,860 kilograms. The bill of lading, however, listed the gross weight as 9,612 kilograms. What happened to the other 3,248 kilograms? Did the seller make a mistake in preparing the commercial invoice? Did the shipping company make a mistake in preparing the bill of lading? Did the seller forget to ship one or more pieces of machinery? Did the shipping company misplace some machinery? Did someone steal the machinery?

---

In the above example, the seller should have noticed the inconsistency before forwarding the documents to the advising bank. The advising bank should have noticed the inconsistency before forwarding the documents to the issuing bank. The issuing bank should have noticed the inconsistency before forwarding the documents to the buyer. The buyer will most certainly reject this documentation.

## Documentation Consistency Checklist

The following is a list of points of consistency buyers, sellers, and banks should all be aware of when preparing, presenting, and checking documents for documentary credit and documentary collection transactions:

1. Name and address of shipper
2. Name and address of buyer/consignee
3. Issuer name and address
4. Description of the goods, quantities, units
5. Country of origin of the goods
6. Country of destination of the goods
7. Invoice numbers, documentary credit numbers
8. Certifications
9. Legalizations
10. Shipping marks and numbers
11. Net weight, gross weight, volume
12. Number of crates, cartons, or containers

## Issues Relating to Documents

### AMBIGUITY AS TO ISSUERS OF DOCUMENTS

If terms such as "first class," "well-known," "qualified," "independent," "official," "competent," or "local" are used in a documentary credit to refer to the issuer of a required document (e.g., inspection certificate or certificate of origin), banks are authorized to accept whatever documents are presented, provided that on their face they appear to be in compliance with the credit and were not issued by the seller (beneficiary).

### ORIGINALS

The originals of specified documents should be provided unless copies are called for or allowed. If more than one set of originals is required, the buyer should specify in the credit how many are necessary.

Unless otherwise noted in the documentary credit, banks are authorized to accept documents as originals, even if they were produced or appear to have been produced on a copy machine, by a computerized system, or are carbon copies, provided they have the notation "Original" and are, when necessary, signed.

### AUTHENTICATION

Unless otherwise noted in the documentary credit, banks are authorized to accept documents that are authenticated, validated, legalized, visaed, or certified so long as the document appears on its face to satisfy the requirement. This means that the banks are not responsible for the verification of the certification or authorized signature. Certificates must usually bear the signature of the issuer.

#### SIGNATURE

Banks are authorized to accept documents that have been signed by facsimile, perforated signature, stamp, symbol, or any other mechanical or electronic method.

#### UNSPECIFIED ISSUERS OR CONTENTS OF DOCUMENTS

If the credit does not name a specific issuer or specific contents of a document (other than transport documents, insurance documents, and the commercial invoice), banks are authorized to accept documents as presented so long as the data contained in the documents are consistent with the credit and other stipulated documents.

#### ISSUANCE DATE VS. DOCUMENTARY CREDIT DATE

Unless otherwise noted in the documentary credit, banks are authorized to accept documents dated prior to the issuance date of the credit, so long as all other terms of the credit have been satisfied.

## Document List

The following is a list of common documents used in international payment transactions. Other documents may be required depending upon unusual or industry-specific transactions.

1. Commercial Invoice
2. Marine/Ocean/Port-to-Port Bill of Lading
3. Non-Negotiable Sea Waybill
4. Charter Party Bill of Lading
5. Multimodal (Combined) Transport Document
6. Air Transport Document (Air Waybill)
7. Road, Rail, or Inland Waterway Transport Documents
8. Courier Receipt
9. Post Receipt
10. Insurance Document (or Certificate)
11. Certificate of Origin
12. NAFTA Certificate of Origin
13. Certificate of Origin Form A
14. Packing List
15. Inspection Certificate
16. Export License
17. Consular Invoice
18. Shipper's Export Declaration (SED)

## Commercial Invoice

### DEFINITION

The commercial invoice is the key accounting document describing the commercial transaction between the buyer and the seller.

### ✔KEY ELEMENTS

The commercial invoice includes the following elements:

1. Name and address of seller
2. Name and address of buyer
3. Date of issuance
4. Invoice number
5. Order or contract number
6. Quantity and description of the goods
7. Unit price, total price, other agreed upon charges, and total invoice amount stated in the currency of the documentary credit (e.g., US$, €, ¥, etc.)
8. Shipping details including: weight of the goods, number of packages, and shipping marks and numbers
9. Terms of delivery and payment
10. Any other information as required in the documentary credit (e.g., country of origin)

### CAUTIONS & NOTES

In transactions involving a documentary credit it is vitally important that the description of the goods in the commercial invoice correspond precisely with the description of goods in the documentary credit.

The invoice amount should match exactly (or at least should not exceed) the amount specified in the credit. Banks have the right to refuse invoices issued for amounts in excess of the amount stated in the credit. For this, as well as other reasons, the invoice should be made out in the same currency as the credit amount.

The exception: when a documentary credit specifies "about" in relation to the currency amount and quantity of merchandise, in which case the invoice may specify an amount equal to plus or minus 10 percent of the stipulated amount of the credit.

Unless otherwise stipulated in the documentary credit, the commercial invoice must be made out in the name of the applicant (buyer). The exception: In a transferable documentary credit the invoice may be made out to a third party.

The buyer, seller, and bank(s) should all carefully check for discrepancies in the invoice. The details specified therein should not be inconsistent with those of any other documents, and should exactly conform to the specifications of the credit.

# Indonesia Coffee Export Co.

Jalan Sudirman
Jakarta 10420, Indonesia

## INVOICE

June 27, 20XX
Invoice No. 98-123456

American Caffeine Import Company
125 Main Street
Seattle, Washington

Description of goods:
15 metric tons of 60-kilo bags of New Crop D.P. Sumatra Mandheling Arabica Grade 1 - Green Coffee - As per buyer's purchase order No. 1234

TOTAL CIF Seattle, Washington, USA US$65,000.00

| | |
|---|---|
| Payment: | By irrevocable documentary letter of credit No. 1234567 dated May 27, 20XX of The American Import Bank, Seattle, Washington USA |
| Payment Terms: | At 120 days' sight, draft drawn on San Francisco International Bank, San Francisco, California, USA |
| Country of Origin: | Indonesia |
| Number of bags: | 250 bags |
| Weights: | Gross 15,000 kilo, Net 15,000 kilo |
| Marks/No.: | USA Made in Indonesia No. 12345.67 |
| Dispatch: | Through ABC Freight Services, by sea from Jakarta via Sea Maritime Steamship Line to Seattle |

Indonesia Coffee Export Co.

*Indonesia Coffee Export Company*

## Transport Documents

Many of the problems arising in payment transactions have to do with transport documents. Often, the buyer stipulates a type of transport document that is not appropriate to the mode(s) of carriage. Other notes and issues:

### BILLS OF LADING

A bill of lading is a document issued by a carrier to a shipper, signed by the captain, agent, or owner of a vessel, furnishing written evidence regarding receipt of the goods (cargo), the conditions on which transportation is made (contract of carriage), and the engagement to deliver goods at the prescribed port of destination to the lawful holder of the bill of lading.

A bill of lading is, therefore, both a receipt for merchandise and a contract to deliver it as freight. There are a number of different types of bills of lading and a number of issues that relate to them as a group of documents.

### STRAIGHT BILL OF LADING (NON-NEGOTIABLE)

A straight bill of lading indicates that the shipper will deliver the goods to the consignee. The document itself does not give title to the goods (non-negotiable). The consignee need only identify himself to claim the goods. A straight bill of lading is often used when payment for the goods has already been made in advance or in cases where the goods are shipped on open account. A straight bill of lading, therefore, cannot be transferred by endorsement.

### SHIPPER'S ORDER BILL OF LADING

A shipper's order bill of lading is a title document to the goods, issued "to the order of" a party, usually the shipper, whose endorsement is required to effect its negotiation. Because it is negotiable, a shipper's order bill of lading can be bought, sold, or traded while goods are in transit. These are highly favored for documentary credit transactions. The buyer usually needs the original or a copy as proof of ownership to take possession of the goods.

### BLANK ENDORSED NEGOTIABLE BILL OF LADING

A blank endorsed negotiable bill of lading is one that has been endorsed without naming an endorsee. In simple terms, the person in possession of a blank endorsed negotiable bill of lading may claim possession of the goods.

### AIR WAYBILL

An air waybill is a form of bill of lading used for the air transport of goods and is not negotiable.

### CLEAN BILL OF LADING

A clean bill of lading is one where the carrier has noted that the merchandise has been received in apparent good condition (no apparent damage, loss, etc.) and that does not bear such notations as "Shipper's Load and Count," etc.

Most forms of payment require a "clean" bill of lading in order for the seller to obtain payment under a documentary credit. There are, however, some circumstances in some trades, in which transport documents with special clauses are acceptable. For example, in the steel trade, such notations are the rule rather than the exception. If this is the case, the credit should explicitly state which clause(s) will be deemed acceptable.

### CLAUSED BILL OF LADING

A claused bill of lading is one which contains notations that specify a shortfall in quantity or deficient condition of the goods and/or packaging. Opposite of clean bill of lading.

### MULTIPLE MODES OF TRANSPORT

If multiple modes of transport are to be permitted, or partial shipments are allowed, and part of the goods will be shipped by one mode of transport and part by another, it is necessary to put "or" or "and/or" between the names of the required transport documents. For example, if the goods are to be shipped by both sea and air, the credit might specify "marine bill of lading and/or air waybill."

### ORIGINALS

In documentary credit transactions the full set of original transport documents (one or more) must be presented to the bank. If the full set of transport documents consists of several originals, all of the originals should be submitted. The buyer (applicant) can stipulate in the credit the number of originals to be issued in a set—but many countries consider a set of one original only to be desirable.

### NAMED CARRIER

A transport document must appear on its face to have been issued by a named carrier, or his agent. This does not mean that the applicant must name the carrier in the documentary credit application. It merely means that the transport document must indicate the name of the carrier. The applicant is, of course, free to stipulate a particular carrier, but this could cause delay in shipping the goods.

### ON DECK

A transport document that specifically states that the goods are loaded "on deck" (subject to wind and weather) will not be acceptable in documentary credit transactions unless specifically authorized. If the transport document shows that the goods are loaded on deck, any accompanying insurance document must show cover against "on deck" risks. Bear in mind, however, that dangerous cargo (including certain chemicals and live animals) are often carried on deck.

### ON BOARD

"On board" is a notation on a bill of lading indicating that the goods have in fact been loaded on board or shipped on a named vessel. This notation may be made by the carrier, his agent, the master of the ship, or his agent. Unless expressly authorized, the transport document issued by the carrier must reflect that it is "on board" in order for the seller to obtain payment under a documentary credit.

## Marine/Ocean/Port-to-Port Bill of Lading

### DEFINITION

A marine bill of lading is a transport document covering port-to-port shipments of goods (for carriage of goods solely by sea).

### ✔KEY ELEMENTS

The marine bill of lading contains the following elements:

1. Name of carrier with a signature identified as that of carrier, or ship's master, or agent for or on behalf of either the carrier or ship's master
2. An indication or notation that the goods have been loaded "on board" or shipped on a named vessel. Also, the date of issuance or date of loading
3. An indication of the port of loading and the port of discharge as specified in the original documentary credit
4. A sole original, or if issued in multiple originals, the full set of originals.
5. The terms and conditions of carriage or a reference to the terms and conditions of carriage in another source or document
6. No indication that the document is subject to a charter party and/or an indication that the named vessel is propelled by sail only
7. Meets any other stipulations of the documentary credit

### CAUTIONS & NOTES

If the document includes the notation "intended vessel" it must also contain an "on board" notation of a named vessel along with the date of loading, even if the named vessel is the same as the intended vessel.

If the document indicates a place where the goods were received by the carrier different from the port of loading, the document must also contain an "on-board" notation indicating the port of loading as named in the credit and the named vessel, along with the date.

If the documentary credit calls for a port-to-port shipment but does not call specifically for a marine bill of lading, the banks will accept a transport document, however named, that contains the above information. Banks will normally accept the following documents under this title: ocean bill of lading, combined transport bill of lading, short form bill of lading, or received for shipment bill of lading, provided it carries the notation "on board."

If the documents are drawn up "to the order of" the exporter or "to order" they must be endorsed.

If the credit prohibits transshipment this document will be rejected if it specifically states that the goods will be transshipped.

Since this is a negotiable instrument, it may be endorsed and transferred to a third party while the goods are in transit.

**Carrier:**
Hapag-Lloyd Container Linie GmbH, Hamburg

# Bill of Lading

Multimodal Transport or Port to Port Shipment

PAGE 2

Hapag-Lloyd

**Shipper:**
WATSON/SHAKLEY RICE INTERNATIONAL
8176 WILLOW STREET
WINDSOR, CALIFORNIA CA 95492-9305

**Hapag-Lloyd Reference:** 14013696
**B/L-No.:** HLCUOAK980300049

**Export References:**
SHPR REF: JFC(UK) LTD
FWDR REF: SF01078226
C.H.B.NO: 5118

**Consignee or Order:**
TO THE ORDER
BANK OF LLOYDS LONDON

L/C# 3892XVGR012965

**Forwarding Agent:** F.M.C.NO: 0087
NALDUZAK ASSOCIATES, INC.
5088A DIAMOND HEIGHTS BLVD.
SAN FRANCISCO, CA 94131-1605

**Consignee's Reference:**

**Notify Address** (Carrier not responsible for failure to notify; see clause 20 (1) hereof):
CONNOLLY (UK) LIMITED
#1 1000 NORTH CIRCLE ROAD EAST
STAPLES CORNER LONDON NW2 7JP
ENGLAND

**Place of Receipt:**

**Pre-Carriage by:**

**Place of Receipt by Pre-Carrier:**

**Place of Delivery:**

**Ocean Vessel:** 50E04 HEIDELBERG EXPRES

**Port of Loading:** OAKLAND, CA

**Port of Discharge:** THAMESPORT

**Place of Delivery by On-Carrier:**

| Container Nos., Seal Nos.; Marks and Nos. | Number and Kind of Packages; Description of Goods | Gross Weight (kg) | Measurement (cbm) |
|---|---|---|---|
| HLCU 2254295<br>SEAL: 136427 | 1 FCL/FCL 20' CONTAINER STC:<br>1420 PACKAGES MILLED RICE<br><br>COMMODITY: 1006000000 | 43020#<br>19513K | |

SHIPPED ON BOARD DATE: MAR/05/1998
PORT OF LOADING: OAKLAND, CA
VESSEL NAME: KOELN EXPRESS

SHIPMENT PURSUANT TO SC NO. 98-302
SHIPPER'S LOAD, STOWAGE AND COUNT
FREIGHT PREPAID - ORIGIN TERMINAL CHARGE PREPAID
NO S.E.D. REQUIRED, SECTION 30.39 FTSR, C.A.S. - JL.
THESE COMMODITIES, TECHNOLOGY OR SOFTWARE WERE EXPORTED FROM THE UNITED STATES IN ACCORDANCE WITH THE EXPORT ADMINISTRATION REGULATIONS. DIVERSION CONTRARY TO U.S. LAW PROHIBITED. NLR

Above Particulars as declared by Shipper. Without responsibility or warranty as to correctness by carrier (see clause 11(1) and 11(2))

ORIGINAL

**Total No. of Containers/Packages received by the Carrier:** 1

**Shipper's declared value** (see clause 7(1) and 7(2) hereof):

**Movement:** FCL/FCL

**Currency:** USD

| Charge | Rate | Basis | WT/MEA/VAL | Payment | Amount |
|---|---|---|---|---|---|
| THO | 420.00 | CTR | 1 | P | 420.00 |
| SEA | 1530.00 | CTR | 1 | P | 1530.00 |
| BAF | 40.00 | CTR | 1 | P | 40.00 |
| CAF | 6.00 | PCT | 1530 | P | 91.80 |
| THD | 185.00 | CTR | 1 | C | 185.00 |

| Total Freight Prepaid | Total Freight Collect | Total Freight |
|---|---|---|
| 2081.80 | 185.00 | 2266.80 |

**Received** by the Carrier from the Shipper in apparent good order and condition (unless otherwise noted herein) the total number or quantity of Containers or other packages or units indicated in the box opposite entitled "Total No. of Containers/Packages received by the Carrier" for Carriage subject to all the terms and conditions hereof **(Including the Terms and Conditions on the Reverse hereof and the Terms and Conditions of the Carrier's Applicable Tariff)** from the Place of Receipt or the Port of Loading, whichever is applicable, to the Port of Discharge or the Place of Delivery, whichever is applicable. One original Bill of Lading, duly endorsed, must be surrendered by the Merchant to the Carrier in exchange for the Goods or a delivery order. In accepting this Bill of Lading the Merchant expressly accepts and agrees to all its terms and conditions whether printed, stamped or written, or otherwise incorporated, notwithstanding the non-signing of this Bill of Lading by the Merchant.

**In Witness whereof** the number of original Bills of Lading stated below all of this tenor and date has been signed, one of which being accomplished the others to stand void.

**Place and Date of Issue:** CORTE MADERA, CA MAR/05/1998

**Freight Payable at:** CORTE MADERA, CA

**Number of original Bs/L:** 3/3

**For above named carrier**
**Hapag-Lloyd (America) Inc.**
**(as agent)** Allen Miller

## Non-Negotiable Sea Waybill

### DEFINITION

A non-negotiable sea waybill is a transport document covering port-to-port shipments. It is not a title document, is not negotiable and cannot be endorsed.

### ✔KEY ELEMENTS

The non-negotiable sea waybill contains the following elements:

1. Name of carrier with a signature identified as that of carrier, or ship's master, or agent for or on behalf of either the carrier or ship's master
2. An indication or notation that the goods have been loaded "on board" or shipped on a named vessel. Also, the date of issuance or date of loading
3. An indication of the port of loading and the port of discharge as specified in the original documentary credit
4. A sole original, or if issued in multiple originals, the full set of originals
5. The terms and conditions of carriage or a reference to the terms and conditions of carriage in another source or document
6. No indication that the document is subject to a charter party and/or an indication that the named vessel is propelled by sail only
7. Meets any other stipulations of the documentary credit

### CAUTIONS & NOTES

If the document includes the notation "intended vessel" it must also contain an "on board" notation of a named vessel along with the date of loading, even if the named vessel is the same as the intended vessel.

If the document indicates a place where the goods were received by the carrier different from the port of loading, the document must also contain an "on-board" notation indicating the port of loading as named in the credit and the named vessel, along with the date.

If the documentary credit calls for a port-to-port shipment but does not call specifically for a marine bill of lading, the banks will accept a transport document, however named, that contains the above information. Banks will normally accept the following documents under this title: ocean bill of lading, combined transport bill of lading, short form bill of lading, or received for shipment bill of lading, provided it carries the notation "on board."

Because they are not title documents, sea waybills eliminate many of the inconveniences of a bill of lading and offer advantages in situations where the rigid security of a bill of lading is not required. Waybills reduce the opportunity for fraud—although they do by no means eliminate it—and they remove the problems of goods arriving ahead of documents.

Sea waybills are appropriate for shipments between associated companies, for shipments to an agent for sale at destination on an open account basis, and for shipments between companies that have established mutual trust.

Express Cargo Bill · Not Negotiable

# Express Cargo Bill

Carrier:
Hapag-Lloyd Container Linie GmbH, Hamburg

Multimodal Transport or Port to Port Shipment

PAGE 2

Hapag-Lloyd

**Shipper:**
ABC WINE COMPANY
1234 SPAIN STREET
SONOMA, CA 96476

**Hapag-Lloyd Reference:** 10347784

**ECB-No.:** HLCUOAK980300071

**Export References:**
USS-NL-000-008
C.H.B.NO: 5118

**Consignee:**
DELAHAY WINE ENTERPRISES, LTD.
HAZELDONK 1408 - 1412
NL 4386 LH BREDA
THE NETHERLANDS

**Forwarding Agent:** F.M.C.NO: 0087
NALDUZAK ASSOCIATES, INC.
5088A DIAMOND HEIGHTS BLVD.
SAN FRANCISCO, CA 94131-1605

**Consignee's Reference:**

**Notify Address** (Carrier not responsible for failure to notify):
DELAHAY WINE ENTERPRISES, LTD.
HAZALDONK 1408 - 1412
NL 4386 LH BREDA
THE NETHERLANDS

**Place of Receipt:**

**Pre-Carriage by:**

**Place of Receipt by Pre-Carrier:**

**Place of Delivery:**

**Ocean Vessel:** 06E07
KOELN EXPRESS

**Port of Loading:** OAKLAND, CA

**Port of Discharge:** ROTTERDAM

**Place of Delivery by On-Carrier:**

| Container Nos., Seal Nos., Marks and Nos. | Number and Kind of Packages; Description of Goods | Gross Weight (kg) | Measurement (cbm) |
|---|---|---|---|
| | 1 X 40' CONTAINER SAID TO CONTAIN: | | |
| HLCU 4073300 | 1246 CS CALIFORNIA WINES | 19872 | |
| SEAL: 2902455 | LESS THAN 14% ALCOHOL | KGM | |
| PO-DS: 3327-04G | COMMODITY: 2204000000 | | |
| PO-C1: EL100093 | | | |

SHIPPED ON BOARD DATE: MAR/06/1998
PORT OF LOADING: OAKLAND, CA
VESSEL NAME: KOELN EXPRESS

SHIPMENT PURSUANT TO SC NO. 98-500
SHIPPER'S LOAD, STOWAGE AND COUNT
FREIGHT COLLECT
PROTECT AGAINST EXTREME TEMPERATURES
THESE COMMODITIES LICENSED BY THE U.S. FOR ULTIMATE DESTINATION
THE NETHERLANDS. DIVERSION CONTRARY TO U.S. LAW PROHIBITED.

Above Particulars as declared by Shipper. Without responsibility or warranty as to correctness by carrier.

RECEIPT

**Total No. of Containers/Packages received by the Carrier:** 1

**Shipper's declared value** (see clause 7(1) and 7(2) hereof):

**Movement:** FCL/FCL

**Currency:** USD

| Charge | Rate | Basis | WT/MEA/VAL. | Payment | Amount |
|---|---|---|---|---|---|
| THD | 500.00 | CTR | 1 | C | 500.00 |
| SEA | 1701.00 | CTR | 1 | C | 1701.00 |
| BAF | 80.00 | CTR | 1 | C | 80.00 |
| CAF | 21.00 | PCT | 1701 | C | 357.21 |
| THD | 343.00 | CTR | 1 | C | 167.33 |

| Total Freight Prepaid | Total Freight Collect | Total Freight |
|---|---|---|
| | 2805.54 | 2805.54 |

RECEIVED by the Carrier from the Shipper in apparent good order and condition (unless otherwise noted herein) the total number or quantity of Containers or other packages or units indicated in the box opposite entitled "Total No. of Containers/Packages received by the Carrier" for Carriage subject to all the terms and conditions hereof (INCLUDING THE TERMS AND CONDITIONS ON THE REVERSE HEREOF AND THE TERMS AND CONDITIONS OF THE CARRIER'S APPLICABLE TARIFF) from the Place of Receipt or the Port of Loading, whichever is applicable, to the Port of Discharge or the Place of Delivery, whichever is applicable. In accepting this Express Cargo Bill the Merchant expressly accepts and agrees to all its terms and conditions whether printed, stamped or written, or otherwise incorporated, notwithstanding the non-signing of this Express Cargo Bill by the Merchant.

**Place and Date of Issue:** CORTE MADERA, CA MAR/05/1998

**Freight Payable at:** BARKING, U.K.

**For above named carrier**
**Hapag-Lloyd (America) Inc.**
**(as agent)**

90116743

Express Cargo Bill · Not Negotiable

## Charter Party Bill of Lading

### DEFINITION

A charter party bill of lading is a transport document covering port-to-port shipments of goods issued by a party chartering a vessel (as opposed to a named carrier or shipping line).

### ✔KEY ELEMENTS

The charter party bill of lading contains the following elements:

1. An indication that the bill of lading is subject to a charter party
2. A signature or authentication by the ship's master or owner, or agent for or on behalf of either the ship's master or owner
3. Unless otherwise stated in the documentary credit, does not name the carrier
4. An indication or notation that the goods have been loaded "on board" or shipped on a named vessel. Also, the date of issuance or date of loading
5. An indication of the port of loading and the port of discharge as specified in the original documentary credit
6. A sole original, or if issued in multiple originals, the full set of originals
7. No indication that the named vessel is propelled by sail only
8. Meets any other stipulations of the documentary credit

### CAUTIONS & NOTES

The charter party bill of lading may have preprinted wording indicating that the shipment has been loaded "on board" the "named vessel," but the document must still be signed as per number two above.

If preprinted wording is used, the date of issuance is deemed to be the date of loading on board. In all other cases the document must contain an "on board" "named vessel" notation along with the date the shipment was loaded on board.

CODE NAME: "CONGENBILL" . EDITION 1978

Shipper

Swiss Export Ltd.
Industriestrasse 200
CH-8050 Zürich-Oerlikon

**BILL OF LADING**
TO BE USED WITH CHARTER-PARTIES

B/L No. GGG/mzf 101

Reference No. 1150.01.23.

Consignee

TO ORDER OF SHIPPER

**SHIPCRAFT TRANSPORT INC.**

General Agents:
SHIPCRAFT A/S
(Hovedgaden 16)
P O Box 142
DK-2970 Hoersholm, Denmark
Phone: 4 2-571033
Telex: 37584 Shpcr Dk
Fax: 4 2-571044

Notify address

1st: ViaMAT (Far East)
1-10-7 Higashi Gotanda
Sinagawa-Ku, TOKYO 141
2nd: Suzuki K.K.
Saitama

**Agent for Switzerland:**

**MAT TRANSPORT AG**
**Erlenstrasse 95**
**P.O. Box**
**CH-4002 Basel, Switzerland**

**Phone: 061 68 68 000**
**Fax: 061 68 68 001**

Vessel: M/V TIGER

Port of loading: Cherbourg

Port of discharge: Yokohama

| Shipper's description of goods | | | Gross weight | |
|---|---|---|---|---|
| 92HBFC0803T<br>1 - 240 | 240 packages | MACHINERY as per contract PQ 733 054 dated 12.10.19..<br>Letter of credit No. MC986CH34 dated 4.12.19.. | 452'500 kg | 1202 m3 |

# ORIGINAL

(of which -0-(none) on deck at Shipper's risk; the Carrier not being responsible for loss or damage howsoever arising)

Freight payable as per CHARTER-PARTY dated 7. March 19..

FREIGHT ADVANCE.
Received on account of freight:
PREPAID AS AGREED

Time used for loading 0 days 23 hours.

**SHIPPED** at the Port of Loading in apparent good order and condition on board the Vessel for carriage to the Port of Discharge or so near thereto as she may safely get the goods specified above.

Weight, measure, quality, quantity, condition, contents and value unknown.

IN WITNESS whereof the Master or Agent of the said Vessel has signed the number of Bills of Lading indicated below all of this tenor and date, any one of which being accomplished the others shall be void.

FOR CONDITIONS OF CARRIAGE SEE OVERLEAF

| Freight payable at | Place and date of issue |
|---|---|
| Basel/Switzerland | Basel, - 6. Mai 19.. |
| **Number of original Bs/L** | **Signature** |
| 3/3 (Three) | **MAT TRANSPORT AG**<br>as agent of the owner<br>i.e. Shipcraft Transport Inc. |

Printed and sold
by Carl Svanberg Tryckeri AB, Box 91, 35103 Vaxjo.
by authority of The Baltic and International Maritime Conference, Copenhagen.

## Multimodal (Combined) Transport Document

### DEFINITION

A multimodal transport document is a bill of lading covering two or more modes of transport, such as shipping by rail and by sea.

### ✔KEY ELEMENTS

The multimodal transport document contains the following elements:

1. Name of carrier or multimodal transport operator with a signature identified as that of carrier, transport operator, or ship's master, or agent for or on behalf of either the carrier, transport operator, or ship's master
2. An indication that the shipment has been "dispatched," "taken in charge," or "loaded on board," along with a date
3. Indication of the place of receipt of the shipment as named in the documentary credit that may be different from the place of actual loading "on board" and the place of delivery of the shipment as named in the documentary credit, which may be different from the place of discharge
4. A sole original, or if issued in multiple originals, the full set of originals
5. The terms and conditions of carriage or a reference to the terms and conditions of carriage in another source or document other than the multimodal transport document
6. No indication that the document is subject to a charter party and/or an indication that the named vessel is propelled by sail only
7. Meets any other stipulations of the documentary credit

### CAUTIONS & NOTES

In multimodal situations the contract of carriage and liability is for a combined transport from the place of shipment to the place of delivery. Thus, the document evidences receipt of goods and not shipment on board.

The date of issuance of the document is deemed to be the date of dispatch unless there is a specific date of dispatch, taking in charge, or loading on board, in which case the latter date is deemed to be the date of dispatch.

Even if a credit prohibits transshipment, banks will accept a multimodal transport document that indicates that transshipment will or may take place, provided that the entire carriage is covered by one transport document.

A combined transport document issued by a freight forwarder is acceptable unless the credit stipulates otherwise or unless the credit specifically calls for a "marine bill of lading." The issuing freight forwarder accepts carrier responsibility for performance of the entire contract of carriage and liability for loss or damage wherever and however it occurs.

As a rule, multimodal transport documents are not negotiable instruments.

# Bill of Lading

Multimodal Transport or Port to Port Shipment

PAGE 2

Hapag-Lloyd

**Carrier:** Hapag-Lloyd Container Linie GmbH, Hamburg

**Hapag-Lloyd Reference:** 10347484

**B/L-No.:** HLCUOAK980204041

**Shipper:**
WILSON COMMODITIES INTERNATIONAL
100 MEADOWCREEK DRIVE
CORTE MADERA, CA 94125

**Export References:**
REF#156008
REF#156008
C.H.B.NO: 12330

**Consignee or Order:**
ZAIDNERS INTERNATIONAL B.V.
POSTBUS 27
4870 AA ETTEN-LEUR
THE NETHERLANDS

**Forwarding Agent:** F.M.C.NO: 0953
NALDUZAK ASSOCIATES, INC.
5088A DIAMOND HEIGHTS BLVD.
SAN FRANCISCO, CA 94131-1605

**Consignee's Reference:**

**Notify Address** (Carrier not responsible for failure to notify; see clause 20 (1) hereof).
GARCIA ROTTERDAM B.V.
POSTBUS 425
3200 AK SPIJKENISSE
THE NTHERLANDS

**Place of Receipt:** FRESNO, CA

**Pre-Carriage by:**

**Place of Receipt by Pre-Carrier:**

**Place of Delivery:**

**Ocean Vessel:** 23E06 ROTTERDAM EXPRESS

**Port of Loading:** OAKLAND, CA

**Port of Discharge:** ROTTERDAM

**Place of Delivery by On-Carrier:**

| Container Nos., Seal Nos.; Marks and Nos. | Number and Kind of Packages; Description of Goods | Gross Weight (kg) | Measurement (cbm) |
|---|---|---|---|
| HLXU 4787302<br>SEAL: 3814 | 1 40' HC REEFER CONTAINER STC:<br>791 CARTONS OF RASPBERRIES<br>SEEDLESS<br><br>COMMODITY: 0811000003<br>MAINTAIN TEMPERATURE AT<br>-18.0 CELSIUS OR LOWER | 42857LBS | |

SHIPPED ON BOARD DATE: FEB/17/1998
PORT OF LOADING: OAKLAND, CA
VESSEL NAME: CAPE HENRY

CARGO STOWED UNDER REFRIGERATION
SHIPPER'S LOAD, STOWAGE AND COUNT
FREIGHT COLLECT
THESE COMMODITIES, TECHNOLOGY OR SOFTWARE WERE EXPORTED FROM THE UNITED STATES IN ACCORDANCE WITH THE EXPORT ADMINISTRATION REGULATIONS. DIVERSION CONTRARY TO U.S. LAW PROHIBITED. NLR

Above Particulars as declared by Shipper. Without responsibility or warranty as to correctness by carrier (see clause 11(1) and 11(2))

ORIGINAL

**Total No. of Containers/Packages received by the Carrier:** 1

**Shipper's declared value (see clause 7(1) and 7(2) hereof):**

**Movement:** FCL/FCL

**Currency:** USD

| Charge | Rate | Basis | WT/MEA/VAL | Payment | Amount |
|---|---|---|---|---|---|
| OLF | 490.00 | CTR | 1 | C | 490.00 |
| THO | 500.00 | CTR | 1 | C | 500.00 |
| SEA | 3805.00 | CTR | 1 | C | 3805.00 |
| BAF | 80.00 | CTR | 1 | C | 80.00 |
| CAF | 21.00 | PCT | 3805 | C | 799.05 |
| THD | 343.00 | CTR | 1 | C | 170.12 |

| Total Freight Prepaid | Total Freight Collect | Total Freight |
|---|---|---|
| | 5844.17 | 5844.17 |

**Received** by the Carrier from the Shipper in apparent good order and condition (unless otherwise noted herein) the total number or quantity of Containers or other packages or units indicated in the box opposite entitled "Total No. of Containers/Packages received by the Carrier" for Carriage subject to all the terms and conditions hereof **(Including the Terms and Conditions on the Reverse hereof and the Terms and Conditions of the Carrier's Applicable Tariff)** from the Place of Receipt or the Port of Loading, whichever is applicable, to the Port of Discharge or the Place of Delivery, whichever is applicable. One original Bill of Lading, duly endorsed, must be surrendered by the Merchant to the Carrier in exchange for the Goods or a delivery order. In accepting this Bill of Lading the Merchant expressly accepts and agrees to all its terms and conditions whether printed, stamped or written, or otherwise incorporated, notwithstanding the non-signing of this Bill of Lading by the Merchant.

**In Witness whereof** the number of original Bills of Lading stated below all of this tenor and date has been signed, one of which being accomplished the others to stand void.

**Place and Date of Issue:** CORTE MADERA, CA FEB/23/1998

**Freight Payable at:** DESTINATION

**Number of original Bs/L:** 3/3

**For above named carrier**
**Hapag-Lloyd (America) Inc.**
**(as agent)**

Allen Miller

90116741

## Air Transport Document (Air Waybill)

### DEFINITION

An air waybill is a non-negotiable transport document covering transport of cargo from airport to airport.

### ✔KEY ELEMENTS

The air waybill contains the following elements:

1. Name of carrier with a signature identified as that of carrier or named agent for or on behalf of the carrier
2. An indication that the goods have been accepted for carriage. Also, the date of issuance or date of loading
3. An indication of the actual date of dispatch if required by the documentary credit, or, if the actual date of dispatch is not required by the credit, the issuance date of the document is deemed to be the date of shipment
4. An indication of the airport of departure and airport of destination
5. Appears on its face to be the original for consignor/shipper regardless of wording in the documentary credit stipulating a full set of originals
6. The terms and conditions of carriage or a reference to the terms and conditions of carriage in another source or document
7. Meets any other stipulations of the documentary credit

### CAUTIONS & NOTES

Information contained in the "for carrier use only" box concerning flight number and date are not considered to be the actual flight number and date.

Since air waybills are issued in three originals—one for the issuing carrier, one for the consignee (buyer), and one for the shipper (seller)—the documentary credit should not require presentation in more than one original. Nor should it call for a "full set of original air waybills."

The air waybill is not a negotiable document. It indicates only acceptance of goods for carriage.

The air waybill must name a consignee (who can be the buyer), and it should not be required to be issued "to order" and/or "to be endorsed." Since it is not negotiable, and it does not evidence title to the goods, in order to maintain some control of goods not paid for by cash in advance, sellers often consign air shipments to their sales agents, or freight forwarders' agents in the buyer's country.

The air waybill should not be required to indicate an "actual flight date" since IATA regulations specify that reservations requested by the shipper shall not be inserted under "Flight/Date."

**085** | BSL | 7260 2751 — 085-7260-2751

NOT NEGOTIABLE
**AIR WAYBILL**
AIR CONSIGNMENT NOTE

swissair

Issued by: Swiss Air Transport Co., Ltd., Zurich, Switzerland
Member of IATA (International Air Transport Association)

Copies 1, 2 and 3 of this Air Waybill are originals and have the same validity

It is agreed that the goods described herein are accepted in apparent good order and condition (except as noted) for carriage SUBJECT O THE CONDITIONS OF CONTRACT ON THE REVERSE HEREOF. THE SHIPPER'S ATTENTION IS DRAWN TO THE NOTICE CONCERNING CARRIERS' LIMITATION OF LIABILITY. Shipper may increase such limitation of liability by declaring a higher value for carriage and paying a supplemental charge if required.

| | |
|---|---|
| Shipper's Name and Address | SWISS EXPORT LTD<br>AIRFREIGHT DIVISION<br>ZUERICH |
| Shipper's account Number | |
| Consignee's Name and Address | IMPORT KONTOR<br>VIENNA<br>Phone: 633 7876 |
| Consignee's account Number | |
| Issuing Carrier's Agent Name and City | FORWARDING LTD<br>BASLE |
| Agent's IATA Code | 81-4 0000 |
| Account No. | |
| Accounting information | |
| Airport of Departure (Addr. of the Carrier) and requested Routing | BSL-VIE |
| to | VIE |
| By first Carrier (Routing and Destination) | SWISSAIR |
| to / by / to / by | |
| Currency | SFR |
| CHGS Code | |
| WT/VAL PPD / COLL | CC |
| Other PPD / COLL | PP |
| Declared Value for Carriage | NVD |
| Declared Value for Customs | |
| Airport of Destination | VIENNA |
| Flight/Date (For Carrier Use only) | SR436/8.7. |
| Flight/Date | |
| Amount of Insurance | |

INSURANCE - If carrier offers insurance and such insurance is requested in accordance with conditions on reverse hereof, indicate amount to be insured in figures in box marked amount of insurance.

Handling Information

| No of Pieces RCP | Gross Weight | kg lb | Rate Class | Commodity Item No. | Chargeable Weight | Rate / Charge | Total | Nature and Quantity of Goods (incl. Dimensions or Volume) |
|---|---|---|---|---|---|---|---|---|
| 8 | 200,6 | K | C | 6750 | 201 | 1.90 | 381.90 | CHEMICALS NOT RESTRICTED<br>CONTRACT No 100-15-2 |
| 8 | 200,6 | | | | | | | |

| | Prepaid | Collect |
|---|---|---|
| Weight Charge | | 381.90 |
| Valuation Charge | | |
| Tax | | |
| Total other Charges Due Agent | 15.00 | |
| Total other Charges Due Carrier | | |
| Total Prepaid / Total Collect | 15.00 | 381.90 |
| Currency Conversion Rates / cc charges in Dest. Currency | | |
| For Carrier's Use only at Destination / Charges at Destination / Total collect Charges | | |

Other Charges: AWA 15.00

Shipper certifies that the particulars on the face hereof are correct and that insofar as any part of the consignment contains dangerous goods, such part is properly described by name and is in proper condition for carriage by air according to the applicable Dangerous Goods Regulations.

SWISS EXPORT LTD / p.o. Forwarding LTD

Signature of Shipper or his Agent

07.07. BASLE Forwarding LTD

Executed on (Date) at (Place) Signature of Issuing Carrier or its Agent

085-7260 2751

**No. 3 - ORIGINAL for SHIPPER**

Form 30.301
Printed in the Fed. Rep. Germany - Bartsch Verlag, Munich-Ottobrunn 600j (III)

## Road, Rail or Inland Waterway Transport Documents

### DEFINITION

Road, rail, or inland waterway bills of lading are transport documents covering transport of cargo from named points via road, rail or inland waterway modes of transport.

### ✔KEY ELEMENTS

In documentary credit transactions road, rail, or inland waterway bills of lading contain the following elements:

1. Name of carrier with a signature or authentication identified as that of carrier or named agent for or on behalf of the carrier and/or a reception stamp or other mark noting receipt by the carrier, or named agent for or on behalf of the carrier
2. An indication that the goods have been accepted for shipment, dispatch or carriage. Also, the date of issuance or date of shipment
3. An indication of the place of shipment and place of destination as specified in the credit
4. Meets any other stipulations of the documentary credit

### CAUTIONS & NOTES

In road, rail, or inland waterway transport documents the date of issuance is considered the date of shipment unless there is a reception stamp, in which case that date is deemed to be the date of shipment.

Unless otherwise stipulated in the documentary credit, banks will accept transport document(s) as presented as a "full set."

Unless otherwise stipulated in the documentary credit, banks will accept road, rail, or inland waterway transport documents as originals whether marked as such or not.

**1** Absender (Name, Anschrift, Land) / Expéditeur (nom, adresse, pays)

METALLWAREN AG

CH-8904 AESCH

INTERNATIONALER FRACHTBRIEF
LETTRE DE VOITURE INTERNATIONAL

Diese Beförderung unterliegt trotz einer gegenteiligen Abmachung den Bestimmungen des Übereinkommens über den Beförderungsvertrag im internat. Straßengüterverkehr (CMR)

Ce transport est soumis. nonobstant toute clause contraire, á la Convention relative au contrat de transport international de marchandises par route (CMR)

**2** Empfänger (Name, Anschrift, Land) / Destinataire (nom, adresse, pays)

CIE PORTUGAISE
D'ALUMINIUM

P-PORTO

**16** Frachführer (Name, Anschrift, Land) / Transporteur (nom, adresse. pays)

TRANSPORT AG

CH-4002 BASEL

**3** Auslieferungsort des Gutes / Lieu prévu pour la livraison de la marchandise

Ort/Lieu PORTO
Land/Pays PORTUGAL

**17** Nachfolgende Frachtführer (Name Anschrift, Land) / Transporteurs successifs (nom, adresse, pays)

**4** Ort und Tag der Übernahme des Gutes / Lieu et date de la prise en charge de la merchandise

Ort/Lieu 8904 AESCH
Land/Pays SCHWEIZ
Datum/Date 18.8.19..

**18** Vorbehalte und Bemerkungen der Frachtführer / Réserves et observations des transporteurs

**5** Beigefügte Dokumente / Documents unnexés

| **6** Kennzeichen u. Nr / Marques et numéros | **7** Anzahl d. Packstücke / Nombre des colis | **8** Art der Verpackung / Mode d'emballage | **9** Bezeichnung des Gutes* / Nature de la marchandise* | **10** Statistik-Nr. / No statistique | **11** Bruttogew. i. kg / Poids brut, kg | **12** Umfang in m³ / Cubage m³ |
|---|---|---|---|---|---|---|
| 95140/1-2 | 2 | CAISSES | FITA DE ALPACA PARA O FABRICO DE COMPONENTES<br>0,6 x 350 x 700<br>(AS PER CONFIRMATION 1182 dd. 15.6.19..) | | 985.- | |

Klasse / Classe — Ziffer / Chiffre — Buchstabe / Lettre — (ADR) / (ADR)

**13** Anweisungen des Absenders (Zoll- und sonstige amtliche Behandlung) / Instructions de l'expéditeur (formalités douanières et autres)

BANK REFERENZ CA 11-8804

| **19** Zu sahlen vom / A payer par | Absender / L'expéditeur | Währung / Monnaie | Empfänger / Le Destinataire |
|---|---|---|---|
| Fracht / Prix de transport | | | |
| Ermäßigungen / Réductions | | | |
| Zwischensumme / Solde | | | |
| Zuschläge / Suppléments | | | |
| Nebengebühren / Frais accessoires | | | |
| Sonstiges + / Divers | | | |
| Zu sahl. Gesamtsum. / Total á payer | | | |

**14** Rückerstattung / Remboursement

**15** Frachtzahlungsanweisungen / Prescription d'affranchissement

Frei / Franco FREIGHT PREPAID
Unfrei / Non franco

**20** Besondere Vereinbarungen / Conventions particulieres

**21** Ausgefertigt in / Etablie á BASEL am / le 18.8. 19..

**24** Gut empfangen / Réception des marchandises — Datum / Date

am / le ............ 19 ............

**22** TRANSPORT AG

Unterschni und Stempeiries Absenders / (Signature et timbre de l'expéditeur)

**23** Unterschrift und Stempel des Frachtführers / (Signature et timbre du transporteur)

Unterschrift und Stempel des Empfängers / (Signature et timbre du destinataire)

**25** Angaben zur Ermittlung der Tarifentfernung mit Grenzübergängen

| von | bis | km |
|---|---|---|
| | | |

**28** Berechnung des Beförderungsentgelts

| frachtpfl. Gewicht in kg | Tarifstelle: Sonderabmachung | Güterarten | Währung | Frachtsatz | Beförderungsentgelt |
|---|---|---|---|---|---|
| | | | | Summe | |

**26** Vertrangspartner des Frachtführers ist - kein - Hilfsgewerbetreibender im Sinne des ansuwendenden Tarifs

| **27** | Amtl. Kennzeichen | Nutzlast in kg |
|---|---|---|
| Kfz | | |
| Anhänger | | |

Benutzte Gen. Nr ........................ National, Bilateral, EG, CEMT

Ausfüllen unter der Verantwortung des Absenders / A remplir sous las responsabilité de l'expéditeur **1 – 15** einschließlich / y compris et **21 + 22** Die mit fett gedruckten Linien eingerahmten Rubriken müssen vom Frachtführer ausgefüllt werden. Les parties encadrées de lignes grasses doivent étre remplies par le transporteur.

## Courier Receipt

DEFINITION

A courier receipt is a document issued by a courier or expedited delivery service evidencing receipt of goods for delivery to a named consignee.

✔KEY ELEMENTS

In documentary credit transactions courier receipts should include the following elements:

1. Appears on its face to name the issuer
2. Appears on its face to be stamped, signed, or authenticated by the service
3. Name and address of the shipper (seller)
4. Name and address of the consignee (buyer)
5. The date of pick-up or receipt of the goods by the service
6. Meets any other stipulations of the documentary credit

CAUTIONS & NOTES

Unless the documentary credit names a specific courier or expedited delivery service, banks will accept a document issued by any courier or service.

## Post Receipt

DEFINITION

A post receipt is a document issued by the postal service of a country evidencing receipt of goods for delivery to a named consignee.

✔KEY ELEMENTS

In documentary credit transactions postal receipts should include the following elements:

1. Appears on its face to be stamped or authenticated by the postal service
2. The date of pick-up or receipt of the goods by the postal service
3. Name and address of the shipper (seller)
4. Name and address of the consignee (buyer)
5. Meets any other stipulations of the documentary credit

## SAMPLE COURIER RECEIPT

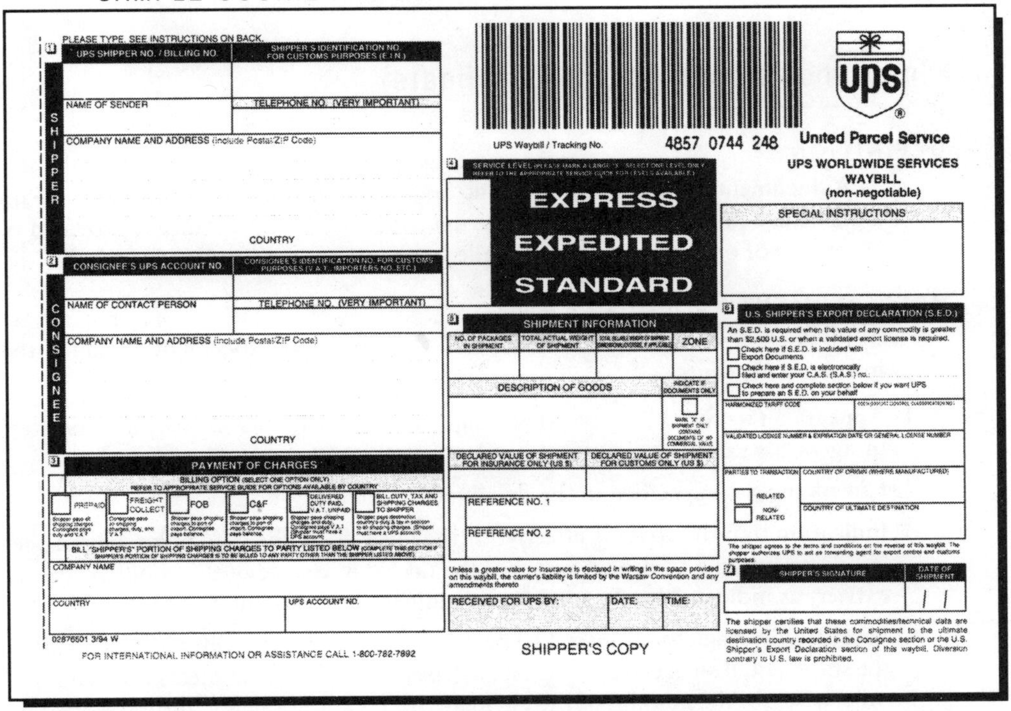
PLEASE TYPE. SEE INSTRUCTIONS ON BACK.

1 SHIPPER: UPS SHIPPER NO. / BILLING NO. | SHIPPER'S IDENTIFICATION NO. FOR CUSTOMS PURPOSES (E.I.N.)

NAME OF SENDER | TELEPHONE NO. (VERY IMPORTANT)

COMPANY NAME AND ADDRESS (Include Postal/ZIP Code)

COUNTRY

2 CONSIGNEE: CONSIGNEE'S UPS ACCOUNT NO. | CONSIGNEE'S IDENTIFICATION NO. FOR CUSTOMS PURPOSES (V.A.T., IMPORTERS NO., ETC.)

NAME OF CONTACT PERSON | TELEPHONE NO. (VERY IMPORTANT)

COMPANY NAME AND ADDRESS (Include Postal/ZIP Code)

COUNTRY

3 PAYMENT OF CHARGES

BILLING OPTION (SELECT ONE OPTION ONLY) REFER TO APPROPRIATE SERVICE GUIDE FOR OPTIONS AVAILABLE BY COUNTRY

PREPAID | FREIGHT COLLECT | FOB | C&F | DELIVERED DUTY PAID, V.A.T. UNPAID | BILL DUTY, TAX AND SHIPPING CHARGES TO SHIPPER

BILL "SHIPPER'S" PORTION OF SHIPPING CHARGES TO PARTY LISTED BELOW

COMPANY NAME

COUNTRY | UPS ACCOUNT NO.

02876501 3/94 W

FOR INTERNATIONAL INFORMATION OR ASSISTANCE CALL 1-800-782-7892

UPS Waybill / Tracking No. 4857 0744 248

United Parcel Service

UPS WORLDWIDE SERVICES WAYBILL (non-negotiable)

4 SERVICE LEVEL: EXPRESS | EXPEDITED | STANDARD

SPECIAL INSTRUCTIONS

5 SHIPMENT INFORMATION

NO. OF PACKAGES IN SHIPMENT | TOTAL ACTUAL WEIGHT OF SHIPMENT | ZONE

DESCRIPTION OF GOODS | INDICATE IF DOCUMENTS ONLY

DECLARED VALUE OF SHIPMENT FOR INSURANCE ONLY (US $) | DECLARED VALUE OF SHIPMENT FOR CUSTOMS ONLY (US $)

REFERENCE NO. 1

REFERENCE NO. 2

Unless a greater value for insurance is declared in writing in the space provided on this waybill, the carrier's liability is limited by the Warsaw Convention and any amendments thereto.

RECEIVED FOR UPS BY: | DATE: | TIME:

SHIPPER'S COPY

6 U.S. SHIPPER'S EXPORT DECLARATION (S.E.D.)

An S.E.D. is required when the value of any commodity is greater than $2,500 U.S. or when a validated export license is required.

Check here if S.E.D. is included with Export Documents

Check here if S.E.D. is electronically filed and enter your C.A.S. (S.A.S.) no.

Check here and complete section below if you want UPS to prepare an S.E.D. on your behalf

HARMONIZED TARIFF CODE

VALIDATED LICENSE NUMBER & EXPIRATION DATE OR GENERAL LICENSE NUMBER

PARTIES TO TRANSACTION: RELATED / NON-RELATED | COUNTRY OF ORIGIN (WHERE MANUFACTURED)

COUNTRY OF ULTIMATE DESTINATION

7 SHIPPER'S SIGNATURE | DATE OF SHIPMENT

The shipper certifies that these commodities/technical data are licensed by the United States for shipment to the ultimate destination country recorded in the Consignee section or the U.S. Shipper's Export Declaration section of this waybill. Diversion contrary to U.S. law is prohibited.

## SAMPLE POST RECEIPT

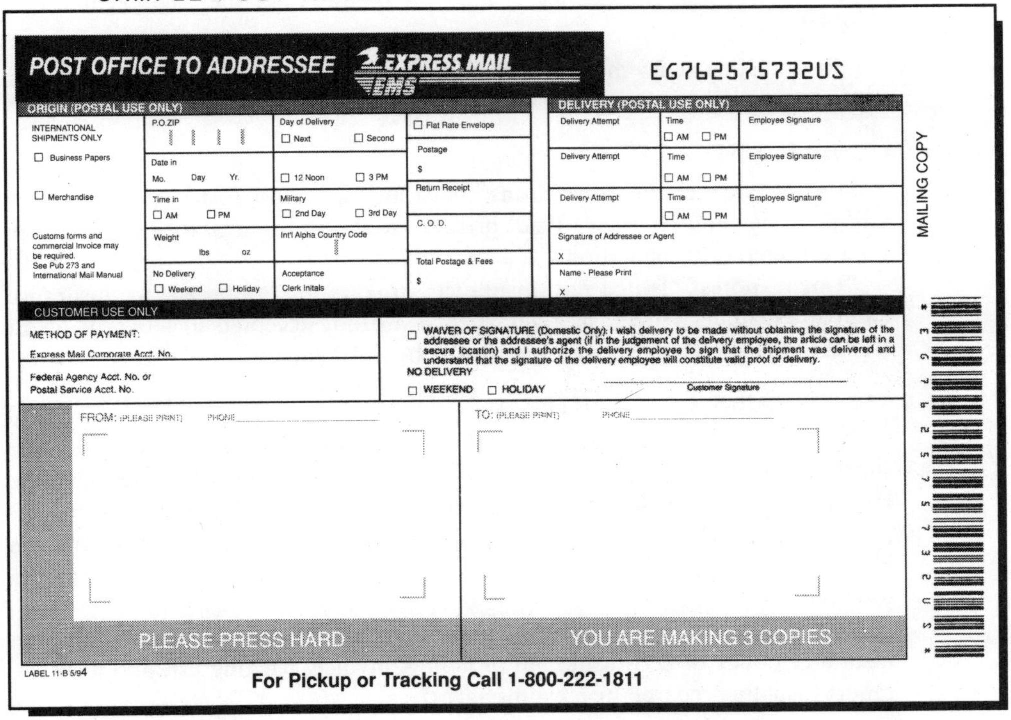
POST OFFICE TO ADDRESSEE — EXPRESS MAIL EMS

EG762575732US

ORIGIN (POSTAL USE ONLY)

INTERNATIONAL SHIPMENTS ONLY: Business Papers; Merchandise

Customs forms and commercial invoice may be required. See Pub 273 and International Mail Manual

PO ZIP | Day of Delivery: Next, Second | Flat Rate Envelope

Date in: Mo. Day Yr. | 12 Noon, 3 PM | Postage $

Time in: AM, PM | Military: 2nd Day, 3rd Day | Return Receipt

Weight: lbs oz | Int'l Alpha Country Code | C.O.D.

No Delivery: Weekend, Holiday | Acceptance Clerk Initials | Total Postage & Fees $

DELIVERY (POSTAL USE ONLY)

Delivery Attempt | Time: AM, PM | Employee Signature

Delivery Attempt | Time: AM, PM | Employee Signature

Delivery Attempt | Time: AM, PM | Employee Signature

Signature of Addressee or Agent X

Name - Please Print X

MAILING COPY

CUSTOMER USE ONLY

METHOD OF PAYMENT:

Express Mail Corporate Acct. No.

Federal Agency Acct. No. or Postal Service Acct. No.

WAIVER OF SIGNATURE (Domestic Only): I wish delivery to be made without obtaining the signature of the addressee or the addressee's agent (if in the judgement of the delivery employee, the article can be left in a secure location) and I authorize the delivery employee to sign that the shipment was delivered and understand that the signature of the delivery employee will constitute valid proof of delivery.

NO DELIVERY: WEEKEND, HOLIDAY — Customer Signature

FROM: (PLEASE PRINT) PHONE

TO: (PLEASE PRINT) PHONE

PLEASE PRESS HARD — YOU ARE MAKING 3 COPIES

LABEL 11-B 5/94

For Pickup or Tracking Call 1-800-222-1811

## Insurance Document (or Certificate)

### DEFINITION

A document indicating the type and amount of insurance coverage in force on a particular shipment. Used to assure the consignee that insurance is provided to cover loss of or damage to cargo while in transit.

### ✔KEY ELEMENTS

In documentary credit transactions the insurance document includes the following elements:

1. Appears on its face to be issued and signed by an insurance carrier, underwriter or agent for same
2. Covers the risks specified in the documentary credit
3. Indication that the cover is effective at the latest from the date of loading of the goods on board a transport vessel or the taking in charge of the goods by the carrier, as indicated by the transport document (bill of lading, etc.)
4. Specifies coverage for at least 110 percent of either: (a) the CIF or CIP value of the shipment, if such can be determined from the various documents on their face, otherwise, (b) the amount of the payment, acceptance or negotiation specified in the documentary credit, or (c) the gross amount of the commercial invoice
5. Is presented as the sole original, or if issued in more than one original, all the originals
6. The insurance currency should be consistent with the currency of the documentary credit

### CAUTIONS & NOTES

Documentary credit transactions indicating CIF (Cost Insurance Freight) or CIP (Carriage and Insurance Paid) pricing should list an insurance document in their required documentation.

"Cover notes" issued by insurance brokers (as opposed to insurance companies, underwriters, or their agents) are not accepted in letter of credit transactions unless authorized specifically by the credit.

### IN CASE OF LOSS OR SHORTFALL

The consignee should always note on the delivery document any damage or shortfall prior to signing for receipt of the goods. The consignee has the responsibility to make reasonable efforts to minimize loss. This includes steps to prevent further damage to the shipment. Expenses incurred in such efforts are almost universally collectible under the insurance policy. Prompt notice of loss is essential.

Copies of documents necessary to support an insurance claim include the insurance policy or certificate, bill of lading, invoice, packing list, and a survey report (usually prepared by a claims agent).

$ ______________ (sum insured)

No. 473301

CERTIFICATE OF MARINE INSURANCE

## WASHINGTON INTERNATIONAL INSURANCE COMPANY

**300 PARK BOULEVARD, SUITE 500, ITASCA, IL 60143-2625**

This is to Certify, *That on the* *day of* *19* *, this Company*

*insured under Policy No.* *made for*

*for the sum of* *Dollars,*

*on*

*Valued at sum insured. Shipped on board the S/S or M/S* *and/or following steamer or steamers*

*at and from* (Initial Point of Shipment) *, via* (Port of Shipment)

*to* (Port or Place of Destination) *and it is understood and agreed, that in case of loss, the same*

*is payable to the order of* *on surrender of this Certificate which conveys the right of collecting any such loss as fully as if the property were covered by a special policy direct to the holder hereof, and free from any liability for unpaid premiums. This certificate is subject to all the terms of the open policy, provided however, that the rights of a bona fide holder of this certificate for value shall not be prejudiced by any terms of the open policy which are in conflict with the terms of this certificate.*

### SPECIAL CONDITIONS

MARKS & NUMBERS

NEW MERCHANDISE shipped subject to an UNDER DECK bill of lading insured–

Against all risks of physical loss or damage from any external cause, irrespective of percentage, excepting those excluded by the F.C. & S., Nuclear Exclusion and S.R. & C.C. Warranties, arising during transportation between the points of shipment and of destination named herein.

The above conditions apply only to New Approved Commodities, properly packed for export, as listed in the Master Policy to which this Certificate is made a part of. Commodities such as, but not limited to, Automobiles, Household Goods and Personal Effects, Wines, Liquors, Beer and Similar Spirits, are subject to further conditions and/or warranties of the policy.

Non-approved commodities are subject to the F.P.A. conditions of the Master Policy unless broader conditions have been approved by these underwriters prior to attachment of risk and so endorsed hereon.

USED MERCHANDISE AND/OR ON DECK SHIPMENTS insured–

Warranted free of particular average unless caused by the vessel being stranded, sunk, burnt, on fire or in collision, but including risk of jettison and/or washing overboard, irrespective of percentage.

| DEDUCTIBLE | COUNTRY CODE |
| --- | --- |
| | |

### TERMS AND CONDITIONS–SEE ALSO BACK HEREOF

WAREHOUSE TO WAREHOUSE: This insurance attaches from the time the goods leave the Warehouse and/or Store at the place named in the Policy for the commencement of the transit and continues during the ordinary course of transit, including customary transhipment if any, until the goods are discharged overside from the overseas vessel at the final port. Thereafter the insurance continues whilst the goods are in transit and/or awaiting transit until delivered to final warehouse at the destination named in the Policy or until the expiry of 15 days (or 30 days if the destination to which the goods are insured is outside the limits of the port) whichever shall first occur. The time limits referred to above to be reckoned from midnight of the day on which the discharge overside of the goods hereby insured from the overseas vessel is completed. Held covered at a premium to be arranged in the event of transhipment, if any, other than as above and/or in the event of delay in excess of the above time limits arising from circumstances beyond the control of the Assured.

NOTE–IT IS NECESSARY FOR THE ASSURED TO GIVE PROMPT NOTICE TO THESE ASSURERS WHEN THEY BECOME AWARE OF AN EVENT FOR WHICH THEY ARE "HELD COVERED" UNDER THIS POLICY AND THE RIGHT TO SUCH COVER IS DEPENDENT ON COMPLIANCE WITH THIS OBLIGATION.

PERILS CLAUSE: Touching the adventures and perils which this Assurer is contented to bear and takes upon itself, they are of the seas, fires, assailing thieves, jettisons, barratry of the masters and mariners, and all other like perils, losses and misfortunes that have or shall come to the hurt, detriment or damage of the said goods and merchandise, or any part thereof, except as may be otherwise provided for herein or endorsed hereon.

SHORE CLAUSE: Where this insurance by its terms covers while on docks, wharves or elsewhere on shore, and/or during land transportation, it shall include the risks of collision, derailment, overturning or other accident to the conveyance, fire, lightning, sprinkler leakage, cyclones, hurricanes, earthquakes, floods (meaning the rising of navigable waters), and/or collapse or subsidence of docks or wharves, even though the insurance be otherwise F.P.A.

BOTH TO BLAME CLAUSE: Where goods are shipped under a Bill of Lading containing the so-called "Both to Blame Collision" Clause, these Assurers agree as to all losses covered by this insurance, to indemnify the Assured for this Policy's proportion of any amount (not exceeding the amount insured) which the Assured may be legally bound to pay to the shipowners under such clause. In the event that such liability is asserted the Assured agrees to notify these Assurers who shall have the right at their own cost and expense to defend the Assured against such claim.

MACHINERY CLAUSE: When the property insured under this Policy includes a machine consisting when complete for sale or use of several parts, then in case of loss or damage covered by this insurance to any part of such machine, these Assurers shall be liable only for the proportion of the insured value of the part lost or damaged, or at the Assured's option, for the cost and expense, including labor and forwarding charges, of replacing or repairing the lost or damaged part; but in no event shall these Assurers be liable for more than the insured value of the complete machine.

LABELS CLAUSE: In case of damage affecting labels, capsules or wrappers, these Assurers, if liable therefor under the terms of this policy, shall not be liable for more than an amount sufficient to pay the cost of new labels, capsules or wrappers, and the cost of reconditioning the goods, but in no event shall these Assurers be liable for more than the insured value of the damaged merchandise.

DELAY CLAUSE: Warranted free of claim for loss of market or inherent vice or nature of the subject matter insured or for loss, damage or deterioration arising from delay, whether caused by a peril insured against or otherwise.

AMERICAN INSTITUTE CLAUSES: This insurance, in addition to the foregoing, is also subject to the following American Institute Cargo Clauses, current forms:

1. **MARINE EXTENSION CLAUSES**
2. **DEVIATION**
3. **CRAFT, ETC.**
4. **CARRIER**
5. **BILL OF LADING, ETC.**
6. **EXPLOSION**
7. **INCHMAREE**
8. **CONSTRUCTIVE TOTAL LOSS**
9. **GENERAL AVERAGE**
10. **SOUTH AMERICA 60 DAY CLAUSE**
11. **S.R. & C.C. ENDORSEMENT**
12. **WAR RISK INSURANCE**

PARAMOUNT WARRANTIES: THE FOLLOWING WARRANTIES SHALL BE PARAMOUNT AND SHALL NOT BE MODIFIED OR SUPERSEDED BY ANY OTHER PROVISION INCLUDED HEREIN OR STAMPED OR ENDORSED HEREON UNLESS SUCH OTHER PROVISION REFERS SPECIFICALLY TO THE RISKS EXCLUDED BY THESE WARRANTIES AND EXPRESSLY ASSUMES THE SAID RISKS:

F.C. & S.: Notwithstanding anything herein contained to the contrary, this insurance is warranted free from capture, seizure, arrest, restraint, detainment, confiscation, preemption, requisition or nationalization, and the consequences thereof or any attempt thereat, whether in time of peace or war and whether lawful or otherwise; also warranted free, whether in time of peace or war, from all loss, damage or expense caused by any weapon of war employing atomic or nuclear fission and/or fusion or other reaction or radioactive force or matter or by any mine or torpedo, also warranted free from all consequences of hostilities or warlike operations (whether there be a declaration of war or not), but this warranty shall not exclude collision or contact with aircraft, rockets or similar missiles or with any fixed or floating object (other than a mine or torpedo), stranding, heavy weather, fire or explosion unless caused directly ( and independently of the nature of the voyage or service which the vessel concerned or, in the case of a collision, any other vessel involved therein, is performing) by a hostile act by or against a belligerent power; and for the purposes of this warranty 'power' includes any authority maintaining naval, military or air forces in association with a power.

Further warranted free from the consequences of civil war, revolution, rebellion, insurrection, or civil strife arising therefrom, or piracy.

NUCLEAR EXCLUSION: Notwithstanding anything to the contrary herein, it is hereby understood and agreed that this Policy shall not apply to any loss, damage or expense due to or arising out of, whether directly or indirectly, nuclear reaction, radiation, or radioactive contamination, regardless of how it was caused. However, subject to all provisions of this Policy, if this Policy insures against fire, then direct physical damage to the property insured located within the United States or Puerto Rico by fire directly caused by the above excluded perils, is insured, provided that the nuclear reaction, radiation, or radioactive contamination was not caused, whether directly or indirectly, by any of the perils excluded by the F.C. & S. Warranty of this Policy.

Nothing in this clause shall be construed to cover any loss, damage, liability or expense caused by nuclear reaction, radiation or radioactive contamination arising directly or indirectly from the fire mentioned above.

S.R & C.C. Warranted free of loss or damage caused by or resulting from:

(a) strikes, lockouts, labor disturbances, riots, civil commotions, or the acts of any person or persons taking part in any such occurrences or disorders.

(b) vandalism, sabotage or malicious act, which shall be deemed also to encompass the act or acts of one or more persons, whether or not agents of a sovereign power, carried out for political, terroristic or ideological purposes and whether any loss, damage or expense resulting therefrom is accidental or intentional.

TIME FOR SUIT: No suit or action against this Assurer for the recovery of any claim by virtue of this insurance shall be sustained in any Court of Law or Equity unless commenced within one (1) year from the time loss occurred or, if such limitation is not valid by the law of the place where the policy is issued, within the shortest contractual period of limitation permitted by such law.

This Certificate is issued in Original and Duplicate, one of which being accomplished the other to stand null and void.

To support a claim local Revenue Laws may require this certificate to be stamped.

Not transferable unless countersigned

Countersigned ______________

Paul D. Amstutz
President

James P. Sheehy
Assistant Treasurer

ADDITIONAL CONDITIONS AND INSTRUCTIONS TO CLAIMANTS ON REVERSE SIDE

ORIGINAL

W-13FF 6/97

## Certificate of Origin

### DEFINITION

A document issued by an authority, as stated in the documentary credit, stating the country of origin of goods.

### ✔KEY ELEMENTS

In documentary credit transactions a certificate of origin should include the following elements:

1. Key details (typically consignor, consignee, and description of goods) regarding the shipment. Also, such details to be in conformity with other documents (e.g., documentary credit, commercial invoice)
2. A statement of origin of the goods
3. The name, signature and/or stamp or seal of the certifying authority

### CAUTIONS & NOTES

The certificate of origin is typically required by the buyer's (importer's) country as a requirement for import processing. If you are the buyer (importer) and your country requires such documentation make sure that you specify in the documentary credit the documentation (in form and content) as specified by your country's customs authority.

A certificate or origin can be the key document required for obtaining special (reduced) tariff rates for imports from countries listed as beneficiaries to programs such as the GSP (Generalized Systems of Preferences). In such a case specific forms (such as the Certificate of Origin Form A—for GSP certification) must be used.

Buyers should avoid the use of such terms as "first class," "well-known," "qualified," "independent," "official," "competent," or "local" when referring to the certifying authority. It is preferable to specifically name the required certifying authority.

Use of vague terminology (as above) will result in the bank's acceptance of any relevant document that appears "on its face" to be in compliance with the documentary credit, so long as it was not issued (signed) by the beneficiary (seller).

In certain countries the certificate of origin is prepared by the seller (beneficiary to the documentary credit) on a standard form and then certified (with a signature, stamp or seal) by the certifying authority.

Certifying authorities most often used are city and regional chambers of commerce and chambers of commerce and industry.

**Exporteur**
Exportateur
Esportatore
Exporter

MUELLER AG
Birsstrasse 26
4132 Muttenz / Switzerland

**Empfänger**
Destinataire
Destinatario
Consignee

ADILMA TRADING CORPORATION
27, Nihonbashi, Chiyoda-Ku
TOKYO 125 / Japan

Nr.
No. 201884

**URSPRUNGSZEUGNIS**
**CERTIFICAT D'ORIGINE**
**CERTIFICATO D'ORIGINE**
**CERTIFICATE OF ORIGIN**

**SCHWEIZERISCHE EIDGENOSSENSCHAFT**
**CONFÉDÉRATION SUISSE**
**CONFEDERAZIONE SVIZZERA**
**SWISS CONFEDERATION**

**Ursprungsstaat**
Pays d'origine
Paese d'origine
Country of origin
SWITZERLAND

**Angaben über die Beförderung (Ausfüllung freigestellt)**
Informations relatives au transport (mention facultative)
Informazioni riguardanti il trasporto (indicazione facoltativa)
Particulars of transport (optional declaration)

**Bemerkungen**
Observations
Osservazioni
Observations

LETTER OF CREDIT NR. 064204

**Zeichen, Nummern, Anzahl und Art der Packstücke; Warenbezeichnung**
Marques, numéros, nombre et nature des colis; désignation des marchandises
Marche, numeri, numero e natura dei colli; designazione delle merci
Marks, numbers, number and kind of packages; description of the goods

ADILMA TRADING 6 cases CYLINDER-
VIA TOKYO PRESS
NR. 1-6 COMPLETELY
ORDER 0-535/1 ASSEMBLED

**Nettogewicht**
Poids net
Peso netto
Net weight
kg, l, $m^3$
etc./ecc.

12'140,0 kg

**Bruttogewicht**
Poids brut
Peso lordo
Gross weight

12'860,0 kg

CHAMBER OF COMMERCE * BASLE *

**Die unterzeichnete Handelskammer bescheinigt den Ursprung oben bezeichneter Ware**
La Chambre de commerce soussignée certifie l'origine des marchandises désignées ci-dessus
La sottoscritta Camera di commercio certifica l'origine delle merci summenzionate
The undersigned Chamber of commerce certifies the origin of the above mentioned goods

Basel, 2 6. 04.

CHAMBER OF COMMERCE * BASLE *

**Basler Handelskammer**
**Chambre de Commerce de Bâle**
**Camera di Commercio di Basilea**
**Basle Chamber of Commerce**

# NAFTA Certificate of Origin

### DEFINITION

The NAFTA (North American Free Trade Agreement) Certificate of Origin is a document prepared by an exporter attesting that the country of origin of goods exported to one of the NAFTA countries is from Canada, the United States, or Mexico.

### ✔KEY ELEMENTS

A NAFTA Certificate of Origin includes the following elements:

1. Name and address of exporter
2. Blanket period of shipment (for multiple shipments of identical goods for a specified period of up to one year)
3. Name and address of importer
4. Name and address of producer
5. Description of goods
6. Harmonized System tariff classification number up to six digits
7. Preference criteria (one of six criteria of rules of origin of the goods)
8. Indication of whether the exporter is the producer of the goods
9. Regional Value Content indication
10. Country of origin of goods
11. Exporter company name, date and authorized signature

### CAUTIONS & NOTES

The NAFTA Certificate of Origin is the key document required for obtaining special (reduced) tariff rates for imports from countries listed as beneficiaries of the North American Free Trade Agreement.

DEPARTMENT OF THE TREASURY
UNITED STATES CUSTOMS SERVICE

Aproved through 12/31/96
OMB No. 1515-0204
See back of form for Paperwork Reduction Act Notice.

NORTH AMERICAN FREE TRADE AGREEMENT

## CERTIFICATE OF ORIGIN

*Please print or type* 19 CFR 181.11, 181.22

| 1. EXPORTER NAME AND ADDRESS | 2. BLANKET PERIOD *(DD/MM/YY)* |
|---|---|
| | FROM |
| TAX IDENTIFICATION NUMBER: | TO |
| 3. PRODUCER NAME AND ADDRESS | 4. IMPORTER NAME AND ADDRESS |
| TAX IDENTIFICATION NUMBER: | TAX IDENTIFICATION NUMBER: |

| 5. DESCRIPTION OF GOOD(S) | 6. HS TARIFF CLASSIFICATION NUMBER | 7. PREFERENCE CRITERION | 8. PRODUCER | 9. NET COST | 10. COUNTRY OF ORIGIN |
|---|---|---|---|---|---|
| | | | | | |

I CERTIFY THAT:

- THE INFORMATION ON THIS DOCUMENT IS TRUE AND ACCURATE AND I ASSUME THE RESPONSIBILITY FOR PROVING SUCH REPRESENTATIONS. I UNDERSTAND THAT I AM LIABLE FOR ANY FALSE STATEMENTS OR MATERIAL OMISSIONS MADE ON OR IN CONNECTION WITH THIS DOCUMENT;
- I AGREE TO MAINTAIN, AND PRESENT UPON REQUEST, DOCUMENTATION NECESSARY TO SUPPORT THIS CERTIFICATE, AND TO INFORM, IN WRITING, ALL PERSONS TO WHOM THE CERTIFICATE WAS GIVEN OF ANY CHANGES THAT COULD AFFECT THE ACCURACY OR VALIDITY OF THIS CERTIFICATE;
- THE GOODS ORIGINATED IN THE TERRITORY OF ONE OR MORE OF THE PARTIES, AND COMPLY WITH THE ORIGIN REQUIREMENTS SPECIFIED FOR THOSE GOODS IN THE NORTH AMERICAN FREE TRADE AGREEMENT, AND UNLESS SPECIFICALLY EXEMPTED IN ARTICLE 411 OR ANNEX 401, THERE HAS BEEN NO FURTHER PRODUCTION OR ANY OTHER OPERATION OUTSIDE THE TERRITORIES OF THE PARTIES; AND
- THIS CERTIFICATE CONSISTS OF [ ] PAGES, INCLUDING ALL ATTACHMENTS.

| 11. | 11a. AUTHORIZED SIGNATURE | | 11b. COMPANY | |
|---|---|---|---|---|
| | 11c. NAME *(Print or Type)* | | 11d. TITLE | |
| | 11e. DATE *(DD/MM/YY)* | 11f. TELEPHONE NUMBER ▷ | *(Voice)* | *(Facsimile)* |

Customs Form 434 (121793)

## Inspection Certificate

### DEFINITION

A document issued by an authority, as stated in the documentary credit, indicating that goods have been inspected (typically according to a set of industry, customer, government, or carrier specifications) prior to shipment and the results of the inspection.

Inspection certificates are generally obtained from neutral testing organizations (e.g., a government entity or independent service company).

### ✔KEY ELEMENTS

In documentary credit transactions an inspection certificate should include the following elements:

1. Key details (typically consignor, consignee, and description of goods) regarding the shipment. Also, such details to be in conformity with other documents (e.g., documentary credit, commercial invoice)
2. Date of the inspection
3. Statement of sampling methodology
4. Statement of the results of the inspection
5. The name, signature and/or stamp or seal of the inspecting entity

### CAUTIONS & NOTES

In the case of certain countries and certain commodities the inspection certificate must be issued by an appropriate government entity.

Buyers should avoid the use of such terms as "first class," "well-known," "qualified," "independent," "official," "competent," or "local" when referring to an acceptable inspection authority. It is preferable to agree beforehand as to a specific inspection organization or entity and for the buyer to name the required certifying organization or entity in the documentary credit.

Use of vague terminology (as above) will result in the bank's acceptance of any relevant document that appears "on its face" to be in compliance with the documentary credit, so long as it was not issued by the beneficiary (seller).

**SGS Supervise (Suisse) S.A.**

May 10, 19..

Hardstrasse 1
Postfach 4149
**CH-4002 Basel**
Tel. (+41-61) 271 36 11
Fax (+41-61) 271 40 48
Telex : 962 457 SGS

## Certificate No 1407/ 012488

| | | |
|---|---|---|
| BUYER | : | TA PING CO. LTD. YACHT BUILDING<br>18-5, HARBOUR STREET, TAIPEI, TAIWAN |
| SELLER | : | SWISS EXPORT LTD. AIRFREIGHT DIVISION<br>8008 ZUERICH,SWITZERLAND |
| LETTER OF CREDIT NBR. | : | FB-03-45786-9 |
| GOODS | : | MACHINERY PARTS, as designated below |
| CONTRACT NBR. | : | FA12345WO79PE |
| IMPORT PERMIT NUMBER | : | TW-2395-497-0006, as declared |
| SERVICES REQUIRED | : | FINAL PRE-SHIPMENT INSPECTION |

This is to certify that, at buyers' request and based on the specifications submitted to us, we have inspected the following goods:

1. MATERIAL DESIGNATION
   1 LOT ACCESSORIES AND SPARE PARTS FOR FOOD PROCESSING MACHINERY, as detailed in seller's commercial invoice and corresponding packing list both dated April 29, 19

2. INSPECTIONS PERFORMED AND FINDINGS
   2.1. Material identification for conformity with the specifications submitted to us.
   2.2. Visual inspection on workmanship, finish and condition.
   2.3. Quantitative and completeness checks.
   2.4. Dimensional checks at random, where applicable.
   2.5. Packing inspection: The packing, consisting of 5 plywood cases, is considered adequate to ship the goods by air to Taipei under normal conditions of transport and handling.
   2.6. Marking inspection: The shipping marks include: **SWISS EXPORT 0405/1-5**
   2.7. Loading details as per Air Waybill No. BSL 122077 issued by PANALPINA LTD BASLE-AIRPORT on 4 MAY ..

3. INSPECTION RESULTS AND CONCLUSION
   Based on the inspections performed, we certify the goods to be new, of good workmanship and finish, free from apparent damage or defect, and that the shipment is fully in compliance with the contract requirements in specification, quantity, quality, proper packing and marking.

5. DATE AND PLACE OF INSPECTION
   April 30, 19.. on seller's premises in Zurich, Switzerland with subsequent review of loading details.

---

This certificate is evidence of and reports on our findings at the time and place of inspection. It does not release buyers or sellers from their contractual obligations.

SGS SUPERVISE (SUISSE) SA
BASLE OFFICE, SWITZERLAND

As Member of SOCIETE GENERALE
DE SURVEILLANCE S.A. (SGS)
Geneva, Switzerland

The issuance of this Certificate does not exonerate buyers or sellers from exercising all their rights and discharging all their liabilities under the Contract of Sale Stipulations to the contrary are not binding on us. – The present inspection has been carried out to the best of our knowledge and ability. and our responsibility is limited to the exercise of reasonable care

# Export License

## DEFINITION

An export license is a document prepared by a government authority of a nation granting the right to export a specific quantity of a commodity to a specified country.

This document is often required for the exportation of certain natural resources, national treasures, drugs, strategic commodities, and arms and armaments.

## ✔KEY ELEMENTS

The export license of each country will have its own form and content. Certain elements are likely to be included in all export licenses:

1. Name and address of seller
2. Name and address of buyer
3. Date of issuance
4. Validity date
5. Description of goods covered by license
6. Name of country of origin
7. Name of country of ultimate destination

## CAUTIONS & NOTES

Some countries require export licenses for virtually all commodities and products. The license is a means of control and taxation. In some cases the lack of an export license can be cited as a reason why goods cannot be shipped, even though payment has been made. Buyers should be especially careful about buying sensitive goods from countries with a demonstrated lack of rule by law.

The export license is typically the responsibility of the seller. However, if the buyer is dealing in sensitive goods, he should research the need for an export license beforehand. Failure to secure such a license can delay or prevent shipment and jeopardize the validity of a documentary credit.

## Consular Invoice

### DEFINITION

A consular invoice is an invoice covering a shipment of goods certified (usually in triplicate) in the country of export by a local consul of the country for which the merchandise is destined.

### ✔KEY ELEMENTS

The consular invoice of each country will have its own form and content. Certain elements are likely to be included in all consular invoices:

1. Name and address of seller
2. Name and address of buyer
3. Date of issuance
4. Country of origin of the goods shipped
5. Country of final destination of the goods
6. Quantity and description of the goods
7. Shipping details including: weight of the goods, number of packages, and shipping marks and numbers

### CAUTIONS & NOTES

This invoice is used by customs officials of the country of entry to verify the value, quantity, country of origin, and nature of the merchandise.

Some countries require that the consular invoice be prepared on their own forms, which are usually supplied by the consul of that country. Some require that they be in the language of their country and officially be certified by that country's consulate in the state or country of export.

In some cases the certification and legalization of these documents can take considerable time, and this should be considered by both buyer and seller when such documents are required.

## Shipper's Export Declaration (SED)

### DEFINITION

An export declaration is a document specifying the particulars of an export transaction.

Note that different countries have different names for the export declaration. In the USA it is called the SED or Shipper's Export Declaration.

### ISSUED BY

The export declaration is issued by the exporter/seller/consignor and presented to the export authority of the country of export. In some cases, it must be certified by the export authority.

### ✔KEY ELEMENTS

Each country has its own export declaration form. The shipper's export declaration typically includes the following elements:

1. Name and address of seller
2. Name and address of buyer
3. Date of issuance
4. Quantity and description of the goods
5. Country of origin of the goods shipped
6. Country of final destination of the goods
7. Quantity and description of the goods
8. Shipping details including: weight of the goods, number of packages, and shipping marks and numbers
9. Statement that the goods will not be diverted to another country contrary to the laws of the exporting country

### ! CAUTIONS & NOTES

The shipper's export declaration is used by a nation's customs authorities to control exports and compile trade statistics. The SED is rarely a requirement of the importer, but rather is required of the exporter by the export authorities.

# SAMPLE EXPORT DECLARATION FOR THE UNITED STATES

U.S. DEPARTMENT OF COMMERCE ó U.S. CENSUS BUREAU ñ Economics and Statistics Administration ó BUREAU OF EXPORT ADMINISTRATION

FORM 7525-V (7-25-2000)

## SHIPPER'S EXPORT DECLARATION

OMB No. 0607-0152

1a. U.S. PRINCIPAL PARTY IN INTEREST (USPPI) (Complete name and address)

ZIP CODE

2. DATE OF EXPORTATION

3. TRANSPORTATION REFERENCE NO.

b. USPPI EIN (IRS) OR ID NO.

c. PARTIES TO TRANSACTION ☐ Related ☐ Non-related

4a. ULTIMATE CONSIGNEE (Complete name and address)

b. INTERMEDIATE CONSIGNEE (Complete name and address)

5. FORWARDING AGENT (Complete name and address)

6. POINT (STATE) OF ORIGIN OR FTZ NO.

7. COUNTRY OF ULTIMATE DESTINATION

8. LOADING PIER (Vessel only)

9. METHOD OF TRANSPORTATION (Specify)

14. CARRIER IDENTIFICATION CODE

15. SHIPMENT REFERENCE NO.

10. EXPORTING CARRIER

11. PORT OF EXPORT

16. ENTRY NUMBER

17. HAZARDOUS MATERIALS ☐ Yes ☐ No

12. PORT OF UNLOADING (Vessel and air only)

13. CONTAINERIZED (Vessel only) ☐ Yes ☐ No

18. IN BOND CODE

19. ROUTED EXPORT TRANSACTION ☐ Yes ☐ No

20. SCHEDULE B DESCRIPTION OF COMMODITIES (Use columns 22ñ24)

| D/F or M (21) | SCHEDULE B NUMBER (22) | QUANTITY ñ SCHEDULE B UNIT(S) (23) | SHIPPING WEIGHT (Kilograms) (24) | VIN/PRODUCT NUMBER/ VEHICLE TITLE NUMBER (25) | VALUE (U.S. dollars, omit cents) (Selling price or cost if not sold) (26) |
|---|---|---|---|---|---|
| | | | | | |

27. LICENSE NO./LICENSE EXCEPTION SYMBOL/AUTHORIZATION

28. ECCN (When required)

29. Duly authorized officer or employee

The USPPI authorizes the forwarder named above to act as forwarding agent for export control and customs purposes.

30. I certify that all statements made and all information contained herein are true and correct and that I have read and understand the instructions for preparation of this document, set forth in the "Correct Way to Fill Out the Shipperís Export Declaration." I understand that civil and criminal penalties, including forfeiture and sale, may be imposed for making false or fraudulent statements herein, failing to provide the requested information or for violation of U.S. laws on exportation (13 U.S.C. Sec. 305; 22 U.S.C. Sec. 401; 18 U.S.C. Sec. 1001; 50 U.S.C. App. 2410).

Signature

Confidential ñ For use solely for official purposes authorized by the Secretary of Commerce (13 U.S.C. 301 (g)).

Title

Export shipments are subject to inspection by U.S. Customs Service and/or Office of Export Enforcement.

Date

31. AUTHENTICATION (When required)

Telephone No. (Include Area Code)

E-mail address

This form may be printed by private parties provided it conforms to the official form. For sale by the Superintendent of Documents, Government Printing Office, Washington, DC 20402, and local Customs District Directors. The "Correct Way to Fill Out the Shipper's Export Declaration" is available from the U.S. Census Bureau, Washington, DC 20233.

## Regional Trade Pact Import/Export Declaration

### DEFINITION

A standardized export/import document used in common by members of a regional trade group containing compliance, administrative and statistical information.

### ISSUED BY

This document is typically issued by the exporter/seller.

### ✔KEY ELEMENTS

The typical trade pact import/export declaration contains the following elements:

1. Name and address of exporter/seller/consignor
2. Name and address of importer/buyer/consignee
3. Description and value of the goods
4. A statement of origin of the goods
5. Country of destination of the goods
6. Carrier and means of transport
7. Other compliance, administrative and statistical information

### ! CAUTIONS & NOTES

This document is used as an export declaration when exporting from any trade pact member country to a non-member country and as both an import and export declaration when transporting goods across country borders within the trade group.

Because of its standardized format, this document is often linked to a computer system for the electronic transfer of information to export and import authorities within the trade group.

### THE EU (EUROPEAN UNION) SAD (SINGLE ADMINISTRATIVE DOCUMENT)

This document is a prime example of a regional trade pact import/export declaration. It was established by the European Community Council in 1988 with the goal of standardizing customs documentation and simplifying international transactions.

This particular document is used as an import/export declaration and also for the declaration of goods in transit within EU and EFTA (European Free Trade Area) countries. It may be submitted by computer directly to the customs authorities in all the 15 EU member nations.

Countries outside of the EU have shown interest in using the SAD and some have already adopted the format for their import documentation (e.g., Bulgaria).

## SAMPLE REGIONAL TRADE PACT DECLARATION FOR THE EU

**THIS SET OF FORMS IS PRINTED ON NCR PAPER. IF COMPLETING BY HAND, WRITE IN BLOCK LETTERS, USING A BALLPOINT PEN AND APPLY MAXIMUM PRESSURE WITH THE SET RESTING ON A FIRM SURFACE.**

**HANDLE WITH CARE**

**EUROPEAN COMMUNITY 1 2 3 4 5 6 7**

A OFFICE OF DISPATCH/EXPORT

1 Copy for the country of dispatch/export 1

2 Consignor/*Exporter* No

1 DECLARATION

3 Forms

4 Loading lists

5 Items

6 Total packages

7 Reference number

8 Consignee No

9 Person responsible for financial settlement No

10 *Country first destin.*

11 *Trading country*

13 *CAP*

14 Declarant/Representative No

15 Country of despatch/*export*

15 C disp. /*exp.* Code a b

17 Country destin. Code a b

16 Country of origin

17 Country of destination

18 Identity and nationality of means of transport at departure

19 Ctr.

20 Delivery terms

21 Identity and nationality of active means of transport crossing the border

22 Currency and total amount invoiced

23 Exchange rate

24 Nature of transaction

25 Mode of transport at the border

26 Inland mode of transport

27 Place of loading

28 Financial and banking data

29 Office of exit

30 Location of goods

31 Packages and description of goods — Marks and numbers — Container No(s) — Number and kind

32 Item No

33 Commodity Code

34 Country origin Code a b

35 Gross mass (kg)

37 PROCEDURE

38 Net mass (kg)

39 *Quota*

40 Summary declaration/Previous document

41 Supplementary units

44 Additional information/Documents produced/Certificates and authorisations

A.I. Code

46 Statistical value

47 Calculation of taxes

| Type | Tax base | Rate | Amount | MP |
|---|---|---|---|---|
| | | | | |
| | Total: | | | |

48 Deferred payment

49 Identification of warehouse

B ACCOUNTING DETAILS

50 Principal No Signature:

represented by

Place and date:

C OFFICE OF DEPARTURE

51 Intended offices of transit (and country)

52 Guarantee not valid for

Code

53 Office of destination (and country)

D CONTROL BY OFFICE OF DEPARTURE Stamp:

Result:

Seals affixed: Number:

Identity:

Time limit (date):

Signature:

54 Place and date:

Signature and name of declarant/representative:

C88 (1-8) PCU(January 1996)

## Packing List

### DEFINITION

A packing list is a document prepared by the shipper listing the kinds and quantities of merchandise in a particular shipment.

A copy of the packing list is often attached to the shipment itself and another copy sent directly to the consignee to assist in checking the shipment when received. Also called a bill of parcels.

### ✔KEY ELEMENTS

The packing list should include the following elements:

1. Name and address of seller
2. Name and address of buyer
3. Date of issuance
4. Invoice number
5. Order or contract number
6. Quantity and description of the goods
7. Shipping details including: weight of the goods, number of packages, and shipping marks and numbers
8. Quantity and description of contents of each package, carton, crate or container
9. Any other information as required in the documentary credit (e.g., country of origin)

### ! CAUTIONS & NOTES

The packing list is a more detailed version of the commercial invoice but without price information. The type of each container is identified, as well as its individual weight and measurements. The packing list is attached to the outside of its respective container in a waterproof envelope marked "packing list enclosed," and is immediately available to authorities in both the countries of export and import.

Although not required in some transactions, it is required by some countries and some buyers.

CHAPTER 17

# Document Checklists

THE FOLLOWING IS a series of checklists for document preparation and examination by the buyer, seller, and advising and issuing banks. They are not fully comprehensive as there are an almost infinite number of transaction variations possible, some of which require specialized procedures and documentation. Therefore, they should be viewed only as a general guide.

## SELLER/EXPORTER/BENEFICIARY

The seller/exporter/beneficiary has the responsibility of preparing and presenting documents in accordance with the terms of the documentary credit or collection. If the documents are incorrect or inconsistent there is a risk of having them refused, wasting time and money, and possibly imperiling the transaction itself.

## ISSUING (BUYER'S) BANK

The issuing (buyer's) bank has the responsibility of examining the documents package presented by the seller/beneficiary to make certain they are consistent with the documentary credit or collection.

## ADVISING BANK

The advising bank (often the confirming bank as well) has the responsibility of examining the documents presented by the issuing bank to determine if they are consistent with the requirements of the documentary credit or collection.

## BUYER/IMPORTER/APPLICANT

The buyer/importer/applicant first has the responsibility of listing documents that are required of the seller in the documentary credit. Upon presentation by the bank the buyer examines documents for consistency and accuracy. Problems with documents often lead to problems securing goods from the shipping company or customs or receiving unwanted or incorrect goods.

## General Consistency Checklist

SELLER BUYER ADVISING BANK ISSUING BANK

The following is a list of points of consistency the seller, buyer, and banks should be aware of when preparing or examining documents for documentary transactions. Does information on all the documents agree as to the following:

1. Name and address of seller/shipper/exporter/beneficiary? ❑
2. Name and address of buyer/consignee/importer? ❑
3. Issuer name and address? ❑
4. Quantities and description of the goods? ❑
5. Country of origin of the goods? ❑
6. Country of destination of the goods? ❑
7. Invoice numbers, documentary credit numbers? ❑
8. Certifications? ❑
9. Legalizations? ❑
10. Shipping marks and numbers? ❑
11. Net weight, gross weight, volume? ❑
12. Number of crates, cartons, or containers? ❑
13. Documents that so require are legally certified or legalized? ❑
14. All documents are in complete sets and of the number specified in the credit? ❑

## Letter of Transmittal

ISSUING BANK ADVISING BANK

TO WHICHEVER BANK(S) RECEIVE THE DOCUMENTS.

1. Is the documentary credit addressed to your bank? ❑
2. Does the documentary credit have a current date? ❑
3. Are the instructions in the letter clear? ❑
4. Are all the listed documents enclosed? ❑
5. Do the values of the documents correspond? ❑
6. Have any discrepancies been noted? ❑

## The Documentary Credit

SELLER

1. Is the documentary credit consistent with the contract or agreement between the buyer and seller? ☐
2. Are the terms of the documentary credit acceptable? ☐
3. Is the documentary credit valid? ☐
4. Is there enough time to satisfy the terms of the documentary credit? ☐
5. Is it reasonably possible to obtain all the documentation required by the documentary credit within the time allotted? ☐
6. Are the quantities of the goods specified in the documentary credit available in time to meet the ship date? ☐
7. Is the documentary credit irrevocable? ☐
8. Is the documentary credit confirmed by a trusted bank? ☐

## The Draft

SELLER BUYER ADVISING BANK ISSUING BANK

1. Is the name of the drawee correct? ☐
2. Is the name of the payee correct? ☐
3. Does the draft contain the "to the order of" notation? ☐
4. Does the draft contain an expiration date? ☐
5. Does the draft contain an unconditional instruction to pay? ☐
6. Are the amounts in words and figures identical? ☐
7. Is the draft drawn on the party named in the documentary credit? ☐
8. If the draft is made out to own order (ourselves), is it endorsed? ☐
9. Does the draft contain any and all notations as stipulated in the credit? (i.e., drawn under credit number ___)? ☐
10. Does the draft name the place and date of issue? ☐
11. Does the draft bear the signature of the issuer? ☐
12. Are the values of the draft, invoices, and the credit consistent? ☐

## Commercial Invoice

SELLER BUYER ADVISING BANK ISSUING BANK

1. Is the invoice issued by the seller/beneficiary as named in the credit?
2. Is the invoice issued to the buyer/applicant as named in the credit?
3. Is the invoice issued to the correct address of the buyer/applicant as stated in the documentary credit?
4. Does the description of the goods in the invoice correspond exactly to their description in the documentary credit?
5. Does the quantity of the goods in the invoice correspond exactly to the quantities specified in the documentary credit?
6. Does the value of the goods (unit price and total price) correspond exactly to the values specified in the documentary credit?
7. Does the invoice amount not exceed the amount of the documentary credit?
8. Is the invoice free of any unauthorized charges?
9. Does the currency used in pricing in the invoice match that of the documentary credit?
10. Does the invoice state the delivery terms (e.g., CIF, EXW)?
11. Do the delivery terms stated in the invoice match those specified in the documentary credit?
12. If required by the documentary credit, is the invoice signed?
13. If required by the documentary credit, does the invoice bear proper certifications, authorizations, or legalizations?
14. If required by the documentary credit, does the invoice contain any special marks, numbers, or other notations?

## The Transport Document(s)

SELLER BUYER ADVISING BANK ISSUING BANK

1. Does the transport document contain the correct consignee name and address as specified in the credit? ☐
2. Does the transport document contain an "on board" notation? ☐
3. Does the transport document contain a notation naming the vessel? ☐
4. Does the transport document contain a notation of the on board date? ☐
5. Does the transport document name the correct port of loading and port of destination as stipulated in the documentary credit? ☐
6. Is the transport document "clean" (without notations for shortage, loss, or damage)? ☐
7. If the transport document states "on deck" stowage, it is allowed by the credit? ☐
8. If required by the documentary credit, is the "notify address" listed? ☐
9. Was the transport document issued within the period specified in the documentary credit? ☐
10. Is the full set of originals being presented? ☐
11. Is the transport document *not* a charter party document, *unless* authorized by the documentary credit? ☐
12. Is the transport document *not* a forwarder's transport document, *unless* authorized by the documentary credit? ☐
13. Is the quantity and description of the goods consistent with that contained in the documentary credit? ☐
14. Are the marks and numbers on the transport document consistent with those on other documents? ☐
15. Are the freight payments terms consistent with those stipulated in the documentary credit? ☐
16. Does the transport document meet the stipulations of the documentary credit with regard to transshipment? ☐
17. Does the transport document meet all other stipulations of the documentary credit? ☐

## Certificate of Origin

SELLER BUYER ADVISING BANK ISSUING BANK

1. Is the name and address of the seller as specified in the credit? ☐
2. Is the name and address of the buyer as specified in the credit? ☐
3. Is the date of issuance correct? ☐
4. Is the quantity and description of the goods in conformity with the documentary credit? ☐
5. Is the country of origin named and in conformity with the documentary credit? ☐
6. Is the issuer named and in conformity with the documentary credit? ☐
7. Does the document bear the signature, stamp, or authentication of the issuer? ☐
8. Is any other information included as required in the documentary credit? ☐

## Inspection Certificate

SELLER BUYER ADVISING BANK ISSUING BANK

1. Does the inspection certificate contain key details of the consignor, consignee, and inspection entity? ☐
2. Does the inspection certificate contain a description of the goods that is consistent with the description of goods in the credit? ☐
3. Does the inspection certificate contain the date of the inspection? ☐
4. Does the inspection certificate contain a statement of the sampling methodology? ☐
5. Does the inspection certificate contain a statement of the results of the inspection? ☐
6. Does the inspection certificate contain the name, signature, and/or stamp or seal of the inspecting entity? ☐

## Insurance Document

SELLER BUYER ADVISING BANK ISSUING BANK

1. Was the insurance document issued as either a policy or as a certificate as stipulated in the credit? ❑
2. Is the insurance document issued and signed by an insurance carrier, underwriter, or their agent (*not* by a broker)? ❑
3. Does the insurance document cover all the risks specified in the credit? ❑
4. Does the insurance document cover the risks resulting from a) the particular mode of shipment, b) the transport route, or c) reloading or "on deck" storage, etc.? ❑
5. Does the insurance document indicate that cover is effective at the latest from the date of loading of the goods on board or the taking in charge of the goods by the carrier, as indicated by the transport document? ❑
6. Is the information in the insurance document concerning mode of transport and transport route consistent with the documentary credit? ❑
7. Does the document specify coverage for at least 110 percent of either a) the CIF or CIP value of the shipment, or, if that information is not provided, b) the amount of the payment, acceptance or negotiation specified in the documentary credit, or c) the gross amount of the invoice? ❑
8. Is the currency of the insurance document consistent with the credit? ❑
9. Have all issued originals of the document been presented? ❑
10. If endorsement is required, is the document properly endorsed? ❑

## Packing List

SELLER BUYER ADVISING BANK ISSUING BANK

1. Is the name and address of the seller as specified in the credit? ❑
2. Is the name and address of the buyer as specified in the credit? ❑
3. Is the date of issuance correct? ❑
4. Are the invoice numbers, contract numbers, order numbers, and any other numbers correct and in conformity with the documentary credit? ❑
5. Is the quantity and description of the goods in conformity with the credit? ❑
6. Are all shipping details correct including: weight of the goods, number of packages, and shipping marks and numbers? ❑
7. Is other information included as required (e.g., country of origin)? ❑

CHAPTER 18

# CyberPayments

INTERNATIONAL TRADE has continued its explosive 1990s growth into the 21st century, and it is now possible to purchase goods and services from many more places and in more ways than ever before. Electronic commerce—the ability to purchase goods and services over the Internet from around the world at any time of day or night—is foremost in that phenomenal growth. The Internet has developed from being an information source to becoming a medium of high-speed digital transactions. A growing number of companies are taking advantage of the Web by selling products and services of all sorts, both to consumers (B2C) and to other businesses. Although electronic commerce does not dominate international trade, all indications are that just about every size firm in a sweeping cross-section of countries are planning and executing e-commerce strategies.

In 1996, Web commerce registered sales of just US$73 million in the consumer market and a mere US$12 million in the business-to-business (B2B) market. The B2B market alone exceeded US$6 trillion by 2007 and is set to grow at a minimum of 15% per year for the next decade.

But before electronic commerce could experience such phenomenal growth patterns, several issues had to be resolved. Privacy, lack of trust, the real potential for fraud, and the difficulty of making or receiving payment over the Internet were among the most commonly cited problems inhibiting early versions of electronic commerce. In response, the industry worked feverishly to remedy these issues, and tremendous strides were made in just a few years. All indications are, that because of this remedial work, the explosive growth predictions for the turn of the century will be close to the mark.

## What is Electronic Commerce?

Electronic commerce includes Internet transactions, certain forms of network electronic commerce, point-of-sale networks, some types of computer-to-computer transactions, select forms of electronic funds transfer, and the sale of information technology hardware, software, and services that assist companies in the development, maintenance, and administration of electronic commerce. This continues to be a highly dynamic area, however, and new methods of conducting commercial transactions are being added all the time to this broad category of trade.

Technology development is moving along at rocket speed as businesses and industries around the world see the many opportunities to create and expand markets with high technology. While information, advertising and research are all conducted electronically, this chapter focuses on electronic payments and the many benefits to international trade of continued development in this area.

## Introducing the Parties

### CARDHOLDER

The cardholder is an authorized holder of a credit or debit card supported by an "issuer," and registered to perform electronic purchase transactions. In simple terms, this simply means someone who holds a Visa, MasterCard, American Express or other such card, or the holder of a bank debit card (sometimes called an ATM card).

Note that many larger retail stores have their own proprietary store credit cards. These cards come in two forms: 1) Cards that may be used solely in transactions with the specific store, either in person or at that store's Web site, and 2) Cards that carry the name of the retail establishment, but which were issued by Visa or MasterCard (for example) and serve as a general credit card usable at any establishment that accepts, in this case, Visa or MasterCard.

### MERCHANT

A merchant is a seller of goods, services, or information who is authorized to accept credit or debit cards in payment for products or services. In the case of e-commerce, this also means a seller authorized to accept these cards through an electronic medium. A merchant may also provide electronic transaction services and/or electronic delivery of items, such as information.

### ISSUER

An issuer is a financial institution that provides credit or debit cards that support cybertransactions. Issuers are generally banks or savings and loans companies that issue magnetic-strip payment cards.

### ACQUIRER

An acquirer is a financial institution that processes payment card transactions. Acquirers of cyberpayment cards must possess the necessary software and support technology to ensure that cyberpayments are effected accurately and securely.

### CERTIFICATION AUTHORITY

A certification authority is an agency that creates and distributes electronic certificates for cardholders, merchants, issuers, and acquirers. Since these certificates are at the very heart of cyberpayment security, certification authorities must be highly trusted, and they must undergo strict checks and periodic inspections to ensure the rigid guidelines for generating and handling certificates are followed.

A significant question is how to decide to trust a given certification authority. A hierarchies of trust model has been utilized by the developers of the Secured Electronic Transactions Standards (SET) protocol to answer this concern. Most transactions will involve five parties: the cardholder, the merchant, the cardholder's bank, the merchant's bank, and the credit card provider. Most other early protocols (e.g., SSL) could only handle one-to-one transactions.

A traditional trust hierarchy begins with a central organization, known as the root authority. This entity establishes policies and procedures for the physical, information, and personnel security of the certification authority function for itself and subsidiary authorities. Although it would seem that national governments should play the role of the ultimate authority, to date only a few private organizations in the United States have taken active measures to be considered this authority. As security and tax issues grow, more governments may go this route rather than private business.

## CyberPayments Today

The growth of e-commerce has been greatly facilitated by the ability and security that has become commonplace in Internet credit-card transactions. Most surprising is the use of credit card transactions in the B2B segment.

The ability to order and pay for products over the Internet has revolutionized international trade. It can provide purchasers in one country with access to goods and services from another of which they might otherwise not even be aware. More importantly, many purchases in the B2B sector can be made without the necessity of cumbersome letter of credit processes.

Since many governments restrict imports of certain products and regulate advertising and other marketing tools within their national borders, purchasers are often forced to choose from a limited—or even monopolistic—supply of a desired product (e.g., Amazon.fr (France) will not permit access to Amazon.com (U.S.) while using a French-based ISP due to book discounting regulations in France). With Internet access, purchasers can scour the world in minutes to find the right product at the best price.

Until recently, however, suppliers used the Internet primarily for advertising purposes. All orders were taken either over the telephone or by mail. While this certainly opened the door and paved the way for Internet commerce, it still required that business be conducted through traditional methods.

Two major issues kept international businesses from flocking en masse to the Internet: trust and security. Both buyers and sellers must have confidence in the infrastructure of the Internet for it to support electronic commerce. It was the advent of SET and its constant updating that has made this possible.

## Secure Electronic Transaction Standards (SET)

SET is a single technical standard for safeguarding credit and debit card purchases made over the open networks of the Internet. It is an international protocol that details how credit and debit card transactions on the Internet are secured using encryption technology and digital certification. Developed by a consortium including IBM, VISA, MasterCard, Microsoft, Netscape Communications, VeriSign and VeriFone, and GTE, among others, SET provides internationally approved and available cryptography that complies with minimum requirements to ensure the effectiveness of a global authentication service. The SET specifications include business requirements, technical specifications, and a programmer's guide.

The publication of the SET standard opened the electronic marketplace to participating banks, and to buyers and sellers around the world. SET continues to be the leader in securing international credit and debit card transactions over the Internet, and it maintains the trust of buyers and sellers conducting electronic commerce in both the B2B and B2C sectors.

### HOW SET WORKS

Instead of providing sellers with access to credit card numbers, SET technology in both the buyer's and the seller's computers encodes the numbers so only the consumer and financial institution have access to them. When a transaction is requested, the credit card information is sent electronically to the seller's bank, where the information is decrypted and verified. The bank then issues a digital certificate ensuring that the parties to the transaction are, indeed, who they claim to be, and that the transaction is legitimate. The bank acts as a sort of virtual escrow with a letter-of-credit style transaction being resolved in nanoseconds rather than days.

SET requires both public and private "key pairs" for every party to a transaction, except the actual cardholder. Every key must be signed by a trusted "certification authority" who creates and distributes electronic certificates for cardholders, merchants, and payment gateways (such as banks). These certificates play a significant role in verifying the identities of users, vendors, and even the certification authorities themselves. Every party to a SET transaction, except the cardholder, is required to have a valid digital certificate issued by a certification authority.

Each nation (and within the US, each state) has their own certification authorities operating within the Public Key Infrastructure (PKI). In general, businesses will purchase certificates from public Certification Authorities (CAs) which must comply with rigid compliance and inspection procedures set forth in the SET Standards. An extensive list of international CAs can be found at <www.pki-page.org>.

There are three types of certificates available:

### CLASS 1 CERTIFICATES

These certificates, issued to individuals only, confirm that a user's name (or registered alias) and electronic mail address do not duplicate a combination of those two items already entered in the certification repository. Class 1 certificates are used modestly to enhance the security of Web browsing and personal electronic mail, but they do not offer any assurances as to a certificate holder's identity.

### CLASS 2 CERTIFICATES

This level certificate, currently issued to individuals only, is allocated only after the Certification Authority has checked an applicant's registration information against trusted third-party consumer information databases, like those used to check credit status. Class 2 certificates are typically used for electronic mail authentication, software validation, and on-line subscription services. Class 2 certificates are reasonable, but not foolproof, assurance of a subscriber's identity.

### CLASS 3 CERTIFICATES

These are high-assurance certificates issued to both individuals and organizations. For individuals to receive Class 3 certificates, they must physically appear before a Class 3 Local Registration Authority and present three forms of identification. Organizations may obtain Class 3 certificates by submitting incorporation documents and other similar public records. The Certification Authority verifies the information through independent call-backs to the organization and queries to third-party corporate or consumer credit databases.

The SET specification requires compatible software in the cardholder's (purchaser's) computer and in the seller's computer. In addition, the computer of the seller's bank must contain technology enabling it to decrypt the financial information, and the certification authority utilizes the same technology to issue the digital certificates. Note: While most of this technology is easily incorporated into existing network browsers and servers it is not universally permitted in the international markets.

### BANK CARDS, DEBIT CARDS AND SET

Since the development of the SET, the protocol has been spearheaded primarily by US, Japan and EU companies and has focused principally on bank card transactions. However, for electronic commerce to become truly international a secure method of conducting transactions must also be developed for traders in countries that are not as bank card centric as these three giants.

Of course, some countries are reluctant to allow their domestic firms access to the ease of SET processes even when the technology is available. Some governments limit e-commerce for political reasons (online information purchase) while others are still trying to come to grips with the tax ramifications of online transactions. Lastly, some nations wish to protect their domestic firms by limiting domestic access to overseas sellers.

## Adaptations of SET

SET is a vast international attempt to impose a single standard for international electronic commercial transactions and it has been widely adapted to a number of payment methods. Below are listed some common and not so common cyberpayment methods that have adapted SET processes:

### SMART CARDS

Just a few years ago only banks in Australia, Europe, and Japan were issuing "smart cards," which combine credit, debit, and stored value on a single card. Smart cards are micro-processor-equipped cards that work with card readers installed in the computers of consumers. These devices are now widely available, although the US market has limited usage of this technology.

The buyer slips the card in a reader (available on office PCs as well) and the transaction is secure and guaranteed, making Internet purchasing tremendously alluring to both businesses and consumers. A single smart card can carry many applications—it can function as a credit, debit, and/or ATM card, while at the same time store a cardholder's medical insurance information, frequent flyer mileage information, and other financial data.

The cardholder's information is accessed by a card acceptance device only if that terminal is programmed to read the card or if the cardholder has authorized access via use of a Personal Identification Number (PIN) or virtual "fingerprint." The security of a chip card is far greater than that of the once popular magnetic strip bank cards because use of the chip allows encryption of the vital information.

Most importantly, smart cards are already being used in international commerce to keep track of transportation records such as bills of lading. They are able to store all the payment information relating to an international trade transaction, thus enabling traders to quickly and effectively undertake secure payment arrangements.

### E-CASH

Most on-line transactions systems involve the debit of a customer's credit or debit account. This type of system works well, but giving away a credit card or bank account number can expose purchasers to unnecessary risk of theft when used in an unsecured medium like some nation-specific Internet gateways. Several companies have developed systems to allow transactions to be conducted entirely over the Internet. In order to be effective, these systems must be able to validate the transaction, provide for nonrepudiation by either party, and ensure at least some level of privacy for the parties to the transaction.

Electronic cash systems use digital signatures, which can be quickly verified with the entity that issued them to validate that the electronic currency represents actual value. A digital signature is a way to encrypt a message so that the recipient can decode it and be certain of the authenticity of the transaction. A measure of privacy can be added to the signature technology by utilizing a blind signature—digital signature with an additional number built-in and known only by the party owning it.

One of the biggest advantages of e-cash also draws much criticism. It offers the user complete anonymity, so the seller never knows who the buyer is—only that the buyer's e-cash is valid. On the other hand, since it is a cash-based system, buyers in countries that restrict capital outflow can more freely purchase goods and services from other countries without detection by the authorities.

Since this system is one of the most technologically simple, and coupled with the complete anonymity it offers, it is well-placed to take advantage of the great increases anticipated in electronic commerce over the next few years. A number of companies have developed systems to facilitate electronic commerce; each system offers some advantages and some disadvantages.

## Barriers to Electronic Payments

For all of its growth in the last few years, there are still some impediments on the super highway of electronic commerce. The Clearing House (www.theclearinghouse.org), an E-payments solutions firm, surveyed companies that use electronic payments to determine their attitudes to the process. The finding produced five main concerns:

### ADEQUATE INFORMATION

Most company representatives stated that lack of information with payments was a key barrier to be overcome, although they varied in the amount of information they need. Currently, one-seventh of all payments are accompanied by enough electronic remittance information for automated reconciliation. The survey also found that across the revenue segments, 65 percent of companies were "likely" to "certain" to adopt a service that integrated the remittance information with the payment.

#### BETTER TO RECEIVE THAN TO GIVE

Companies have shown they are more interested in receiving payments electronically than in sending them. This is partially due to the perceived loss of check float associated with making electronic payments. Since automated clearing house (ACH) transactions and bank wires settle within one or two days, funds are moved earlier than with checks, unless the terms of payments are renegotiated.

#### CASH FLOW TIMING

There is often an assumption that the electronic payment was a debit transaction initiated by their trading partner. Results show that while they do like using direct debits for collections, businesses do not like being debited by other companies as a form of payment. Instead, they prefer to control the timing and amount of payments. Direct debits are used primarily out of pressure from large customers or limited to well-established business partners, due to the lack of security and the difficulty in resolving issues.

#### SHOW ME YOUR'S FIRST

The beneficiary's bank and account number must be known in order to initiate electronic payments. Many companies said they were reluctant to give out their account numbers, which are required to initiate electronic payments. This points to an overriding security concern that many companies have with their accounts. The survey showed that 38 percent of large revenue companies had experienced unauthorized debits to their accounts in the past six months.

#### BACK OFFICE SOFTWARE

Another barrier is the lack of functionality and integration in cash management and accounting systems. Existing business software is not designed to easily send or receive payments, nor is it integrated with the payment systems in other parts of many companies.

## The Future of CyberPayments

While nobody is certain what the future will bring, we do know that the Internet recognizes no national borders. Electronic commerce is global in nature, so the Internet cannot help but to dramatically increase international trade. As trust and security issues are resolved—as they continue to be each day—companies around the world will add the software and hardware tools required to conduct their business on-line.

The ever-changing technology in electronic commerce and the introduction of new hardware, software, and service technologies forces market participants to quickly and readily adjust their basic business strategies. Companies who want to participate in the worldwide electronic commerce revolution must adapt their electronic commerce service capabilities and product offerings to the requirements of the electronic commerce marketplace, or rely on revenues from more traditional business services, hoping these continue to be profitable (or even exist in ten years).

There is an active movement under way to enable intermediaries such as banks and other financial institutions to underwrite electronic transactions by offering guarantees and recourse, much as they do with today's documentary letters of credit. The bill of lading, which is almost universally used in international sales transactions and operates as the document of title, has become a fully electronic document, although the digital version is not universally accepted. The Bolero project (www.bolero.net or www.boleroassociation.org/dow_docs.htm) has already allowed many global distribution firms to establish completely paperless transactions. Such innovation comes in the wake of United Nation's reports that the cost of using paper for all aspects of an international transaction exceeds US$420 billion per year.

One of the key issues that will determine the future for cyberpayments will be the rise or demise of fraud in electronic transactions. International trade using paper documents has seen many enormous acts of fraud over the centuries and has produced many cases (some in excess of US$1 billion) such as that involving RBG Resources of London. Two of the main components that served to deceive legitimate parties to the transaction were the destruction of documents and the time delay inherent in the use of paper-based transactions. Both attributes, common possibilities when using paper, are difficult if not impossible when electronic transactions are utilized. Certainly, no one is saying that cyberpayments are "fraud proof," but they are certainly a major step in the direction of fraud reduction. Technology to secure the "electronic signature" has made these advances in communications and fraud reduction possible.

CHAPTER 19

# Glossary

THE FOLLOWING TERMS are excerpted from the *Dictionary of International Trade*, also by World Trade Press. Note: the terms documentary credit, credit, and letter of credit are used interchangeably.

**ABOUT** In connection with letters of credit, "about" means a tolerance of plus/minus 10 percent regarding the documentary credit value, unit price or the quantity of the goods, depending on the context in which the tolerance is mentioned.

**ACCEPTANCE LETTER OF CREDIT** A letter of credit that, in addition to other required documents, requires presentation of a term draft drawn on the bank nominated as the accepting bank under the letter of credit.

**ACCEPTED DRAFT** A bill of exchange accepted by the drawee (acceptor) by putting his signature (acceptance) on its face. In doing so, he commits himself to pay the bill upon presentation at maturity.

**ACCEPTING BANK** A bank that by signing a time draft accepts responsibility to pay when the draft becomes due. In this case the bank is the drawee (party asked to pay the draft) but only becomes the acceptor (party accepting responsibility to pay) upon acceptance (signing the draft). See ACCEPTANCE; BILL OF EXCHANGE.

**ACCEPTOR** The party that signs a draft or obligation, thereby agreeing to pay the stated sum at maturity. See ACCEPTANCE; BILL OF EXCHANGE.

**ACCOUNT PARTY** The party that instructs a bank (issuing bank) to open a letter of credit. The account party is usually the buyer or importer. See LETTER OF CREDIT.

**ADVANCE AGAINST COLLECTION** A short term loan or credit extended to the seller (usually the exporter) by the seller's bank once a draft has been accepted by the buyer (generally the importer) of the seller's goods. Once the buyer pays, the loan is paid off. If the buyer does not pay the draft, the seller must still make good on the loan. See BILL OF EXCHANGE.

**ADVICE** (banking/letters of credit) The forwarding of a letter of credit, or an amendment to a letter of credit to the seller, or beneficiary of the credit, by the advising bank (typically the seller's bank).
The term "advice" connotes several types of forms used on the banking field. Generally speaking, an advice is a form of letter that relates or acknowledges a certain activity or result with regard to a customer's relations with a bank. Examples include credit advice, debit advice, advice of payment, and advice of execution. In commercial transactions, information on a business transaction such as shipment of goods.

**ADVICE OF FATE** A bank's notification of the status of a collection that is still outstanding.

**ADVISED CREDIT** A letter of credit whose terms and conditions have been forwarded by a bank. See ADVICE.

**ADVISING BANK** The bank (also referred to as the seller's or exporter's bank) that receives a letter of credit or amendment to a letter of credit from the issuing bank (the buyer's bank) and forwards it to the beneficiary (seller/exporter) of the credit.

**AFTER DATE** A notation used on financial instruments (such as drafts or bills of exchange) to fix the maturity date as a fixed

number of days past the date of drawing of the draft. For example, if a draft stipulates "60 days after date," it means that the draft is due (payable) 60 days after the date it was drawn. This has the effect of fixing the date of maturity of the draft, independent of the date of acceptance of the draft.
See ACCEPTANCE; BILL OF EXCHANGE.

AFTER SIGHT A notation on a draft that indicates that payment is due a fixed number of days after the draft has been presented to the drawee. For example, "30 days after sight" means that the drawee has 30 days from the date of presentation of the draft to make payment.
See ACCEPTANCE; BILL OF EXCHANGE.

AGENT BANK (1) A bank acting for a foreign bank. (2) A bank handling administration of a loan in a syndicated credit.

AIR WAYBILL (also airbill) (shipping) A shipping document used by airlines for air freight. It is a contract for carriage that includes conditions of carriage including such items as limits of liability and claims procedures. The air waybill also contains shipping instructions to airlines, a description of the commodity, and applicable transportation charges. Air waybills are used by many truckers as through documents for coordinated air/truck service.
Air waybills are not negotiable. The airline industry has adopted a standard formatted air waybill that accommodates both domestic and international traffic. The standard document was designed to enhance the application of modern computerized systems to air freight processing for both the carrier and the shipper. See BILL OF LADING; NEGOTIABLE.

ALL RISK (insurance) Extensive insurance coverage of cargo, including coverage due to external causes such as fire, collision, pilferage etc., but usually excluding "special" risks such as those resulting from acts of war, labor strikes, and the perishing of goods, and from internal damage due to faulty packaging, decay, or loss of market.

AMENDMENT (law/general) An addition, deletion or change in a legal document.
(banking/letters of credit) A change in the terms and conditions of a letter of credit (e.g., extension of the letter of credit's validity period, shipping deadline, etc.), usually to meet the needs of the seller. The seller requests an amendment of the buyer who, if he agrees, instructs his bank (the issuing bank) to issue the amendment. The issuing bank informs the seller's bank (the advising bank) who then notifies the seller of the amendment. In the case of irrevocable letters of credit, amendments may only be made with the agreement of all parties to the transaction.

APPROVAL BASIS (banking/letters of credit) If documents containing discrepancies are presented to the nominated bank under a letter of credit, the bank can forward the documents to the issuing bank for approval, with the beneficiary's agreement. Because of the risk of loss in transit and delays resulting in interest loss, however, it is recommended that the beneficiary first try to correct the documents; but, if that is not possible, the beneficiary asks the nominated bank to contact the issuing bank for authorization to accept the discrepancies.

APPROXIMATELY See ABOUT.

ARRIVAL NOTICE (shipping) A notice furnished to the consignee and shipping broker alerting them to the projected arrival of freight and its availability for pickup.

ASSIGNMENT (law/shipping/banking) The transfer of rights, title, interest, and benefits of a contract or financial instrument to a third party.
(banking/letters of credit) The beneficiary of a letter of credit is entitled to assign his/her claims to any of the proceeds that he/she may be entitled to, or portions thereof, to a third party. Usually the beneficiary informs the issuing or advising bank that his/her claims or particle claims under the letter of

credit were assigned and asks the bank to advise the assignee (third party) that it has acknowledged the assignment. The validity of the assignment is not dependent on bank approval. In contrast, the transfer requires the agreement of the nominated bank. An assignment is possible regardless of whether the letter of credit is transferable.

ASSIGNMENT OF PROCEEDS See ASSIGNMENT.

AT SIGHT Terms of a financial instrument that is payable upon presentation or demand. A bill of exchange may be made payable, for example, at sight or after sight, which (respectively) means it is payable upon presentation or demand or within a particular period after demand is made. See BILL OF EXCHANGE.

AVAILABILITY (banking/letters of credit) In letters of credit, refers to the availability of documents in exchange for payment of the amount stated in the letter of credit. Availability options are:
(1) By *sight payment*: payment on receipt of the documents by the issuing bank or the bank nominated in the letter of credit.
(2) By *deferred payment*: payment after a period specified in the letter of credit, often calculated as number of days after the date of presentation of the documents or after the shipping date.
(3) By *acceptance*: acceptance of a draft (to be presented together with other documents) by the issuing bank or by the bank nominated in the letter of credit, and the payment thereof at maturity.
(4) By *negotiation*: meaning the giving of value by the nominated bank to the beneficiary for the documents presented, subject to receipt of cover from the issuing bank. See LETTER OF CREDIT; BILL OF EXCHANGE; NEGOTIATION.

BACK-TO-BACK LETTER OF CREDIT A new letter of credit opened in favor of another beneficiary on the basis of an already existing, non-transferable letter of credit. For example, a British merchant agrees to buy cotton in Egypt for sale to a Belgian shirtmaker. The Belgian establishes a non-transferable letter of credit for payment to the British merchant who then uses the strength of the letter of credit as a security with his bank for opening a new letter of credit to finance payment to the Egyptian cotton producer or dealer.

BANK ACCEPTANCE A bill of exchange drawn on or accepted by a bank to pay specific bills for one of its customers when the bill becomes due. Depending on the bank's creditworthiness, the acceptance becomes a financial instrument that can be discounted for immediate payment. See BILL OF EXCHANGE.

BANK DRAFT A check drawn by one bank against funds deposited to its account in another bank.

BANKER'S BANK A bank that is established by mutual consent by independent and unaffiliated banks to provide a clearinghouse for financial transactions.

BANKER'S DRAFT A draft payable on demand and drawn by, or on behalf of, a bank upon itself. A banker's draft is considered cash and cannot be returned unpaid.

BANK RELEASE A document issued by a bank, after it has been paid or given an acceptance, giving authority to a person to take delivery of goods.

BEARER (general) The person in possession. (banking/finance/law/shipping) A person who possesses a bearer document and who is entitled to payment of funds or transfer of title to property on presentation of the document to the payee or transferor. A buyer, for example, who presents bearer documents of title (such as a bill of lading) to a shipper that transported the goods is entitled to receive the shipment. A seller who presents to a bank a negotiable instrument, such as a check, that is payable to the bearer is entitled to payment of the funds. See BEARER DOCUMENT; ENDORSEMENT.

BEARER DOCUMENT (banking/finance/law/shipping) A negotiable instrument, commercial paper, document of title, or security that is issued payable or transferable on demand to the individual who holds the instrument, or one that is endorsed in blank. A bearer document authorizes the payment of funds or the transfer of property to the bearer when the bearer presents the document to the person, such as a bank or a shipper, that is holding the funds or property. See BLANK ENDORSEMENT, BEARER; ENDORSEMENT.

BEARER INSTRUMENT
See BEARER DOCUMENT.

BENEFICIARY (banking/letter of credit) The individual or company in whose favor a letter of credit is opened.
(insurance) The person or legal entity named to receive the proceeds or benefits of an insurance policy.

BILL OF EXCHANGE An unconditional order in writing, signed by a person (drawer) such as a buyer, and addressed to another person (drawee), typically a bank, ordering the drawee to pay a stated sum of money to yet another person (payee), often a seller, on demand or at a fixed or determinable future time. The most common versions of a bill of exchange are:
(1) A draft, wherein the drawer instructs the drawee to pay a certain amount to a named person, usually in payment for the transfer of goods or services. Sight drafts are payable when presented. Time drafts (also called usance drafts) are payable at a future fixed (specific) date or determinable (30, 60, 90 days etc.) date. Time drafts are used as a financing tool (as with Documents against Acceptance, D/A terms) to give the buyer time to pay for the purchase.
(2) A promissory note, wherein the issuer promises to pay a certain amount.

BILL OF LADING (shipping) A document issued by a carrier to a shipper, signed by the captain, agent, or owner of a vessel, furnishing written evidence regarding receipt of the goods (cargo), the conditions on which transportation is made (contract of carriage), and the engagement to deliver goods at the prescribed port of destination to the lawful holder of the bill of lading. A bill of lading is, therefore, both a receipt for merchandise and a contract to deliver it as freight. There are a number of different types of bills of lading.
(1) A *straight bill of lading* indicates that the shipper will deliver the goods to the consignee. The document itself does not give title to the goods (non-negotiable). The consignee need only identify him- or herself to claim the goods. A straight bill of lading is often used when payment for the goods has been made in advance.
(2) A *shipper's order bill of lading* is a title document to the goods, issued "to the order of" a party, usually the shipper, whose endorsement is required to effect its negotiation. Because it is negotiable, a shipper's order bill of lading can be bought, sold, or traded while goods are in transit and is commonly used for letter-of-credit transactions. The buyer usually needs the original or a copy as proof of ownership to take possession of the goods.
(3) An *air waybill* is a form of bill of lading used for the air transport of goods and is not negotiable. See AIR WAYBILL for a fuller explanation.
(4) A *clean bill of lading* is a bill of lading where the carrier has noted that the merchandise has been received in apparent good condition (no apparent damage, loss, etc.) and which does not bear such notations as "Shipper's Load and Count," etc.
(5) A *claused bill of lading* is a bill of lading that contains notations which specify deficient condition(s) of the goods and/or packaging.

BLANK ENDORSEMENT (law/banking/shipping) The signature or endorsement of a person or firm on any negotiable instrument (such as a check, draft, or bill of lading), usually on the reverse of the document, without designating another person to whom the endorsement is made. The document therefore becomes bearer

paper. In shipping, for example, the holder of a blank endorsed bill of lading can take possession of the shipment.
See ENDORSEMENT; BEARER DOCUMENT.

CARRIAGE AND INSURANCE PAID TO . . . (CIP) See Chapter 6: Incoterms 2000 starting on page 24.

CARRIAGE PAID TO . . . (CPT) See Chapter 6: Incoterms 2000 starting on page 24.

CERTIFICATE OF ANALYSIS A document issued by a recognized organization or governmental authority confirming the quality and composition of goods listed in the certificate. Certificates of analysis are often required by authorities in importing countries for animal and plant products for consumption and for pharmaceuticals.
See CERTIFICATE OF INSPECTION; PHYTOSANITARY INSPECTION CERTIFICATE.

CERTIFICATE OF INSPECTION A document certifying that merchandise (such as perishable goods) was in good condition at the time of inspection, usually immediately prior to shipment. Preshipment inspection is a requirement for importation of goods into many developing countries. Often used interchangeably with certificate of analysis. See PHYTOSANITARY INSPECTION CERTIFICATE; CERTIFICATE OF ANALYSIS.

CERTIFICATE OF INSURANCE See INSURANCE CERTIFICATE.

CERTIFICATE OF MANUFACTURE A document (often notarized) in which a producer of goods certifies that the manufacturing has been completed and the goods are now at the disposal of the buyer.

CERTIFICATE OF ORIGIN (customs) A document attesting to the country of origin of goods. A certificate of origin is often required by the customs authorities of a country as part of the entry process. Such certificates are usually obtained through an official or quasiofficial organization in the country of origin such as a consular office or local chamber of commerce. A certificate of origin may be required even though the commercial invoice contains the information.

CERTIFICATE OF ORIGIN FORM A A document required by the customs authority in developed countries to prove eligibility of merchandise under duty-free import programs such as the Generalized System of Preferences (GSP) and the Caribbean Basin Initiative.

CERTIFICATE OF WEIGHT (shipping) A document stating the weight of a shipment.

CERTIFICATION (LEGALIZATION) Official certification of the authenticity of signatures or documents in connection with letter of credits, such as certificates or origin, commercial invoices, etc. by chambers of commerce, consulates, and similar recognized government authorities.

CLAUSED BILL OF LADING (shipping) Notations on bills of lading that specify deficient condition(s) of the goods and/or the packaging.

CLEAN BILL OF EXCHANGE A bill of exchange having no other documents, such as a bill of lading affixed to it.

CLEAN BILL OF LADING (shipping) A bill of lading receipted by the carrier for goods received in "apparent good order and condition," without damages or other irregularities, and without the notation "Shippers Load and Count."

CLEAN COLLECTION A collection in which the demand for payment (such as a draft) is presented without additional documents. See BILL OF EXCHANGE.

CLEAN DRAFT A sight or time draft that has no other documents attached to it. This is to be distinguished from documentary draft. See BILL OF EXCHANGE.

CLEAN LETTER OF CREDIT A letter of credit against which the beneficiary of the credit may draw a bill of exchange without presentation of documents.

CLEAN ON BOARD BILL OF LADING (shipping) A document evidencing cargo laden aboard a vessel with no exceptions as to cargo condition or quantity.

COLLECTING BANK The bank that acts as agent for the seller and seller's bank in collecting payment or a time draft from the buyer to be forwarded to the remitting bank (usually the seller's bank).

COLLECTION (general) The presentation for payment of an obligation and the payment thereof. The receipt of money for presentation of a draft or check for payment at the bank on which it was drawn or presentation of any item for deposit at the place at which it is payable.

COLLECTION ENDORSEMENT See ENDORSEMENT.

COLLECTION PAPERS All documents (invoices, bills of lading, etc.) submitted to a buyer for the purpose of receiving payment for a shipment. See DOCUMENTARY COLLECTION.

COMBINED BILL OF LADING (shipping) A bill of lading covering a shipment of goods by more than one mode of transportation.

COMBINED TRANSPORT (shipping) Consignment (shipment) sent by means of various modes of transport, such as by rail and by ocean.

COMBINED TRANSPORT BILL OF LADING (shipping) A bill of lading covering a shipment of goods by more than one mode of transportation.

COMMERCIAL INVOICE (general) A document identifying the seller and buyer of goods or services, identifying numbers such as invoice number, date, shipping date, mode of transport, delivery and payment terms, and a complete listing and description of the goods or services being sold including quantities, prices, and discounts.

(customs) A commercial invoice is often used by governments to determine the true transaction value of goods for the assessment of customs duties and also to prepare consular documentation. Governments using the commercial invoice to control imports often specify its form, content, number of copies, language to be used, and other characteristics.

CONFIRMED LETTER OF CREDIT A letter of credit that contains a guarantee on the part of both the issuing and advising banks of payment to the seller so long as the terms and conditions of the letter of credit are satisfied.

Confirmation is only added to irrevocable letters of credit, usually available with the advising bank. If confirmation of the letter of credit is desired, the applicant must state this expressly in his/her letter of credit application. The confirming bank assumes the credit risk of the issuing bank as well as the political and transfer risks of the purchaser's country.

If a letter of credit does not contain a confirmation request by the issuing bank, in certain circumstances the possibility exists of confirming the letter of credit "by silent confirmation," i.e., without the issuing bank's knowledge.

Without confirmation of the letter of credit, the advising bank will forward the letter of credit to the beneficiary without taking on its own commitment.

CONSIGNEE (shipping) The person or firm named in a freight contract to whom goods have been shipped or turned over for care.

CONSIGNEE MARKS (shipping) A symbol placed on packages for export, generally consisting of a square, triangle, diamond, circle, cross, etc., with designed letters and/or numbers for the purpose of identification.

CONSIGNMENT (shipping) Shipment of one or more pieces of property, accepted by a carrier for one shipper at one time, receipted for in one lot, and moving on one bill of lading.

(commerce) Delivery of merchandise from an exporter (the consignor) to an agent (the consignee) under agreement that the agent sell the merchandise for the account of the exporter. The consignor retains title to the goods until sold. The consignee sells the goods for commission and remits the net proceeds to the consignor.

CONSOLIDATOR'S BILL OF LADING (shipping) A bill of lading issued by a consolidating freight forwarder to a shipper.

CONSULAR INVOICE (customs) An invoice covering a shipment of goods certified (usually in triplicate) by the consul of the country for which the merchandise is destined. This invoice is used by customs officials of the country of entry to verify the value, quantity, country of origin, and nature of the merchandise imported. See COMMERCIAL INVOICE.

COST AND FREIGHT . . . (CFR) See Chapter 6: Incoterms 2000 starting on page 24.

COST, INSURANCE, FREIGHT...(CIF) See Chapter 6: Incoterms 2000 starting on page 24.

DEFERRED PAYMENT LETTER OF CREDIT A letter of credit that enables the buyer to take possession of the title documents (and therefore delivery of the goods) by agreeing to pay the issuing bank at a fixed time in the future. This credit gives the buyer a grace period for payment.

DELIVERED AT FRONTIER. . . (DAF) See Chapter 6: Incoterms 2000 starting on page 24.

DELIVERED DUTY PAID. . . (DDP) See Chapter 6: Incoterms 2000 starting on page 24.

DELIVERED DUTY UNPAID. . . (DDU) See Chapter 6: Incoterms 2000 starting on page 24.

DELIVERED EX QUAY (DUTY PAID)... (DEQ) (duty paid) See Chapter 6: Incoterms 2000 starting on page 24.

DELIVERED EX SHIP . . . (DES) See Chapter 6: Incoterms 2000 starting on page 24.

DISCREPANCIES (banking/letters of credit) The noncompliance of documents with the terms and conditions of a letter of credit. Information (or missing information or missing documents/papers, etc.) in the documents submitted under a letter of credit, that: (1) is not consistent with its terms and conditions; (2) is inconsistent with other documents submitted; (3) does not meet the requirements of the Uniform Customs and Practice for Documentary Credits (UCPDC), Brochure No. 500, 1993 revision.

If the documents show discrepancies of any kind, the issuing bank is no longer obliged to pay and, in the case of a confirmed letter of credit, neither is the confirming bank (strict documentary compliance).

DOCUMENTARY COLLECTION A method of effecting payment for goods whereby the seller/exporter ships goods to the buyer, but instructs his bank to collect a certain sum from the buyer/importer in exchange for the transfer of title, shipping, and other documentation enabling the buyer/importer to take possession of the goods. The two types of documentary collection are:

(1) Documents against Payment (D/P) where the bank releases the documents to the buyer/importer only against a cash payment in a prescribed currency; and

(2) Documents against Acceptance (D/A) where the bank releases the documents to the buyer/importer against acceptance of a bill of exchange (draft) guaranteeing payment at a later date.

In documentary collections, banks act in a fiduciary capacity and make every effort to ensure that payment is received but are liable only for the correct execution of the collection instructions and do not make any commitment to pay the seller/exporter themselves.

Documentary collections are subject to the Uniform Rules of Collections, Brochure No. 322, revised 1978, of the International Chamber of Commerce (ICC) in Paris. See UNIFORM RULES FOR COLLECTIONS; INTERNATIONAL CHAMBER OF COMMERCE.

DOCUMENTARY CREDIT The formal term for letter of credit.

DOCUMENTARY LETTER OF CREDIT See DOCUMENTARY CREDIT.

DOCUMENTARY INSTRUCTIONS The formal list and description of documents (primarily shipping documents) a buyer requires of the seller, especially in a documentary letter of credit.

DOCUMENTATION (general) All or any of the financial and commercial documents relating to a transaction. Documents in an international trade transaction may include: commercial invoice, consular invoice, customs invoice, certificate of origin, bill of lading, inspection certificates, bills of exchange and others.
(banking/documentary credits or collections) The documents required for a letter of credit or documentary collection (documents against payment or documents against acceptance) transaction.
(customs) The documents required by the customs authority of a country to effect entry of merchandise into the country.
(shipping) The function of receiving, matching, reviewing, and preparing all the paperwork necessary to effect the shipment of cargo. This includes bills of lading, dock receipts, export declarations, manifests, etc.

DOCUMENTS AGAINST ACCEPTANCE (D/A) See DOCUMENTARY COLLECTION.

DOCUMENTS AGAINST PAYMENT (D/P) See DOCUMENTARY COLLECTION.

DRAFT See BILL OF EXCHANGE.

ENDORSEMENT (banking/law) (In UK, indorsement) The act of a person who is the holder of a negotiable instrument in signing his or her name on the back of that instrument, thereby transferring title or ownership. An endorsement may be made in favor of another individual or legal entity, resulting in a transfer of the property to that other individual or legal entity.
(1) A *blank endorsement* is the writing of only the endorser's name on the negotiable instrument without designating another person to whom the endorsement is made, and with the implied understanding that the instrument is payable to the bearer.
(2) A *collection endorsement* is one that restricts payment of the endorsed instrument to purposes of deposit or collection.
(3) A *conditional endorsement* is one that limits the time at which the instrument can be paid or further transferred or that requires the occurrence of an event before the instrument is payable.
(4) A *restrictive endorsement* is one that directs a specific payment of the instrument, such as for deposit or collection only, and that precludes any other transfer.

EX . . . (NAMED POINT OF ORIGIN) (trade term) A term of sale where the price quoted applies only at the point of origin and the seller agrees to place the goods at the disposal of the buyer at the specified place on the date or within the period fixed. All other charges are for the account of the buyer. See EX WORKS. See also Chapter 6: Incoterms 2000 starting on page 24.

EXCHANGE CONTROL(S) (foreign exchange) The rationing of foreign currencies, bank drafts, and other monetary instruments for settling international financial obligations by countries seeking to ameliorate acute balance of payments difficulties. When such measures are imposed, importers must apply for prior authorization from the government to obtain the foreign currency required to bring in designated amounts and types of goods. Since such measures have the effect of restricting imports, they are considered non-tariff barriers to trade.

EXCHANGE RATE (foreign exchange) The price of one currency expressed in terms of another, i.e., the number of units of one currency that may be exchanged for one unit of another currency. For example, \$/SwF = 1.50, means that one US dollar costs 1.50 Swiss francs.
(1) In a system of free exchange rates, the actual exchange rate is determined by supply and demand on the foreign exchange market.
(2) In a system of fixed exchange rates, the

exchange rate is tied to a reference (e.g., gold, US dollars, Japanese yen, etc.). Influences on exchange rates include differences between interest rates and other asset yields between countries, investor expectations about future changes in a currency's value, investors' views on the overall quantity of assets in circulation, arbitrage, and central bank exchange rate support.

EX FACTORY (trade term) A term of sale where the buyer takes title to the goods when they leave the vendor's dock. See EX WORKS. See also Chapter 6: Incoterms 2000 starting on page 24.

EXPIRATION DATE In letter of credit transactions, the final date the seller (beneficiary of the credit) may present documents and draw a draft under the terms of the letter of credit. Also called expiry date. See LETTER OF CREDIT.

EX WAREHOUSE See Chapter 6: Incoterms 2000 starting on page 24.

EX WORKS . . . (NAMED PLACE) See Chapter 6: Incoterms 2000 starting on page 24.

FINANCIAL INSTRUMENT (banking/finance) A document that has monetary value or is evidence of a financial transaction. Examples of financial instruments are: checks, bonds, stock certificates, bills of exchange, promissory notes, and bills of lading.

FOB (trade term) An abbreviation used in some international sales contracts, when imports are valued at a designated point, as agreed between buyer and seller, that is considered "Free on Board." In such contracts, the seller is obligated to have the goods packaged and ready for shipment from the agreed point, whether his own place of business or some intermediate point, and the buyer normally assumes the burden of all inland transportation costs and risks in the exporting country, as well as all subsequent transportation costs, including the costs of loading the merchandise on the vessel. However, if the contract stipulates "FOB vessel" the seller bears all transportation costs to the vessel named by the buyer, as well as the costs of loading the goods on to that vessel. The same principle applies to the abbreviations "FOR" (free on rail) and "FOT" (free on truck). See Chapter 6: Incoterms 2000 starting on page 24.

FOREIGN BILLS Bills of exchange or drafts drawn on a foreign party and denominated in foreign currency. See BILL OF EXCHANGE.

FOREIGN EXCHANGE (banking/foreign exchange) Current or liquid claims payable in foreign currency and in a foreign country (bank balances, checks, bills of exchange). Not to be confused with foreign bank notes and coin, which are not included in this definition.

FOREIGN EXCHANGE MARKET (foreign exchange) (1) The worldwide system of contacts, either by telephone, teleprinter or in writing, that take place between non-bank foreign exchange dealers and foreign exchange traders at banks as well as foreign exchange traders amongst themselves, where the monies of different countries are bought and sold.
(2) Wherever foreign exchange rates are determined.

FOREIGN EXCHANGE RATE (foreign exchange) The price of one currency in terms of another.

FORWARD FOREIGN EXCHANGE (foreign exchange) An agreement to purchase foreign exchange (currency) at a future date at a predetermined rate of exchange. Forward foreign exchange contracts are often purchased by international buyers of goods who wish to hedge against foreign exchange fluctuations between the time the contract is negotiated and the time payment is to be made.

FORWARD MARKET (foreign exchange) The market for the purchase and sale of forward foreign exchange. Forward dates are usually one, three, six or twelve months in the future. See FORWARD FOREIGN EXCHANGE.

FORWARD OPERATIONS (foreign exchange) Foreign exchange transactions, on which the fulfillment of the mutual delivery obligations is made on a date later than the second business day after the transaction was concluded.

FORWARD RATE (foreign exchange) A contractually agreed upon exchange rate for a forward foreign exchange contract.

FORWARD RATE AGREEMENTS (FRA) (Also known as future rate agreements) An agreement whereby two counterparties hedge themselves against future interest rate changes by agreeing upon an interest rate for a future period within a specific currency segment, which is valid for a predetermined amount. In contrast to futures, FRA's are not standardized and are not traded on exchanges but are used in interbank trading.

FOT See FREE ON RAIL; FREE ON TRUCK; see also Chapter 6: Incoterms 2000 starting on page 24.

FREE ALONGSIDE SHIP . . . (FAS) See Chapter 6: Incoterms 2000 starting on page 24.

FREE CARRIER . . . (NAMED PLACE) (FCA) See Chapter 6: Incoterms 2000 starting on page 24.

FREELY NEGOTIABLE When a letter of credit is stated as "freely negotiable," the beneficiary of the letter of credit has the right to present his documents at a bank of his choice for negotiation.

FREE ON BOARD (FOB) See FREE CARRIER; see also Chapter 6: Incoterms 2000 starting on page 24.

FREE ON RAIL; FREE ON TRUCK (FOR/FOT) (trade terms) These terms are synonymous, since the word "truck" relates to the railway wagons. The terms should only be used when the goods are to be carried by rail. See FREE CARRIER; see also Chapter 6: Incoterms 2000 starting on page 24.

HEDGE A type of economic insurance used by dealers in commodities, foreign exchange, securities, manufacturers, and other producers to prevent loss due to price fluctuations. Hedging consists of counterbalancing a present sale or purchase by a purchase or sale of a similar or different commodity, usually for delivery at some future date. The desired result is that the profit or loss on a current sale or purchase be offset by the loss or profit on the future purchase or sale.

HOUSE AIR WAYBILL (HAWB) (shipping) A bill of lading issued by a freight forwarder for consolidated air freight shipments. In documentary letter of credit transactions HAWBs are treated exactly the same as conventional air waybills, provided they indicate that the issuer itself assumes the liability as carrier or is acting as the agent of a named carrier, or if the credit expressly permits the acceptance of a HAWB. See AIR WAYBILL; BILL OF LADING.

INCOTERMS 2000 A codification of international rules for the uniform interpretation of common contract clauses in export/import transactions. Developed and issued by the International Chamber of Commerce (ICC) in Paris. The version which is currently valid is Publication No. 560 from 2000. The thirteen Incoterms 2000 are:
(1) Ex Works (EXW),
(2) Free Carrier (FCA),
(3) Free Alongside Ship (FAS),
(4) Free On Board (FOB),
(5) Cost and Freight (CFR),
(6) Cost, Insurance and Freight (CIF),
(7) Carriage Paid To (CPT),
(8) Carriage and Insurance Paid To (CIP),
(9) Delivered At Frontier (DAF),
(10) Delivered Ex Ship (DES),
(11) Delivered Ex Quay (DEQ),
(12) Delivered Duty Unpaid (DDU), and
(13) Delivered Duty Paid (DDP).
See Chapter 6: Incoterms 2000 starting on page 24. For a book fully describing responsibilities of the seller and the buyer in

each term, contact: ICC Publishing, Inc., 156 Fifth Avenue, New York, NY 10010; Tel: (212) 206-1150; Fax: (212) 633-6025 or the International Chamber of Commerce (ICC), 38, Cours Albert 1er, 75008 Paris, France; Tel: [33] (1) 49-53-28-28; Fax: [33] (1) 49-53-29-42.

INSPECTION CERTIFICATE A document confirming that goods have been inspected for conformity to a set of industry, customer, government, or carrier specifications prior to shipment. Inspection certificates are generally obtained from independent, neutral testing organizations.

INSURANCE CERTIFICATE (insurance) A document indicating the type and amount of insurance coverage in force on a particular shipment. Used to assure the consignee that insurance is provided to cover potential loss of, or damage to, the cargo while in transit.

In some cases a shipper may issue a document that certifies that a shipment has been insured under a given open policy and that the certificate represents and takes the place of such open policy, the provisions of which are controlling.

Because of the objections that an instrument of this kind did not constitute a "policy" within the requirements of letters of credit, it has become the practice to use a special marine policy. A special marine policy makes no reference to an open policy and stands on its own as an obligation of the underwriting company.

INSURANCE DOCUMENT See INSURANCE CERTIFICATE.

INSURANCE POLICY (insurance) Broadly, the entire written contract of insurance. More specifically, the basic written or printed document, as well as the coverage forms and endorsement added to it.

INSURANCE PREMIUM (insurance) The amount paid to an insurance company for coverage under an insurance policy.

INSURED (insurance) The person(s) protected under an insurance contract (policy).

INSURED VALUE (insurance) The combined value of merchandise, inland freight, ocean freight, cost of packaging, freight forwarding charges, consular fees, and insurance cost for which insurance is obtained.

INSURER (insurance) The party to the insurance contract who promises to indemnify losses or provide service; the insurance company.

INTERNATIONAL CHAMBER OF COMMERCE (ICC) A nongovernmental organization serving as a policy advocate for world business. Members in 110 countries comprise tens of thousands of companies and business organizations. The ICC aims to facilitate world trade, investment, and an international free market economy through consultation with other intergovernmental organizations.

The ICC was founded in Atlantic City (USA) in 1919. It now encompasses associations and companies from all branches of industry. As an institution of international economic self-administration, it operates through expert commissions, subcommittees, and working groups to address questions that are of importance for the international business community. These include, for example, contract and delivery clauses (Incoterms); standardization of means of payment, (Uniform Rules for Collection, Uniform Customs and Practice for Documentary Credits, Uniform Rules for Demand Guarantees); arbitral jurisdiction (Rules of Conciliation and Arbitration); questions relating to such issues as competition, foreign investments, and transportation.

The ICC also offers various services to the business community such as the ATA Carnet system. The ICC publishes many books and references that are valuable to the international trade community. Address: International Chamber of Commerce, 38 Cours Albert 1er, 75008 Paris, France; Tel: [33] (1) 49-53-28-28; Fax: [33] (1) 49-53-29-42. For US representative, contact: US Council for International Business, 1212

Avenue of the Americas, New York, NY 10036; Tel: (212) 354-4480, or, for ICC publications in the United States contact ICC Publishing, Inc., 156 Fifth Avenue, New York, NY 10010; Tel: [1] (212) 206-1150; Fax: [1] (212) 633-6025. Refer to Chapter 20: Resources for a list of ICC publications.

INVOICE A document identifying the seller and buyer of goods or services, identifying numbers such as invoice number, date, shipping date, mode of transport, delivery and payment terms, and a complete listing and description of the goods or services being sold including quantities, prices, and discounts. See COMMERCIAL INVOICE.

IRREVOCABLE LETTER OF CREDIT A letter of credit that cannot be amended or canceled without prior mutual consent of all parties to the credit. Such a letter of credit guarantees payment by the bank to the seller/exporter (beneficiary) provided the beneficiary complies with all stipulated conditions. This credit cannot be changed or canceled without the consent of both the buyer and the seller. As a result, this type of credit is the most widely used in international trade. Irrevocable credits are more expensive because of the issuing bank's added liability in guaranteeing the credit. There are two types of irrevocable credits:

(1) The *irrevocable credit not confirmed* (unconfirmed credit). This means that the buyer's bank that issues the credit is the only party responsible for payment to the supplier, and the supplier's bank is obliged to pay the supplier only after receiving payment from the buyer's bank. The supplier's bank merely acts on behalf of the issuing bank and therefore incurs no risk.

(2) The *irrevocable, confirmed credit*. In a confirmed credit, the advising bank adds its guarantee to pay the supplier to that of the issuing bank. If the issuing bank fails to make payment, the advising bank will pay. If a supplier is unfamiliar with the buyer's bank that issues the letter of credit, he may insist on an irrevocable confirmed credit. These credits may be used when trade is conducted in a high-risk area where there are fears of outbreak of war or social, political, or financial instability. Confirmed credits may also be used by the supplier to enlist the aid of a local bank to extend financing to enable him to fill the order. A confirmed credit costs more because the bank has added liability.

Documentary letters of credit issued subject to the Uniform Customs and Practice for Documentary Credits (UCPDC) Publication No. 500 are deemed to be irrevocable unless expressly marked as revocable.

ISSUANCE The establishment of a letter of credit by the issuing bank (buyer's bank) based on the buyer's application and credit relationship with the bank.

ISSUANCE DATE OF THE DOCUMENTS (shipping) Unless otherwise stipulated in a transport document, the date of issuance is deemed to be the date of shipment or loading on board of the goods.

Unless prohibited by the documentary letter of credit, documents bearing a date of issuance prior to that of the letter of credit are acceptable.

ISSUING BANK The buyer's bank that opens a letter of credit at the request of the buyer, in favor of the beneficiary (seller/exporter). Also called the buyer's bank or the opening bank. See also ADVISING BANK; NEGOTIATING BANK.

LETTER OF CREDIT Formal term: documentary credit or documentary letter of credit.

A letter of credit is a document issued by a bank stating its commitment to pay someone (supplier/exporter/seller) a stated amount of money on behalf of a buyer (importer) so long as the seller meets the specific terms and conditions of the credit. Letters of credit are more formally called documentary letters of credit because the banks handling the transaction deal in documents as opposed to goods.

The terms and conditions listed in the credit all involve presentation of specific documents within a stated period of time, hence the formal name—documentary credits.

The documents the buyer requires in the credit may vary, but at a minimum include an invoice and a bill of lading. Other documents the buyer may specify are certificate of origin, consular invoice, insurance certificate, inspection certificate, and others.

Letters of credit are the most common method of making international payments, because the risks of the transaction are shared by both the buyer and the supplier. Documentary letters of credit are subject to the Uniform Customs and Practice for Documentary Credits (UCPDC), Brochure No. 500, of the International Chamber of Commerce (ICC) in Paris. See UNIFORM CUSTOMS AND PRACTICE.

NEGOTIABLE BILL OF LADING (shipping) A bill of lading transferable by endorsement. There are three possibilities: (1) to XY & Co. or their order; (2) to the order of XY & Co.; and (3) to order, without the name of the party. In the latter case the bill remains to the order of the shipper until he endorses it.

These types of bills of lading are usually endorsed on the reverse. The opposite of a negotiable bill of lading is the straight bill of lading See BILL OF LADING; ENDORSEMENT.

NEGOTIABLE INSTRUMENT (law/banking/shipping) A written document (instrument) that can be transferred merely by endorsement (signing) or delivery. Checks, bills of exchange, bills of lading, and warehouse receipts (if marked negotiable), and promissory notes are examples of negotiable instruments.

(USA) The Uniform Negotiable Instruments Act states: "An instrument, to be negotiable, must conform to the following requirements: (1) it must be in writing and signed by the maker or drawer; (2) it must contain an unconditional promise or order to pay a certain sum in money; (3) it must be payable on demand, or at a fixed or determinable future time; (4) it must be payable to order or to bearer; and (5) where the instrument is addressed to a drawee, he must be named or otherwise indicated therein with reasonable certainty."

NEGOTIATING BANK In a letter of credit transaction, the bank (generally the seller's or exporter's bank), that receives documentation from the exporter after he has shipped goods, examines the documents for adherence to the terms and conditions of the letter of credit, and forwards them to the issuing bank (the buyer's or importer's bank). Depending upon the type of letter of credit, the negotiating bank will either credit or pay the exporter immediately under the terms of the letter of credit or credit or pay the exporter once it has received payment from the issuing bank. See ADVISING BANK; ISSUING BANK.

NEGOTIATION (1) The action by which a negotiable instrument is circulated (bought and sold) from one holder to another. (2) In letter of credit transactions, the examination of seller's documentation by the bank to determine if they comply with the terms and conditions of the letter of credit.

NEGOTIATION CREDIT A documentary letter of credit available by negotiation.

NON-NEGOTIABLE (law) Not transferable from one person to another. Usually refers to the transferability of a title document (e.g., non-negotiable bill of lading). Possession of a non-negotiable title document alone does not entitle the holder to receive the goods named therein (e.g., non-negotiable sea waybill, air waybill, forwarder's receipt, etc.). See NEGOTIABLE; NEGOTIABLE INSTRUMENT.

OCEAN BILL OF LADING A receipt for cargo and a contract for transportation between a shipper and the ocean carrier. It may also be used as an instrument of ownership (negotiable bill of lading) that

can be bought, sold, or traded while the goods are in transit. To be used in this manner, it must be a negotiable "order" bill of lading.
(1) A *clean bill of lading* is issued when the shipment is received in good order. If damaged or a shortage is noted, a clean bill of lading will not be issued.
(2) An *on board bill of lading* certifies that the cargo has been placed aboard the named vessel and is signed by the master of the vessel or his representative. In letter of credit transactions, an on board bill of lading is usually necessary for the shipper to obtain payment from the bank. (When all bills of lading are processed, a ship's manifest is prepared by the steamship line. This summarizes all cargo aboard the vessel by port of loading and discharge.)
(3) An *inland bill of lading* (a waybill on rail or the "pro forma" bill of lading in trucking) is used to document the transportation of goods between the port and the point of origin or destination. It should contain information such as marks, numbers, steamship line, and similar information to match with a dock receipt. See also BILL OF LADING.

ORIGINAL DOCUMENTS (banking/letters of credit) Unless otherwise stated in the letter of credit, the requirement for an original document may also be satisfied by the presentation of documents produced or appearing to have been produced:
(1) reprographically,
(2) by automated or computerized systems, or
(3) as carbon copies,
and marked as "originals" and where necessary appearing to be signed.

PACKING LIST A document prepared by the shipper listing the kinds and quantities of merchandise in a particular shipment. A copy is usually sent to the consignee to assist in checking the shipment when received. Also referred to as a bill of parcels.

PARTIES TO THE CREDIT (banking/letters of credit) At least the following three parties are involved in a documentary letter of credit transaction:
(1) Applicant (buyer/importer),
(2) Issuing bank (buyer's bank), and
(3) Beneficiary (seller/exporter).
As a rule, however, the issuing bank will entrust a correspondent bank with the task of advising and authenticating the credit and, if applicable, with payment, acceptance, or negotiation. The issuing bank may also request the advising bank to add its confirmation. See LETTER OF CREDIT.

PAYEE The person or organization to whom a check or draft or note is made payable. The payee's name follows the expression "pay to the order of." See also PAYER; NEGOTIABLE; NEGOTIABLE INSTRUMENT.

PAYER The party primarily responsible for the payment of the amount owed as evidenced by a given negotiable instrument. See also PAYEE.

PHYTOSANITARY INSPECTION CERTIFICATE A certificate, issued by the government authority of an exporting nation to satisfy import regulations of foreign countries, indicating that an export shipment has been inspected and is free from harmful pests and plant diseases.

PRINCIPAL In a documentary collection, an alternate name given to the seller who forwards documents to the buyer through banks. Also called remitter. See DOCUMENTARY COLLECTION.

PRO FORMA INVOICE An invoice provided by a supplier prior to a sale or shipment of merchandise, informing the buyer of the kinds and quantities of goods to be sent, their value, and important specifications (weight, size, and similar characteristics). A pro forma invoice is used: (1) as a preliminary invoice together with a quotation; (2) for customs purposes in connection with shipments of samples, advertising material, etc.

RAIL WAYBILL Freight document that indicates goods have been received for shipment by rail. A duplicate is given to the shipper as a receipt for acceptance of the goods (also called duplicate waybill). See BILL OF LADING.

RED CLAUSE (LETTER OF CREDIT) A special clause included in a documentary letter of credit that allows the seller to obtain an advance on an unsecured basis from the correspondent bank to finance the manufacture or purchase of goods to be delivered under the documentary letter of credit. Liability is assumed by the issuing bank rather than the corresponding bank. It is called red clause because red ink used to be used to draw attention to the clause. The credit may be advanced in part or in full, and the buyer's bank finances the advance payment. The buyer, in essence, extends financing to the seller and incurs ultimate risk for all advanced credits. See LETTER OF CREDIT.

REIMBURSING BANK The bank named in a documentary letter of credit from which the paying, accepting, or negotiating bank may request cover after receipt of the documents in compliance with the documentary credit. The reimbursing bank is often, but not always, the issuing bank. If the reimbursing bank is not the issuing bank, it does not have a commitment to pay unless it has confirmed the reimbursement instruction. The issuing bank is not released from its commitment to pay through the nomination of a reimbursing bank. If cover from the reimbursing bank should not arrive in time, the issuing bank is obliged to pay (including any accrued interest on arrears).

REMITTANCE Funds forwarded from one person to another as payment for bought items or services purchased.

REMITTANCE FOLLOWING COLLECTION (shipping) In instances when the shipper has performed services incident to the transportation of goods, a carrier will collect payment for these services from the receiver and remit such payment to the shipper. Carriers charge nominal fees for this service.

REMITTER In a documentary collection, an alternate name given to the seller who forwards documents to the buyer through banks. See DOCUMENTARY COLLECTION.

REMITTING Paying, as in remitting a payment; also canceling, as in remitting a debt.

REMITTING BANK In a documentary collection, a bank that acts as an intermediary, forwarding the remitter's documents to, and payments from the collecting bank.

RESTRICTED LETTER OF CREDIT A letter of credit, the negotiation of which is restricted to a bank specially mentioned.

REVOCABLE LETTER OF CREDIT A letter of credit which can be canceled or altered by the drawee (buyer) after it has been issued by the drawee's bank. Due to the low level of security of this type of credit, they are extremely rare in practice.
This credit can be changed or canceled by the buyer without prior notice to the supplier. Because it offers little security to the buyer, revocable credits are generally unacceptable to the buyer and are rarely used.

REVOLVING LETTER OF CREDIT A letter of credit that is automatically restored to its full amount (value) after the completion of each documentary exchange.
The number of utilizations and the period of time within which these must take place are specified in the letter of credit. The revolving letter of credit is used when a purchaser wishes to have certain partial quantities of the ordered goods delivered at specified intervals (multiple delivery contract) and when multiple documents are presented for this purpose.
This credit is a commitment on the part of the issuing bank to restore the credit to the original amount after it has been used or drawn down. The number of times it can be utilized and the period of validity is stated in the credit. The credit can be

cumulative or noncumulative. Cumulative means that unutilized sums can be added to the next installment, whereas noncumulative means that partial amounts not utilized in time expire.

ROLLOVER CREDIT Any line of credit that can be borrowed against up to a stated credit limit and into which repayments go for crediting.

SEA WAYBILL A non-negotiable transport document for carriage of goods by sea. The sea waybill indicates the "on board" loading of the goods and can be used in cases where no ocean bill of lading, (i.e., no document of title) is required. For receipt of the goods, presentation of the sea waybill by the consignee named therein is not required, which can speed up processing at the port of destination.

SHIPMENT Except as otherwise provided, cargo tendered by one shipper, on one bill of lading, from one point of departure, for one consignee, to one destination, at one time, via a single port of discharge.

SIGHT DRAFT A financial instrument payable upon presentation or demand. A bill of exchange may be made payable, for example, at sight or after sight, which means it is payable upon presentation or demand, or within a particular period after demand is made. See BILL OF EXCHANGE.

SPOT CASH Immediate cash payment in a transaction, as opposed to payment at some future time.

SPOT EXCHANGE (foreign exchange) The purchase and sale of foreign exchange for delivery and payment at the time of the transaction.

SPOT EXCHANGE RATE (foreign exchange) The price of one currency expressed in terms of another currency at a given moment in time.

SPOT MARKET (foreign exchange) The market (or exchange) for a commodity or foreign exchange available for immediate delivery (usually one or two days after the transaction date).

STANDBY LETTER OF CREDIT This credit is primarily a payment or performance guarantee. It is used primarily in the United States because US banks are prevented by law from giving certain guarantees. Standby credits are often called nonperforming letters of credit because they are only used as a backup payment method if the collection on a primary payment method is past due.
Standby letters of credit can be used, for example, to guarantee the following types of payment and performance:
(1) repay funds borrowed or advanced,
(2) fulfill subcontracts, and
(3) undertake payment of invoices made on open account. The beneficiary to a standby letter of credit can draw from it on demand, so the buyer assumes added risk. See LETTER OF CREDIT.

STRAIGHT BILL OF LADING (shipping) A non-negotiable bill of lading that designates a consignee who is to receive the goods and that obligates the carrier to deliver the goods to that consignee only. A straight bill of lading cannot be transferred by endorsement. See BILL OF LADING.

SWIFT (banking) An acronym for Society for Worldwide Interbank Funds Transfer.

TENOR (banking) The maturity date of a financial instrument. Usually 30, 60, 90 days, etc.

TRANSFERABLE LETTER OF CREDIT A letter of credit where the beneficiary specified in the credit has the option of instructing his bank to transfer the credit fully or in part to another beneficiary.
A letter of credit can only be transferred if it is expressly designated as "transferable" by the issuing bank. This type of letter of credit enables intermediaries (first beneficiaries) to offer security in the form of a letter of credit to their suppliers (second beneficiaries).
This credit allows the supplier to transfer all or part of the proceeds of the letter of credit to a second beneficiary, usually the ultimate supplier of the goods.

TRAVELER'S LETTER OF CREDIT
A letter of credit issued by a bank to a customer preparing for an extended trip. The customer pays for the letter of credit, which is issued for a specified period of time in the amount purchased. The bank furnishes a list of correspondent banks or its own foreign branches at which drafts drawn against the letter of credit will be honored.

UNCLEAN BILL OF LADING
See CLAUSED BILL OF LADING; BILL OF LADING.

UNIFORM CUSTOMS AND PRACTICE (UCP) Full name: Uniform Customs and Practice for Documentary Credits. The internationally recognized codification of rules unifying banking practice regarding documentary credits (letters of credit). The UCPDC was developed by a working group attached to the International Chamber of Commerce (ICC) in Paris, France. It is revised and updated from time to time and the current valid version is ICC Publication 500, which is the 1993 edition.

UNIFORM RULES FOR COLLECTIONS (URC) The internationally recognized codification of rules unifying banking practice regarding collection operations for drafts, their payment or nonpayment, protest, and for documentary collections, (documents against payment, D/P, and documents against acceptance, D/A). The URC was developed by a working group attached to the International Chamber of Commerce (ICC) in Paris, France. It is revised and updated from time to time and the current valid version is ICC Publication 322.

US FOREIGN TRADE DEFINITIONS
An obsolete standard of trade terms, although they are sometimes specified in US domestic contracts. The international standard of trade terms is Incoterms 2000. Chapter 6: Incoterms 2000 starting on page 24.

UNRESTRICTED LETTER OF CREDIT
A letter of credit that may be negotiated through any bank of the beneficiary's choice.

USANCE The time allowed for payment of an international obligation. A usance credit is a credit available against time drafts. See LETTER OF CREDIT; USANCE LETTER OF CREDIT.

USANCE LETTER OF CREDIT
A documentary letter of credit that is not available by sight payment and that is therefore available against
(1) acceptance of a term bill of exchange, or
(2) by deferred payment. See LETTER OF CREDIT.

VALIDITY The time period for which a letter of credit is valid. After receiving notice of a letter of credit opened in his/her behalf, the seller/exporter/beneficiary must meet all the requirements of the letter of credit within the period of validity. See LETTER OF CREDIT.

WAYBILL (shipping) A document prepared by a transportation line at the point of a shipment, showing the point of origin, destination, route, consignor, consignee, description of shipment, and amount charged for the transportation service, and forwarded with the shipment, or direct by mail, to the agent at the transfer point or waybill destination. See BILL OF LADING; AIR WAYBILL; OCEAN BILL OF LADING.

CHAPTER 20

# Resources

## The International Chamber of Commerce (ICC)

The ICC is an excellent source of information on documentary letters of credit, documentary collections, and Incoterms (trade terms). It is also the world's premier business organization that advocates and promotes open international trade and investment systems and the market economy worldwide.

### ICC PUBLICATIONS

Incoterms 2000
Guide to Incoterms 2000
Incoterms in Practice
Software for Incoterms 2000
Incoterms Questions and Answers
Export-Import Basics
Keywords in International Trade
Uniform Customs and Practice for Documentary Credits
UCP 500 Diskette
UCP 500 and 400 Compared
Guide to Documentary Credit Operations
Standard Documentary Credit Forms
Case Studies on Documentary Credits under UCP 500
Opinions of the ICC Banking Commission
Documentary Credits Insight: The most authoritative newsletter on L/Cs

### HOW TO OBTAIN ICC PUBLICATIONS

ICC publications are available from ICC National Committees or Councils which exist in some sixty countries, or from

ICC Publishing, Inc.
156 Fifth Avenue, Suite 308
New York, NY 10010 USA
Tel: 212-206-1150
Fax: 212-633-6025
E-mail: iccpub@interport.net

ICC Publishing, S.A.
38, Cours Albert,1er
75008 Paris, France
Tel: [33] (1) 49 53 29 23
Fax: [33] (1) 49 53 29 02
E-mail: pub@iccwbo.org

**Visit the ICC Web Site at: http://www.iccwbo.org**